Cocke County
Tn.
Survey Book
"A"
1822-1854

W.P.A. Transcription

Retyped By Wayne A. Shaw

COCKE COUNTY, TENNESSEE

SURVEY BOOK "A"

Copied in longhand from the original which has since burned, by A.R. Mews [?] and Heber [?] Parrott

Dec. 1936 - April 1938

Typed by Agnes Mattux and Willis Hutcherson

3

JOHN NEFF 56 ACRES

State of Tennessee Cocke County

By virtue of an entry Made in the Entry Takers office for Cocke county at Newport of No. 4 dated 5th day of April 1824 Founded on rights of Occupancy I have surveyed and laid off for JOHN NEFF fifty six and one fourth acres of land, situate lying and being in the County and state aforesaid, on the west side of Big Pigeon river bounded as follows Vis. Beginning at a stake said to be a corner of JOHN GORMANS deeded land running therewith MARY FINES line south twenty poles to her corner thence the same course seventy four poles and eighty hundredths of a pole to a stake near a sink hole thence East Ninety four poles and thence North Ninety four poles and eighty six hundredths of a pole to a stake Near a Marked red oak bush thence North Ninety four poles and eighty six hundredths of a pole to the beginning. Surveyed the 6th day of April 1824. BY

JAMES JENNINGS)		Jonathan Wood
SAMUEL BOYER)	C.C.	Principal Surveyor of Cocke County

4

JAMES JENNINGS 24 ACRES AND 46 POLES

State of Tennessee Cocke County

By virtue of an entry Made in the Entry takers office for Cocke County at Newport of No. 32 dated the 5th day of April 1824 Founded on right of occupancy I have surveyed and laid off for JAMES JENNINGS twenty four acres and forty six poles of land situate lying and being in the county and state aforesaid on the west side of big Pigeon river. Bounded as follows vis. Beginning at three black oak saplins Near JOHN GORMANS fence south thirty six west fourteen poles to a stake Near a black Oak saplin corner to JOHN GORMAN thence sixty and one half deg. West one hundred and seventy one poles with a conditional line between the said JENNINGS and JOHN GORMAN a post oak near the forks of a road thence with a conditional line between JENNINGS and R. HENRY South fifty deg. East twenty six poles to a stake corner to ADAM GAN thence with his line North sixty two deg. East one hundred and forty five poles to a stake on said JENNINGS deeded land thence with the same North sixty deg. west forty poles to the beginning. Surveyed the 5th day of April 1824.

JOHN NEFF)		Jonathan Wood
THOMAS JENNINGS)	C.C.	Principal Surveyor of Cocke County

5

ADAM GANN 50 ACRES

State of Tennessee Cocke County

By virtue of an Entry Made in the Entry takers office for Cocke County at Newport of No. 31 dated the 5th day of April 1824. Founded on the right of occupancy. I have surveyed and laid off fifty acres of land for ADAM GANN lying and being in the County and state aforesaid on the west side of Big Pigeon River. Bounded as follows Viz. Beginning at two poplars and a black oak corner to JAMES JENNINGS Pattented land running thence due south with RICHARD CROSS line of seventy two poles to a poplar in a hollow corner to FRILANIG SAMPLES thence with his conditional line between the said GANN and SAMPLES due west Ninty six poles to a black oak on the top of a ridge thence with another conditional line between the same south seven degrees East twenty eight poles to a hickory corner to said SAMPLES deeded land, Thence with a conditional line between the said GANN and TOBERTH HENRY North fifty degrees - west sixty five to a stake corner to JAMES JENNINGS New survey Thence with the line of said New survey North sixty two degrees East one hundred and forty five poles to a stake on a line of JAMES JENNINGS deeded land thence with said line south sixty deg. East sixteen poles to the beginning. Surveyed the 7th day of April 1824 by

THOMAS JENNINGS) Jonathan Wood
JAMES JENNINGS) C.C. Principal Surveyor of Cocke County

6
ROBERT HENRY 73 ACRES

State of Tenn. Cocke County
By virtue of an Entry Made in the Entry takers office for Cocke County at Newport of No. 31 dated the 5th day of April 1824. Founded on the right of occupancy I have surveyed and laid off seventy three acres of land for ROBERT HENRY in said county and state on the west side of Big Pigeon River. Beginning on a hickory corner to SAMPLES then with a conditional line between the said HENRY and ADAM GANN, North fifty West Ninty two poles to a post oak then with GORMANS line North seventy six West two poles and eleven links to a stake at NEFFS' line then with DELTOS - South fourteen poles and tenlinks to a stake west Ninty four poles and eighty one hundredths to a stake then with HOODS lines west seven poles to a locust stump - West seventy one poles to a stake then a conditional south fifty two poles to a stake - East ninty six poles to some pine bushes at the forks of a road - South Eighty eight East seventy six poles to a pine stump corner to McSWAIN then with his lines south twenty eight and an half - East Nineteen poles to a stake North sixty five East sixty poles to a stake on SAMPLES line then with Ditto a direct line to the beginning. Surveyed the 8th of April 1824 by

GEORGE WALKER) Jonathan Wood
JOHN FRACHUR) C.C. Principal Surveyor of Cocke County

RICHARD GRANTS 160 ACRES

State of Tenn Cocke County
By virtue of an Entry Made in the Entry takers office for said County at Newport of No. 1 dated the 5th day of April 1824. I have surveyed for RICHARD GRANTS one hundred and sixty acres of land in said county on the waters of Sinking Cove [Cave] Creek. Beginning at a pine tree on JAMES SWAGERTYS line near McPHEARSON'S oak North twenty one West eighty five poles to a stake North fifty East one hundred and two poles to a stake corner to RICHARD GRANT, then with his line a direct course to the beginning. Surveyed the 10th of April 1824 by

JAMES SWAGERTY SR.) Jonathan Wood, Principal
SPENCER FAUBION) C.C. Surveyor of Cocke County

16 [sic]
ANTHONY CHRISTIAN 50 ACRES

State of Tennessee Cocke County
By virtue of an Entry Made in the Entry Takers office for said county at Newport of No. 40 dated the 7th day of April 1824. Founded on right of Occupancy. I have surveyed for ANTHONY CHRISTIAN fifty acres of land on the waters of Clear Creek. Beginning at a Black Oak and white Oak corner to a tract of land belonging to said CHRISTIAN running thence with the same South forty two West twenty four poles to a stake South twenty three poles to a grave or line of another tract of one hundred acres belonging to the same thence with the same West twenty eight poles to a stake South thirty seven and an half poles to a stake thence west sixty six poles to a stake on WILLIAM W. BIBEES line thence North one hundred two an half poles to a stake thence direct line to the beginning. Surveyed the 12th day of April 1824. by
JOHN HALL) Jonathan Wood
JAMES CHRISTIAN) C.C. Principal Surveyor of Cocke County

16 [sic]
H. SHANNON 20 ARES

State of Tennessee Cocke County
By Virtue of an Entry Made in the Entry Takers office for the aforesaid County at Newport of 240 dated the 23rd day of July 1824. I have surveyed for HUGH SHANNON twenty acres of land in said county on the waters of Sinking Creek. Beginning at a Black oak corner to JOHN ROGERS ISAAC ALLEN and JAMES ELLIS running thence with a conditional line with ELLIS South fifteen deg. East sixty six poles to a white Oak thence with conditional lines with JOHN ROGERS south eighty four deg. East forty four poles to a dog wood North sixty four poles to a stake on said ROGERS line thence with Ditto North eighty four deg. West sixty two poles to the beginning. Surveyed 18th of November 1824 by
WM T. ELLIS) Jonathan Wood
SAMUAL JACK) C.C. Principal Surveyor for Cocke County

17 [sic]
JOHN WOOD 50 ACRES

State of Tenn. Cocke County
By Virtue of an Entry Made in the Entry Takers Office for Cocke County at Newport of No. 5 dated the 15th day of April 1824. Founded on rights of Occupancy. I have surveyed for JOHN WOOD fifty acres of land situate in the county and state aforesaid on the North side of French Broad River near the dry fork of Clay Creek on the South side thereof. Beginning at a large white Oak corner to a 20 acre tract belonging to said WOOD. Granted to him by the State of Tenn. running thence with the same North 15 poles to a stake thence East sixty poles and two links to a stake thence with a conditional line between said WOOD and WM BIBEE south thirty seven and an half deg. East fifty four to a hickory thence with another conditional line between the same East thirty two poles to a white Oak thence with vacant land south fifty one poles and six tenths to a stake thence west one hundred and ten poles to a stake on a line of said WOODS. Deeded land then with the lines of the same North forty three and one tenth poles to a stake in said WOODS field East twelve poles to a hickory thence North ten poles to a White oak East ten poles to a stake thence north twenty six poles to a stake West forty poles to the beginning. Having such form as represented by the above platt. Surveyed the 13th April 1824 By
WM W. BIBEE) Jonathan Wood
WM RAY) C.C. Principal Surveyor for Cocke County

18
W. W. BIBEE 100 ACRES

State of Tennessee Cocke County
By Virtue of an Entry made in the Entry Takers office for Cocke County at Newport of No 36 dated the 6th of April 1824. Founded on the rights of occupancy. I have surveyed for WILLIAM W. BIBEE one hundred acres of land situate - lying and being in the county and state aforesaid on each side of the dry fork of Clay Creek. Beginning on a post oak and your corner to said BIBEE Thence with his lines South fifty nine polesto a stake East twenty six poles to a stake-South six poles to a stake stake [sic] East thirty nine poles an an [sic] half to a stake South twenty three poles to a stake-West seven poles to a stake-South nineteen poles to a White oak. Thence with a conditionallines with JOHN WOOD-North seventy seven deg. East sixty one poles to a white oak - thence thirty seven an a half-East thirty poles to a stake corner to a twenty acre tract of said WOOD. thence with the same East thirty seven to a stake said WOOD corner-thence the same course with his nero survey made this day sixty poles further to a stake- thence with Ditto-South thirty seven and an half Deg. East fifty four poles to a hickory. Thence with Ditto Eat [sic] fifteen poles to a stake North forty five poles to a stake on THOMAS CHRISTIANs line-thence with his line North fifty five degrees-West sisteen poles to a stake-North forty two deg. West twenty two poles to a Spanish oak-North eighty six deg. West sixty eight poles to a gum and white oak on the bank of a small branch-North thirty two deg. West sixty poles to a small white Oak bush- thence with a conditional line with MRS. KELLY- South eighty two deg. West one hundred and fifty six poles to the beginning. Having such form and as represented by the above. Surveyed the 13th day of April 1824 by
JOHN WOOD)   Jonathan Wood Principal
DAVID ONEIL) C.C.   Surveyor of Cocke County

JOHN GILLETT 50 ACRES

State of Tenn. Cocke County
By Virtue of an Entry made in the Entry Takers Office for said county at Newport of No 7 dated the 5th day of April 1824. Founded on rights of Occupancy. I have surveyed and laid off for JOHN GILLETT fifty acres of land situated lying and being in county and state of Tenn. on the waters of Clay Creek. Beginning at a grave and white Oak on the North bank of the Dry fork of said Creek running thence with a conditional line with HOLT North sisty seven West forty poles to three post Oakes South forty six West twenty two poles to a white Oak and Dog wood thence with A. DRISKILLS lines south thirteen and an half degrees East eighty three poles to a stake East eighty five poles to a stake North eighty two poles to a stake near a marked piece thence a direct line to the beginning. Having such form a represented by the above plate surveyed the 14th day of April 1824 by
WILLIAM BIBEE   )   Jonathan Wood
WILLIAM P. GILLETT) C.C.   Principal Surveyor for Cocke County

20
ALEXANDER DRISKILL 50 ACRES

State of Tenn. Cocke County
By Virtue of an Entry made in the Entry Takers Office for said county at Newport of No 9 dated the 5th day of Aril 1824 Founded on rights of Occupancy. I have surveyed and laid off for ALEXANDER DRISKILL fifty

Acres of land situate Lying and being in the county and state aforesaid on the waters of little Clay Creek. Beginning at a pear tree on a hill on a line of said DRISKILL deeded land running thence North forty eight degrees East fifty two poles to two Post Oakes on JOHN GILLETTS line thence with the same North thirteen and an half deg. west fifty seven and an half poles to a White Oak and Dogwood corner to said GILLETT thence with another of his lines North forty six deg. East thirty poles to a stake thence with a conditional line between ASY HOLT and DRISKILL North forty four degrees west one hundred and thirteen poles to a stake thence south forty six degrees west forty two poles to a stake thence with CUPS lines south thirty five degrees East forty six poles to a hickory thence South thirty six and an half deg. West twenty two poles to a stake on a line of said DRISKILL's deeded land thence with the same a direct line to the beginning. Having such form as represented by the above Plate. Surveued the 15th day of April 1824 By

JESSE DRISKILL) Jonathan Wood
BERRY HOLT) C.C. Principal Surveyor for Cocke County

21
LUCY KELLY 100 ACRES

State of Tennessee Cocke County
By Virtue of an Entry made in the Entry takers Office for said county at Newport of No 51 dated the 9th day of April 1824. Founded on the right of occupancy. I have surveyed and laid off for LUCY KELLY one hundred acres of land situate in said county on Campbells Branch waters of Clay Creek. Beginning at a small pine at the foot of a Nobb corner to a ten acre tract on which CHARLES KELLY before his deed laid a warrant running thence with said Nobb North eight West West[sic] sixty six poles to a sugar tree- North eleven West with Ditto twenty eight poles to a stake in the public road leading from Newport through the narrows- North with said hill sixty nine poles to a stake South Eighty eight West twenty two poles to a stake- South sixty nine poles with a steep hill to a pone- thence then with Ditto South nineteen and an half- West forty two poles to a stake- thence with conditional lines with GOOCH South forty west fifty eight poles to a stake corner to a tract that formerly belonged to LOFTY- thence with the same- East fifty poles to a stake near a branch- South fifty poles to a black oak Thence South forty one- West twenty two to a post oak and double beech corner to WILLIAM W. BIBEE- Thence with a conditional line with the said BIBEE North eighty two- East one hundred and fifty six poles to a white Oak crossing the aforesaid road at fifty poles- thence with CHRISTIANs lines North thirty two West forty five poles thence to a stake north ten East thirty seven poles to a Dogwood corner to said KELLYS land thence with his lines west fifty six poles to a black Oak south sixteen poles to a sour wood West fifteen poles to a stake thence a direct line to the beginning. Surveyed the 14th day of April 1824 by

WM GILLETT) Jonathan Wood
WILLIAM GOOCH) C.C. Principal Surveyor for Cocke County

D. WOODS 50 ACRES

State of Tenn. Cocke County
By Virtue of an Entry made in the Entry takers office for the aforesaid county of Cocke at Newport of No 22 dated the 5th day of April 1824. I have surveyed for DAVID WOOD fifty acres of land in said county on the waters of Clay Creek. Beginning at a White Oak corner to THOMAS CHRISTIAN on said WOODS line running thence with said CHRISTIANS line North thirty seven East fifty poles to a stake North seventy One and one half East forty

six poles to a black Oak North fourteen and one fourth deg. East sixty Nine poles to a dogwood and black Oak Near the margin of a wood thence with Conditional lines with JOHN WOODS North three West forty five poles to a stake South sixty seven West sixty six to a stake on a line of said WOODS then with the same a direct line to the beginning. Having such form as represented by the above platt. Surveyed the 15th day of April 1824 By
JOHN WOOD)
Jonathan Wood
WM RAY) C.C. Principal
Surveyor for Cocke County

23
MARY TURNER 50 ACRES
State of Tennessee Cocke County
By virtue of an Entry made in the Entry takers Office for Cocke County at Newport of No. 25 dated the 5th day of April 1824. Founded on rights of occupancy. I have surveyed and laid off for MARY TURNER fifty acres of land situate and lying and being in the county and state aforesaid on the waters of Neelys Creek. Beginning at a dog wood on SAMUEL MARTINS line one hundred and seven poles to a stake thence East seventy four poles and eight tenths to a stake on the side of a hill thence South one hundred and seven poles to a stake thence West seventy four and Eight tenths poles to the beginning. Having such form as represented by the above platt. Surveyed the 19th day of April 1824.
WILLIAM TALLY) Jonathan
Wood
JESSEE SMITH) C.C. Principal Surveyor for Cocke County

24
THOMAS FOWLER 80 ACRES
State of Tenn Cocke County
By Virtue of an Entry made in the Entry takers office for Cocke County at Newport of no. 35 dated the 6th day of April 1824. Founded on right of Occupanch. I have surveyed and laid off for THOMAS FOWLER eighty acres of land situate lying and being in the county and state aforesaid on the waters of Clear Creek. Beginning on a marked pine on a line of a tract of land belonging to JOHN SWAGERTY running thence with the same North forty three deg. West Ninety poles to a White Oak on a LINDSEYS line thence with the same South four Deg. West one hundred and seven poles to four hickorys thence west sixty four poles with LINDSEYS Ditto to a stake entry line poles PARROTTS Deed South fifty two poles with Sw Ps line to a post Oak corner to a tract of land containing 20 acres of land belonging to said FOWLER thence with lines of the same Nine and one half poles to a stake South Eighty poles to a pine thence West forty two and one half poles to a stake in a flat thence South seventy four deg. East with vacant land Ninety five poles to a stake North twenty Nine West thirty poles to a black Oak a conditional between him and SWAGERTY thence with Ditto North four and an half deg. Eat[sic] twelve poles and Nine links to a post Oak North seventy two East twenty two poles to a post Oak, North thence North thirty two deg. East Ninety five poles to the beginning. Having such form as represented by the above platt. Surveyed the 28th day of April 1824 by
JOHN FOWLER) Jonathan
Wood
SAMUEL FOWLER) C.C. Principal Surveyor for Cocke County

25
THOMAS FOWLER 80 ACRES
State of Tenn. Cocke County
By virtue of an entry made in the Entry takers Office for Cocke County at Newport of No. 35 dated the 6th day of April 1824. Founded on rights of occupancy I have surveyed and laid off for THOMAS FOWLER eighty acres of land situate lying and being in the county and state aforesaid on the waters of Clear creek. Beginning on a Marked pine on a line of tract of land belonging to JOHN SWAGERTY running thence with the same North-forty-three

North forty three deg. West Ninety poles to a White oak on LINDSEYS line thence with the same South four deg. West one hundred and seven poles to four hickorys thence West sixty four poles with LINDSEYS Ditto to a stake on a line of PARROTTS Deed South fifty two poles with Sd P's line to a post oak corner to a tract of land containing 20 acres belonging to s'd FOWLER thence with the lines of the same Nine and an half poles to a stake South eighty poles to a pine thence West forty two and an half poles to a stake in a flat thence South seventy four deg. East with vacant land ninety five poles to a stake. North twenty Nine west thirty poles to a black oak a Conditional between him and SWAGERTY thence South Ditto North four and an half Deg. East twelve poles and Nine links to a Post Oak North seventy two East twenty two poles to a pine North one West twenty one poles to a post oak North fourteen West Sixty six and an half poles to two Spanish Oaks North thence North two deg. East Ninety five poles to the beginning. Having such form as represented by the above plate. Surveyed 28th day of April 1824

JNO FOWLER)

Jonathan Wood

SAMUEL FOWLER) C.C. Principal

Surveyor for Cocke County

THOS. FOWLER 50 ACRES

State of Tenn. Cocke County

By virtue of an Entry made in the Entry Takers Office for the County aforesaid at Newport of No 17 dated the 5th day of April 1824. Founded or entered to enlarge a deeded tract containing 20 acres. I have surveyed and laid off fifty acres of land for THOMAS FOWLER situate lying and being in the county of Cocke and state aforesaid on the North side of Clear Creek. Beginning at a stake on a conditional line with JACOB BOYER near a marked white Oak running thence north fifty nine degrees West seventy one and one tenth poles to a stake thence north thirty one degrees East one hundred and twenty six poles and six tenths poles to a stake on the side of a hill thence south fifty nine deg. East seventy one poles and one tenth to a stake thence south thirty one deg. West thirty four poles to the line of the above named 20 acre tract thence with the lines of the same south seventy three deg. West twenty poles to a red Oak south thirty five deg. West sixty poles to a stake thence a direct line to the beginning.

Having such form as represented by the above plate.

Surveyed the 27th April 1824 by

SOLOMON COWARD)

Jonathan Wood

JNO. F. FOWLER) C.C. Principal

Surveyor for Cocke County

27

ISAAC BOYER 75 ACRES

State of Tenn. Cocke County

By virtue of an Entry made in the Entry Takers office for Cocke County at Newport of No 12 Founded on right of Occupancy. I have surveyed for ISAAC BOYER seventy five acres of land in said county on the waters of Clear Creek. Beginning at a Ironwood on the North bank of Clear Creek on THOS. FOWLERS line running with the same North fifty nine degrees West one hundred and seventy five poles to a stake south thirty six West Ninety poles to a stake south fifty nine East seventy eight poles to a stake on BOYERS line East sixty eight poles to a stake on JAC BOYERS line thence with his lines North twenty five and three fourth poles to a white Oak East fifty one poles to a stake south twenty five and three tenths poles to a sower wood East fourteen poles and an half to an Oak stump North two and an half west seven poles to a white Oak North thirty one East seventeen poles to the beginning. Having such form as represented by the above plate. Surveyed the 29th April 1824 by

AARON BOYER)

Jonathan Wood

LOUIS BOYER) C.C. Principal

Surveyor for Cocke County

JACOB BOYERS 50 ACRES
State of Tenn. Cocke County
By Virtue of an Entry made in the Entry Takers office for Cocke County at Newport of No 13 dated the 5th of April 1824. I have surveyed for JACOB BOYER fifty acres of land in the aforesaid county on the North side of French Broad River. Beginning at a post Oak Grub near the margin of the road leading from Newport to Greenville the said Grub being a corner of a tract of land belonging to said BOYER running thence East crossing said road at two poles in all sixty thence and one fourth poles to a Cocke County at Newport of No 54 dated the 9th day of April 1824. Founded on right of occupancy. I have surveyed and laid off for ARDEN MASON fifty acres of land lying and being in the County and state aforesaid on the waters of McCowans Creek. Beginning at a black gum and beach on the bank of McCowans Creek running thence North thirty and an half deg. West one hundred poles crossing the public road to a small Post oak on the top of a ridge thence North nine and an half East sixty six and an half poles to an elm, iron wood and white oak near the top of a ridge thence South thirty and an half degrees-East one hundred and twenty poles crossing said road to a stake South fifty nine and an half degrees-West sixty six poles to the beginning. Having such a form as represented by the above plate.
Surveyed the 29th of April by
SIMON SMITH)
Jonathan Wood Principal
JOHN SMITH) C.C. Surveyor of
Cocke County

29
SIMON SMITH 50 ACRES
State of Tennessee, Cocke County
By Virtue of an Entry made in the Entry takers office for Cocke County at Newport of No 56 dated the 9th day of April 1824. Founded on the right of occupancy. I have surveyed and laid off for SIMON SMITH fifty acres of land Situate lying and being in the County and State of aforesaid on the waters of McCowans Creek beginning at a chestnut oak running thence South forty three degrees West sixty three and two tenth poles to a stake on the side of a hill-thence South forty seven degrees East one hundred and twenty six and four tenths poles to a stake near some small white oaks- thence North forty three degrees- East sixty three and two tenth poles to a small white Oak, black oak and dogwood- thence North forty seven degrees- West one hundred and twenty six poles and four tenths of poles to the beginning.
Having such form as represented by the above plate.
Surveyed to 30th of April 1824 by
ARDEN SMITH)
Jonathan Wood Principal
JOHN SMITH) C.C. Surveyor
for Cocke County

SIMON SMITH 150 ACRES

State of Tennessee Cocke County
By virtue of an entry made in the Entry takers office at Newport of No. 55 dated the 5th of April 1824. Founded on the rights of occupancy. I have surveyed and laid off for SIMON SMITH one hundred and fifty acres of land - Situate lying and being in the County and state aforesaid on the waters of McCowans Creek - Beginning on a black oak and dogwood on the North side of said creek - running thence South fifty three degrees West two hundred and nineteen poles to a stake on the side of a hill - thence South thirty seven degrees - East crossing said creek twenty five poles in all one hundred and nine poles and five tenths to a stake on a South side of a hill - thence North fifty three degrees - East two hundred and nineteen poles and an half to a stake thence North thirty seven degrees - West one hundred and nine poles and five tenths of a poles to the beginning. Having such form as represented by the above platt.
Surveyed the 30th of April 1824.
AIDEN MASON)
Jonathan Wood
JOHN SMITH) C.C. Principal
Surveyor of Cocke County

ISAAC SMITH 125 ACRES

State of Tennessee Cocke County
By virtue of an entry made in the Entry takers office for the aforesaid County at Newport of No. 64 dated the 20th of April 1824. I have surveyed for ISAAC SMITH 125 acres of land on the waters of McCowans Creek. Beginning at a hickory running South thirty four East one hundred poles crossing the public road from Newport to a stake at the foot of a steep hill thence with the same South fifty two West thirty two poles to a spanish Oak South forty two and an half poles West twenty two poles to a dogwood on said SMITHS line of a tract containing fifteen acres then with the lines of the same North forty West twenty two poles to a stake West thirty five and an half poles to a White Oak South sixty poles to a stake crossing the aforesaid road thence South seventy West one hundred and four poles to a stake thence with NABBS South thirty four West one hundred poles to a stake Near an Ash thence a direct line to the beginning. Having such form as represented by the above platt.
JAMES MASON)
Jonathan Wood
NATHAN TYNY) C.C. Principal
Surveyor for Cocke County

ABNER HARRISON 4 ACRES

By virtue of an Entry Made in the Entry takers office for said county at Newport on No. 28 dated the 5th of April 1824. I have surveyed for ABNER HARRISON 4 acres of land on the south side of Nolochucky river. Beginning at a sickamore on the bank of said river running down the Meadows beside the said river South eighty two deg. West Nineteen poles North eighty Nine West twenty five poles North eighty seven West sixteen poles South seventy three West four poles and seven links to an elm said to be a corner to a tract of land belonging to the HEIRS OF BENJAMIN DEED then with same south twenty poles to a stake at the foot of a steep hill then with Ditto the same North eighty two East twenty eight poles to a sickamore North sixty two East fourteen poles to a poplas then a direct line to the beginning - Having such form as represented by the above platt. Surveyed the 16th day of April 1824 by
JAMES HARRISON)
Jonathan Wood
WILLIAM DAVIS) C.C. Principal
Surveyor of Cocke County

32
NATHAN TYNY [TYRY] 100 ACRES

State of Tenn. Cocke County
By Virtue of an Entry made in the Entry Takers office for said county at Newport of No 53 dated 9th of April 1824. Founded on rights of Occupancy. I have surveyed and laid off for NATHAN TYNY [Tyry] 100 acres of land lying and being in the county, state aforesaid on the waters of Neelys Creek beginning at a Black Oak on JANE JESTER'S line running thence south sixteen West one hundred and sixteen poles near a large marked White Oak on the top of a ridge thence south seventy four deg. East one hundred and seven poles to a stake thence with a conditional line with SIMON SMITH north twenty one and an half degrees East one hundred and sixty five poles to a stake thence a direct line to the beginning Having such form as represented by the above plate
Surveyed the 1st day of May 1824
SIMON SMITH)
Jonathan Wood
JAMES MASON) C.C. Principal
Surveyor for Cocke County

33
<u>H. REEVES 100 ACRES</u>

State of Tenn. Cocke County
By Virtue of an Entry made in the Entry Takers office for said county at Newport of No 60 dated the 16th of April 1824. Founded on rights of occupancy. I have surveyed and laid off for HARRISON REEVES one hundred acres of land situate lying and being in the county and state aforesaid on the waters of Neelys Creek beginning at a White Oak bush on SAMUAL MASTERS line running thence with the same North eighty five and an half poles to a stake thence East one hundred and sixty poles to a stake in a steep hollow near a marked bush and White Oak thence south One hundred and four poles and eight tenths to an Elm and Ash thence ninety two poles to a stake on MARY TURNERS land then with the same North nineteen poles to a stake thence a direct line with hers to the beginning. Having such form as represented by the above plate.
Surveyed the 3rd day of May by
JESSE SMITH)
Jonathan Wood
GEORGE REED) C.C. Principal
Surveyor for Cocke County

33
<u>GEORGE REED 50 ACRES</u>

State of Tennessee - Cocke County
By virtue of an Entry made in the Entry takers office for Cocke County at Newport of No 29 dated the 5th day of April 1824. Founded on the right of Occupancy. I have surveyed and laid off fifty acres of land for GEORGE REED situate lying and being in the county and state aforesaid on the waters Neelys creek. Beginning at an elm on JESSE SMITHS line running thence with the same South sixty four and an half degree East fifty nine poles to a stake North seventy seven degrees East thirty poles to a stake. Thence with vacant land North one hundred and one poles to a stake thence West eighty five poles to a stake Thence South seventy nine poles to the beginning. Having such form represented as the above plate.
Surveyed the third day of May 1824 by
JESSE SMITH)
Jonathan Wood - Principal
WM B. TOLLEY) C.C. Surveyor of
Cocke County

34
WM HARRISON 100 ACRES
State of Tennessee Cocke County
By virtue of an Entry made in the Entry takers office for said county at Newport on No 30 dated the 5th day of April 1824. Founded on the right of occupancy. I have surveyed and laid off for WILLIAM HARRISON one hundred acres of land Situate lying and being in the county and state aforesaid on the South side of Nolochucky river. Bounded as follows viz. Begining at a forked called bark hickory on top of a ridge said to be on a line of BENJAMIN HARRISON running thence with the same North seventy two degrees west one hundred and seventy nine poles to a stake near a branch- Thence North eighteen degrees- west eighty nine and an half poles to a stake near a marked hickory on top of a ridge South seventy two degrees- East one hundred and seventy nine poles ti two hickorys Thence a direct line to the beginning. Having such form as represented by the above plate.
Surveyed the 4th day of May 1824 by
AMBER HARRISON)
Jonathan Wood - Principal
JAMES HARRISON) C.C. Surveyor of
Cocke County

35
WM BRAGG 100 ACRES
State of Tenn Cocke County
By Virtue of an Entry made in the Entry Takers office for Cocke County at Newport of No 18 dated the 5th day of April 1824. Founded on rights of Occupancy. I have surveyed and laid off for WM BRAGG one hundred acres of land situate lying and being in the county and state aforesaid on both sides of Neelys Creek. Beginning at a Beech Tree and BENJAMIN DOUGHTYS line near the aforesaid creek running thence south thirty one degrees west eighty and four tenths poles to three hickorys on the side of a hill thence north fifty nine deg. West one hundred and seventy eight and eight tenths poles to a stake on top of the dividing ridge between Neelys Creek and Chucky thence North thirty one East eighty nine poles and four tenths to a small lynn near the bank of said creek thence a direct line to the beginning. Having such form as represented by the above plate.
Surveyed the 5th day of May 1824 by
WILLIAM SOLOMON)
Jonathan Wood
BENJAMIN DOUGHTY) C.C. Principal
Surveyor for Cocke County

JOHN SMITH 100 ACRES
State of Tenn. Cocke County
By Virtue of an entry made in the Entry Takers office for Cocke County at Newport of No 27th dated the 5th day of April 1824. Founded on rights of Occupancy. I have surveyed and laid off for JOHN SMITH one hundred acres of land situate lying and being in the county and state aforesaid on the south side of Nolochucky River adjoining the forty acre tract belonging to the said Smith beginning on a black Oak a corner thereof running thence East with INMANS line seventy four poles to two White Oaks on said line thence with a conditional line between the said SMITH and JAMES DAVIS South fourteen degrees East one hundred and seventy eight poles to GEORGE JORDONS line thence with the same west one hundred and eighteen poles to a stake thence with his own line North one hundred and sixty six poles to the beginning. Having such form as represented by the above plate
Surveyed the 4th day of May 1824 by
HENRY SMITH)
Jonathan Wood
SAMUEL SMITH) C.C. Principal
Surveyor of Cocke County

36
JAMES ROMINES 70 ACRES

State of Tenn. Cocke County

By Virtue of an Entry made in the Entry Takers Office for Cocke County at Newport of No 63 dated the 19th day of April 1824. Founded on rights of occupancy. I have surveyed and laid off for JAMES ROMINES seventy acres of land situate lying and being in the county and state aforesaid on West side of Big Pigeon River. Beginning at a large black Oak in the margin of the Cosby's Creek road running thence with a conditional line between him and ABRAHAM FINE North forty three degrees East seventy nine poles to a stake thence with McCOYS line North ninety three poles to a hickory on RINCHOWS line thence with the same south fifty nine deg. West forty three poles to a large pine thence with another of his lies West crossing the Cosbys Creek road at thirty three the Jones Cave road at Ninety two three road leading from FREES mill at 139 poles containing in all one hundred and ninty six poles to a whitewood thence with GRAYS line South nine East twenty eight poles to a post Oak Grapes[Grasses?] then with his lines East one hundred and seventy one and an half poles crossing the aforesaid roads to a pine thence south ninety nine poles to the beginning. Having such form as represented by the above plate
Surveyed the 7th of May 1824 by
THOMAS LACY)
Jonathan Wood
ROBERT HOOD) C.C. Principal
Surveyor of Cocke County

37
ISAAC BUELISON 50 ACRES

State of Tennessee Cocke County

By virtue made in the Entry takers office for Cocke County at Newport of No 45 dated the 8th day of April 1824. Founded on the right of occupancy I have surveyed and laid off for ISAAC BUELISON fifty acres of land situate lying and being in the county and state aforesaid on two forks of Cosbys creek. Beginning at a mountain oak on a spur of a mountain running thence with a conditional line between him and HOLLOWAY GILES - South eighty five and an half degrees - East sixty poles to a sake crossing the Briar fork of Cosbys creek at fifty five poles Thence nine and an half East forty poles to a bush and sourwood - Thence North eleven degrees West nineteen poles to a forked dogwood - North eighty two degrees. East forty poles to the same pine - Thence South eighty seven - East crossing the grassy fork of said creek at four poles in all nineteen poles to a large white oak - Then with GREENS± line North twenty three West thirty four poles to a beech between the forks of a small branch thence with conditional lines with him and GREEN West twenty three poles to a sourwood crossing the creek at twenty poles North sixty degrees West forty one poles to a dogwood and birch South seventy four and an half deg. West fifty four poles to a stake on a line of McADAMS deeded land thence with the same a direct line to the beginning. Having such form as represented by the above plate.
Surveyed the 11th day of May 1824 by
HOLLOWAY GILES)
Jonathan Wood Principal
WM GREEN) C.C. Surveyor of
Cocke County

38
ROBIN HOOD 50 ACRES
State of Tennessee Cocke County
By virtue of an Entry made in the Entry takers Office Cocke County at Newport of No 52 dated the 9th day of April 1824. Founded on the right of occupancy. I have surveyed and laid off for ROBIN HOOD fifty acres of land. Situate lying and being in the county and state aforesaid on the west side of Big Pigeon River. Bounded as follows viz. begining at a hickory MARY FINES corner running thence South with JOHN NEFFS line eighty two poles to a small white wood near a locust stump thence west with a conditional line between him and ROBERT HENRY one hundred and nine poles and five tenths to a stake thence North sixty one and an half poles to his deeded land-thence East with the lines of said tract forty eight poles to a hickory North twenty poles to two black oaks thence East sixty poles to the beginning. Having such form as represented in the above plate.
Surveyed the 10th day of May 1824
JNO. BOYER)
Jonathan Wood - Principal
GEO. NELSON) C.C. Surveyor of
Cocke County

39
WILLIAM GRAY 110 ACRES
State of Tennessee Cocke County
By virtue of an Entry made in the Entry takers office for the county aforesaid at Newport of No 19 dated the 5th day of April 1824 I have surveyed for WILLIAM GRAY one hundred and ten acres of land on the waters of Queens Branch Beginning at a white oak THOMAS STUARTS North corner running with the same STUARTS line South nineteen poles to a black oak East seventy poles to two black oaks then with HENRYS line North sixty eight poles to a Post oak, then with ROMINES line North nine deg. West twenty eight poles to FINES line thence with the same North eighty one poles to a stake West one hundred and twenty four and an half poles to a stake South eighty six poles to a stake near the above named STUARTS line thence with ditto a direct line to the beginning. Having such form as represented by the above plate.
Surveyed the 8th day of May 1824
ABRAM FINE)
Jonathan Wood - Principal
WILLIS GRAY) C.C. Surveyor of
Cocke County

40
JOHN NEFF 50 ACRES
State of Tenn. Cocke County
By Virtue of an entry made in the Entry Takers office for the county aforesaid at Newport of No 6 dated the 5th day of April 1824. Founded on rights of Occupancy. I have surveyed and laid off fifty acres of land situate lying and being in the county aforesaid on the waters of Sinking Creek. Beginning at a stake near a Marked Red Bud bush among some limestone rocks near a branchrunning forty two poles to a white Oak thence with the course of a rocky hill and with a conditional [line] with NELSON South fifty nine and one fourth West forty seven poles to the foot of a steep hill thence with the same as a natural boundary South eighty three and an half West fifty seven poles to a white Oak North sixty six west seven and an half poles to a white Oak thence with a conditional with JOHN FREE North eighteen and an half deg. East eighty nine poles to a stake thence a direct line to the beginning.

Having such form as represented by the above plate.
Surveyed the 10th day of May by
ROBIN HOOD)
Jonathan Wood
GEORGE NELSON) C.C. Principal
Surveyor for Cocke County

41
JOHN BOYER 70 ACRES
State of Tenn. Cocke County
By Virtue of an entry made in the Entry Takers office for the county and state aforesaid at Newport No 49 dated the 9th day of April 1824. Founded on rights of Occupancy. I have surveyed and laid off for JOHN BOYER seventy acres of land lying and being in the county and state aforesaid on the waters of Sinking Creek. Beginning at a Spanish Oak on the South side of a branch on the top of a hill running thence East thirty one poles to a small White Oak grub on eyed the 10th day of May by
ROBIN HOOD)
Jonathan Wood
GEORGE NELSON) C.C. Principal
Surveyor of Cocke County

JAMES BAXTER 50 ACRES
By virtue of an entry made in the Entry takers office for Cocke County at Newport of No 48 dated the 8th day of April 1824. Founded on the right of occupancy. I have surveyed and laid off for fifty acres of land for JAMES BAXTER. situate lying and being in the county and state aforesaid on the cany fork of Cosbys Creek. Beginning at a large white oak on the bank of said creek running thence down the creek by the side of a mountain North sixteen deg. West crossing said creek at twenty six poles containing the same in all sisty eight poles to three spruce pines at the foot of a mountain (Smokey) thence with the course of said Mountain North seventy four and an half degrees West crossing said creek at thirteen poles containing the course in all fifty six poles to a large hickory thence south one hundred and fifty poles to a stake thence North sixty eight East eighty one poles to a stake thence North forty poles to the beginning. Having such form as represented by the above plate.
Surveyed the 12th day of May 1824 by
HENRY VALENTINE)
Jonathan Wood - Principal
ROBERT McGOHE) C.C. Surveyor of
Cocke County

42
HOLLOWAY GILES 25 ACRES
State of Tennessee Cocke County
By virtue of an entry made in the Entry takers office for said county at Newport of No 47 dated the 8th day of April 1824. Founded on right of occupancy. I have surveyed and laid off for HOLLOWAY GILES twenty five acres of land situate lying on the waters of Cosbys Creek. Beginning at a beech tree the N.W. corner of the tract of land belonging to H. GILES near the foot of a Mountain running thence with the same East twenty eight poles and four tenths to a stake then with BUELISONS conditional line North fifty six deg. East forty two poles to a stake thence twelve

West ninety four to the same spruce pine bushes corner to BEULISONS survey thence with the lines thereof South eighty two West forty poles to a forked dogwood South eleven East nineteen poles to a sourwood South nine and an half West forty poles to a stake near the Briar fork of said creek near a mountain thence with the same five poles to the beginning. Having such form as represented by the above plate.
Surveyed the 12th day of May 1824.
JAMES BEULISON)
Jonathan Wood - Principal
WM VALENTINE) C.C. Surveyor of
Cocke County

43
FRANCIS GREEN 25 ACRES
By virtue of an entry made in the Entry takers office for Cocke County at Newport of No 37 dated the 6th day of April 1824. Founded on the rights of occupancy. I have surveyed and laid off for FRANCIS GREEN twenty five acres of land in said county on waters of Cosbys creek. Beginning at white oak the corner of a tract of land belonging to said GREEN running thence with the same North forty six West thirty two poles to a chesnut North seventy East fourteen poles to a stake South eighty four East fifteen and three fourths poles to a dogwood North thirteen East crossing Mohawns road at thirty eight poles and the Cany fork of Cosbys creek at eight poles further in all fifty one and an half poles to a beech at the foot of a mountain. Then with ditto North sixty three West forty six poles to a stake on the side of a Mountain South twenty seven and an half West with vALENTINES line crossing the road at fifty six poles and creek at sixty in all seventy six poles to a stake then with BUELISONS line a direct course to the beginning. Having such form as represented by the above plate.
Surveyed the 12th day of May 1824 by
WILLIAM GREEN)
Jonathan Wood - Principal
HENRY VALENTINE) C.C. Surveyor of
Cocke County

44
GEORGE GRAY 109 ACRES
State of Tenn. Cocke County
By Virtue of an entry made in the Entry Takers office for the county of Cocke at Newport of No 68 dated the 11th day of May 1824. Founded on rights of Occupancy. I have surveyed and laid off for GEORGE GRAY 109 acres of land in the said county on the west side of Pigeon River. Beginning at a white oak, chesnut Oak and black Oak on ABRAM FINE'S line then with his line north one hundred and twenty nine poles to a dead post oak and sourwood, North fifty six East thirty eight poles to a black Oak on ABRAM FINE'S line thence with his line North one hundred and twenty nine poles North fifty six East thirty eight poles to a black oak then with conditional lines to SAMUEL BOYER North sixty five West ninety two poles to a Black Oak, hickory and Red Bud in a sink hole South thirty one West ninety five poles to a White Oak on or near HURBY SMITH'S line then with the same south twenty two East thirty nine poles to a white Oak and black Oak South forty west forty three poles to a black Oak South forty six East fifty seven poles to a black Oak thence a direct line to the beginning. Having such form as represented by the above plate.
Surveyed the 14th of May 1824 by
ABRAM FINE)
Jonathan Wood
WILLIAM GRAY) C.C. Principal
Surveyor for Cocke County

45
JOHN BOYER 50 ACRES
By virtue of an entry made in the Entry Takers office for the county and state aforesaid at Newport of No 50 dated the 9th of April. Founded on rights of Occupancy. I have surveyed and laid off for JOHN BOYER fifty acres of land situated lying and being in the county and state aforesaid on the waters of Sinking Creek. Beginning at a small post oak on the side of a hill running thence South eighty four degrees East sixty three poles and three tenths poles to a black Walnut and White Oak thence South six West one hundred and twenty six poles and eight tenths to a stake by a large limestone rock on the top of a hill thence North eighty four degrees West sixty three poles and three tenths poles to a hickory and black Oak saplins thence North six degrees East one hundred and twenty six poles and eight tenths of a pole to the beginning. Having such form as represented by the above plate
Surveyed the 14th of May 1824 by
ROBIN HOOD)
Jonathan Wood
JAMES STRANGE) C.C. Principal
Surveyor

45
GEORGE MILLER 50 ACRES
State of Tennessee Cocke County
By virtue of an entry made in the Entry takers office of the county aforesaid at Newport of No 20 dated the 5th of April 1824. Founded on rights of occupancy. I have surveyed and laid off for GEORGE MILLER fifty acres of land situate in said county on the waters of Sinking creek. Beginning at a small white oak on the side of a ridge ten links East of a Marked maples running thence East eighty nine and four tenths poles to a beech corner to ALEXANDER SMITH then with his line North eighty nine poles and four tenths to two white oaks near a dry branch West eighty nine and for tenths poles to two chesnuts South eighty nine and four tenths poles to the beginning. Having such form as represented by the above plate.
Surveyed the 15th of May 1824 by
ISAAC ALLEN)
Jonathan Wood - Principal
WM MILLER) C.C. Surveyor of
Cocke County

46
RUSSELL JONES 50 ACRES
State of Tennessee Cocke County
By virtue of an entry made in the Entry takers office for the aforesaid county at Newport of No 38 dated 7th day of April 1824. Founded on right of occupancy. I have surveyed and laid off for RUSSEL JONES fifty acres of land situate lying and being in the county and state aforesaid On the waters of Big Creek. Beginning at a beech on his North and lower line of a deeded tract running thence with the same North eighty poles to a stake on the side of a mountain thence west one hundred poles to two beeches and a forked hickory near the top of a hill-thence South eighty poles to a stake-thence East one hundred poles to the beginning. The said tract having such form as represented by the above plate
Surveyed the 19th May 1824 by
JOHN ELLISON)
Jonathan Wood - Principal
JOHN COX) C.C. Surveyor of
Cocke County

47
RUSSELL JONES 50 ACRES
State of Tennessee Cocke County
By virtue of an entry made in the Entry takers office for the county and state aforesaid at Newport of No 39 dated the 7th of April. Founded on right of occupancy. I have surveyed and laid off for RUSSELL JONES fifty acres of land situate lying and being in the county and state aforesaid on the South side of French Broad river on the waters of Big Creek. Beginning at a beech a corner to his deeded tract marked 1796 running thence with the same (viz. his line) West one hundred and twenty six poles and an half to a small dogwood bush-Thence South sixty three and one fourth poles to a chesnut grub East one hundred and twenty six poles and an half to a stake-thence North sixty three and one fourth poles to the beginning. Having such form as represented by the above plate.
Surveyed the 19th day of May 1824 by
JOHN ELLISON)
Jonathan Wood
JOHN COX) C.C. Principal
Surveyor of Cocke County

48
ANTHONY CHRISTIAN 100 ACRES
State of Tenn. Cocke County
By virtue of an entry made in the Entry Takers office for said county at Newport of No 8 dated the 5th of April 1824. Founded on rights of occupancy. I have surveyed and laid off for ANTHONY CHRISTIAN one hundred acres of land situate lying and being in the county and state aforesaid on the North East side of French Broad River. Beginning at a Gum on ANTHONY CHRISTIANS line running thence South thirty two and an half deg. East forty seven and one fourth poles to a chesnut Oak thence with KINDRICKS conditional lines South eighty six and an half East seventy six poles to a White Oak and locust South forty four and an half deg. East thirty poles to a stake North sixty East forty five and three fourths poles to a small chesnut Oak. South seventy and one half deg. East twenty five poles to an Ironwood and dogwood by a branch thence North sixty four poles to a stake North sisty three and an half West one hundred and twenty two and half poles to a stake thence South thirty four poles to a stake on ANTHONY CHRISTIANS line Thence with his lines South seventy five West thirty seven and an half poles to a White Oak stump thence a direct line to the beginning. Having such form as represented by the above plate.
Surveyed the 8th day of June 1824 by
JOHN HALL) Jonathan
Wood
ANTHONY CHRISTIAN) C.C. Principal Surveyor of Cocke County

49
DAVID JONES 35 ACRES
State of Tenn. Cocke County
By virtue of an entry made in the Entry takers office for said county at Newport of No 70 dated the 14th day of May 1824. Founded on rights of priority to increase a deeded tract of 125 acres. I have surveyed and laid off for DAVID JONES thirty five acres of land situate lying and being in the county and state aforesaid on the South side of Nolochucky River. Beginning at a beech Marked R.J. and a white oak corner to the aforesaid tract one hundred and twenty five acres running thence East one hundred poles to a stake near a Lynn thence South fifty six poles to a small dogwood and black oak near a dry branch thence West one hundred poles to two

white oaks and an ash thence North fifty five polesa to the beginning. Having such form as represented by the above plate.
Surveyed the 12th day of June 1824 by
BENJAMIN DOOIS[Davis?]) Jonathan Wood
WILLLIAM P. JONES) C.C. Principal Surveyor of Cocke County

D. MOORE, D. MOORE AND WILLIAM SMITH 50 ACRES
State of Tenn. Cocke County
By virtue of an entry made in the Entry takes office for said county at Newport of No 87 dated the 5th day of June 1824. Founded on the right of Occupancy. I have surveyed and laid off for DUMSEY MOORE, DAVID MOORE and WILLIAM SMITH-Situate lying and being in said county on the South side of Nolochucky River. Beginning at a red Oak running thence North twenty two and an half degrees East one hundred and eighteen poles to the bank of said river Crossing the public road from Newport to Chucky the same course continued eight and four tenths poles further to a stake which eight poles represented in the palte is covered with the waters of said river North sixty seven and an half West sixty three and two tenths of a pole to a stake on the side of a hill near said river South twenty two and an half-West one hundred and twenty six and four tenths poles to a stake on the side of a steep hill crossing the aforesaid road ar fifty poles South sixty seven and an half-East sixty three and two tenths poles to the beginning. Having such form as represented by the above plate.
Surveyed the 11th day of June 1824 by
DAVY DRISKILL)
Jonathan Wood - Principal
SIMON SMITH) C.C. Surveyor of
Cocke County

50
DEMPSEY MOORE 50 ACRES
By virtue of an entry made in the Entry takers office for said county at Newport of No 83 dated the 3rd day of June 1824. Founded on rights of occupancy. I have surveyed and laid off for DEMPSEY MOORE fifty acres of land lying and being in the county and state aforesaid on the South side of Nolochucky River. Beginning at a black Walnut and running thence North eighty three deg. East eighty six poles to a stake on ROBERT MOORES line thence with the same south ninety three poles to a stake near a marked sowerwood thence West Nineteen five poles to a stake thence a direct line to the beginning. Having such form as represented by the above plate.
Surveyed the 11th day of June 1824 by
DAVID MOORE)
Jonathan Wood - Principal
DAVY DRISKILL) C.C. Surveyor of
Cocke County

JOSHUA DRISKILL 75 ACRES
State of Tennessee Cocke County
By Virtue of an entry made in the Entry takers office for said County at Newport of No 85 dated the 4th day of June 1824. Founded on right of Priorty to increase a deeded tract. I have surveyed and laid off for JOSHUA DRISKILL seventy five acres of land situate in said county of Cocke on the waters of Clay creek. Beginning at a Spanish oak-a corner of said deeded tract running thence with the same South one hundred and fifty five poles to two spanish oaks thence West leaving said tract seventy seven and an half poles to three white oaks and a dogwood thence North one hundred and fifty five poles to two spanish oaks thence East seventy seven and an half poles to the beginning. Having such form as represented by the above plate.
Surveyed the 9th day of June by
[No chain carriers given] Jonathan Wood Principal Surveyor
for Cocke County

51
JAMES BUCKNER 50 ACRES
State of Tenn. Cocke County
By virtue of an entry made in the Entry Takers Office for Cocke County at Newport No 3 dated 5th day of April 1824. Founded on rights of Occupancy. I have surveyed for JAMES BUCKNER fifty acres of land in the county and state aforesaid on South side of Nolochucky River. Beginning at a sixteen acre tract of said BUCKNERS running thence with the same West forty poles to a state South sixty three and two tenths poles to some red bud bushes in a steep hollow. Thence with vacant land East sixty eight poles to a White Oak then with said BUCKNERS and DRISKILLL North seven and one fourth deg. East one hundred and Nineteen poles to a stake on said BUCKNERS line of the aforesaid sixteen acre tract thence with the same South twenty five East fifty four poles to the beginning. Having such form as represented by the above plate
Surveyed the 15th day of June 1824 by
JOHN SMITH)
Jonathan Wood
EDWARD BUCKNER) C.C. Principal
Surveyor for Cocke County

52
JAMES BUCKNER 60 ACRES
State of Tennessee Cocke County
By virtue of an entry made in the Entry takers office for said county at Newport of No 5 dated the 5th day of April 1824. Founded on right of occupancy. I have surveyed and laid off for JAMES BUCKNER sixty acres of land situate lying and being in the said county on the South side of Nolochucky River. Beginning at a plum tree marked B. the third corner of a 16 acre tract belonging to said BUCKNER running thence with JOHN SMITHS line North forty West thirty four and an half poles to a Walnut corner to COLEMAN SMITH thence with his line West sixteen poles to DAVID JONES line. thence with the same South thirty six and an half poles to two dogwoods corner to said JONES thence with another of his lines-West one hundred and thirty one and an half poles to an ash on the side of a ridge-thence South one hundred and sixty poles to a stake-thence East one hundred and forty five poles to a stake thence a direct line to the beginning. Having such form as represented by the above plate.
Surveyed the 15th day of June 1824 by

Jonathan Wood
[No chain carriers given] Principal Surveyor of Cocke County

53
WILLIAM TALLY 60 ACRES
State of Tenn. Cocke County
By Virtue of an entry made in the Entry takers office for said County at Newport of No 100 dated the 16th day of June 1824. Founded on rights of Occupancy. I have surveyed and laid off sixty acres of land for WILLIAM TALLY situate lying and being in the county and state aforesaid on the waters of Neelys Creek. Beginning on a White Oak and black Oak on JOHN BRIZEN lines [or John Brizendines] running thence with JAMES TURNERS line North eighty three and an half poles to a stake on MARTINS line thence with the same West one hundred and fifteen poles to two hickorys thence south Eighty three and an half poles to a large beech marked W.B.T. Thence East one hundred and fifteen poles to the beginning. Having such form as represented by the above platt.
Surveyed the 18th day of June 1824 by
JAMES TURNER)
Jonathan Wood
JESSEE SMITH) C.C. Principal
Surveyor of Cocke County

54
B. HARLE 60 ACRES

State of Tennessee Cocke County
By virtue of an entry made in the Entry takers office for said County at Newport of No 61 dated the 17th April 1824 - Founded on rights of priority to increase a tract of land containing one hundred and sixty Pursuant to the same. I have surveyed and laid off for BALDWIN HARLE sixty acres of land situate lying and being in the county and state aforesaid on the waters of Nolochucky river. Beginning at a stake 20 poles from a White Oak the second corner of his old tract on a line thereof running thence with
WILLIAM BROGG)
Jonathan Wood
JAMES SOLOMON) C.C. Principal
Surveyor of Cocke County

ABRAHAM LOFTY 60 ACRES

State of Tennessee Cocke County
By virtue of an entry made in the Entry takers office for the county aforesaid at Newport of No 21 dated the ?th day of May 1824. Founded on rights of Occupancy. I have surveyed and laid off for ABRAHAM LOFTY sixty acres of land situate lying and being in the county and state aforesaid on the waters of Slate creek. Beginning at a White oak Marked A. L. on a conditional line with SHADRACK GOINS thence with the same South one and an half deg. East one hundred and thirty poles to a hollow beech on a ___?__ of a nobb near a branch thence South Eighty eight and an half West seventy four poles to 2 dogwoods on the side of a hill North one and an half west seventy three poles to the public road leading from Newport to Chucky the same course continued in all one hundred and thirty poles to a small cherry tree and white oak thence a direct line to the beginning. Having such form as represented by the above platt.
Surveyed 16th June 1824 by
JOHN WORTH)
Jonathan Wood
PAGE LOFTY) C.C.
Principal Surveyor of Cocke County

55
ABRAHAM AARON 160 ACRES

State of Tennessee
Cocke County
By virtue of an entry made in the Entry takers office for said county at Newport of No 76 dated the 25th of May 1824. Founded on rights of Occupancy. I have surveyed and laid off for ABRAHAM AARON one hundred and sixty acres of land situate lying and being in the County and State aforesaid on the waters of Nolochucky river. Beginning at a Whiteoak near a branch running thence North seventy one deg. East one hundred and sixty eight poles to two beeches on THOMPSONS line thence with the same North fifty five West one hundred and Ninety poles to two white oak bushes thence south seventy one West one hundred and sixty eight poles to three hickorys thence a direct line to the beginning. Having such form as represented by the above platt.

Surveyed the 10th day of June 1824 by
JOHN WORTH)
Jonathan Wood
PAGE LOFTY) C.C.
Principal Surveyor of Cocke County

56
DAVID OTTINGER 50 ACRES
State of Tennessee Cocke County
By virtue of an entry made in the Entry takers office for sd. County at Newport of No. 88, dated the 5th day of June 1824. Founded on rights of Occupancy. I have surveyed and laid off for DAVID OTTINGER fifty acres of land situate lying and being in the County and State aforesaid on the waters of Meadow Creek. Beginning at a black gum corner to said OTTINGERS deeded land running thence West seventy Nine poles to a stake on POTTERS line thence with the same North eleven and an half East forty four poles to a large black Oak POTTERS corner thence North twenty nine poles to a small post Oak thence with a conditional line with HENDERSON North sixty seven and an half deg. East thirty poles to a black oak and pine on HENDERSONS line thence with the same East Ninety three poles to a stake thence a direct line to the beginning. Having such form as represented by the above platt.
Surveyed the 20th day of June A.D. 1824 by
HENRY OTTINGER)
Jonathan Wood
ADAM OTTINGER) C.C. Principal
Surveyor of Cocke County

57
JESSE McPIKE 50 ACRES
State of Tennessee Cocke County
By virtue of an entry made in the Entry Takers office for the aforesaid County of Cocke at Newport on No 2 dated the 5th day of April 1824, Founded on rights of Occupancy. I have surveyed and laid off for JESSE McPIKE fifty acres of land situate lying and being in the county State aforesaid on a branch of Long Creek. Beginning at a sickamore stump on a line of a thirty acre tract belonging to said McPIKE running thence south forty two East one hundred and twenty six and six tenths poles to a stake on the side of a Mountain thence North forty eight degrees East sixty three and three tenths poles to a stake in the margin of the road leading from Newport to Warm Springs thence North forty two deg. West crossing the said road at seventeen poles the same course. continued in all one hundred and twenty and six tenths poles to a sassafras bush thence a direct line crossing said road to the beginning. Having such form as represented by the above platt.
Surveyed the 24th of June 1824 by
JAMES McPIKE)
Jonathan Wood
*WILLIAM LORY) C.C. Principal
Surveyor of Cocke County

*Lory, Tory, Fory?

58
ABRAHAM BOOKER 58 3/4 ACRES

State of Tennessee Cocke County
By virtue of an entry made in the Entry takers office for Cocke County aforesaid at Newport of No 66 dated the 23rd of April 1824. Entered to enlarge or increase a tract containing one hundred one and one fourth acres. I have surveyed and laid off for ABRAHAM BOOKER fifty eight acres and three fourths of an acre of land lying and being in the county and state aforesaid on the South side of French Broad River. Beginning at a White Oak, spanish Oak and hickory corner to said BOOKER running thence with his line South Nineteen and an half deg. East fifty six poles to a beech stump corner to FRANCIS CARTER. Then with his line South

Eleven and an half deg. East seventy three poles to a boxelder North seventy eight and an half East eighty one poles to a stake eleven and one third poles from a black oak marked with three notches thence North eleven and an half West one hundred and twenty poles to a stake near a Marked locust thence south seventy eight and an half West thirty five poles to a bush, thence with conditional lines with ___?___ south forty seven West fifty four poles to a White oak south twelve and an half West ten and an half poles to a stake in said BOOKERS line thence with the same a direct line to the beginning. Having such form as represented by the above platt.
Surveyed the 25th of June 1824 by
ISAAC BOOKER)
Jonathan Wood
OLIVER DAFFIN) C.C. Principal
Surveyor of Cocke County

58
WILLIAM JAMES 50 ACRES

State of Tennessee Cocke County
By virtue of an entry made in the Entry takers office for said county at Newport of No 109 dated the 23rd of June 1824. Founded on rights of occupancy. I have surveyed and laid off for WILLIAM JAMES fifty acres of land situate in the county and State aforesaid in the South side of French Broad river. Beginning at a black Oak on or near the top of a ridge running thence south forty six and an half degrees West Ninety four poles and an half to a black Oak thence south forty three and an half East eighty five poles to a hickory bush thence North forty six and an half East Ninety four and an half poles to a black Oak on the side of a ridge thence a direct line to the beginning. Having such form as represented by the above platt.
Surveyed the 26th of June 1824 by
ISAAC A. MASSY)
Jonathan Wood
DAVID FRANCIS) C.C. Principal
Surveyor of Cocke County

59
LEVI SMITH 50 ACRES

State of Tennessee Cocke County
By virtue of an entry made in the Entry takers office for said County at Newport of No 109 dated the 23rd of June 1824. Founded on rights of occupancy. I have surveyed and laid off for LEVI SMITH fifty acres of land situate lying and being in the County and State aforesaid on the waters of Slate Creek. Beginning on a hickory near an old field running thence South ten and an half degrees west eighty six poles to a hickory near the top of a ridge by a road thence south seventy Nine and an half degrees East eighty three poles to a stake near a Marked hickory & dogwood. Thence North ten and an half deg. East eighty six poles to a chestnut tree and hickory. Thence a direct line to the beginning. Having such form as represented by the above platt. Surveyed the 16th day of June 1824 by
THOMAS DRISKILL)
Jonathan Wood
THOMAS SMITH) C.C. Principal
Surveyor of Cocke County

60
THOMAS DRISKILL 116 ACRES

State of Tennessee Cocke County
By virtue of an entry made in the Entry takers office for said county at Newport of No 57 dated the 9th day of April 1824. Founded on rights of

Occupancy. I have surveyed and laid off for THOMAS DRISKILL one hundred acres of land situate lying and being in the County and State aforesaid on the waters of Slate Creek. Beginning at an elm running thence West seventy two poles to a hickory bush on WORTHS line. Then with his lines South forty One poles to a beech on the bank of a creek, West seventy two poles to sassafras. Thence south seventy eight poles to WORTHS corner the same course continued in all one hundred and eight poles and an half to a stake near the top of a hill. East one hundred and forty four poles to a stake thence a direct line to the beginning. Having such form as represented by the above platt.
Surveyed the 16th Day of June A.D. 1824 by
LEVI SMITH)
Jonathan Wood
THOMAS SMITH) C.C. Principal
Surveyor of Cocke County

JOHN BRIZENDINE 75 ACRES

State of Tennessee Cocke County
By virtue of an entry made in the Entry takers office of said County at Newport of No 24 dated the 5th day of April 1824. Founded on rights of Occupancy I have surveyed for JOHN BRIZENDINE seventy five acres of land situate lying and being in the County and State aforesaid on the waters of Neelys Creek. Beginning at an elm & blackgum between him and WILLIAM TALLY running thence South eighty Nine deg. and fifty Minutes West seventy seven & an half poles to a post Oak and dogwood thence south one hundred and fifty five poles to a stake thence East seventy seven and an half poles to three white Oaks on JESTERS line thence with ditto and TURNERS line North one hundred and fifty five poles to the beginning. Having such form as represented by the above platt.
Surveyed the 18th day of June A.D. 1824 by
JAMES TURNER)
Jonathan Wood
JESSE SMITH) C.C. Principal
Surveyor of Cocke County

61
JOHN SMITH JR. 50 ACRES

State of Tennessee Cocke County
By Virtue of an entry made in the entry takers office for Cocke County at Newport of No 59 of the 13th of April 1824. Founded on right of occupancy. I have surveyed for JOHN SMITH JR. fifty acres of land in said county on the south side of Nolochucky River. Beginning at a hickory COOLMAN SMITH's corner thence with his line south one hundred poles to a walnut then with conditional lines with BUCKNERS south thirty Nine degree and forty five Minutes East thirty four and half poles to a plumb tree Marked B. then North 89 East seventy four poles to a stake North thirty one East to a sugar tree North twenty seven East fifty four poles to beech on STEPH. SMITH's line thence with the same West fifty six poles to a stake thence North twenty two poles to a stake thence a direct line to the beginning. Having such form as represented by the above platt.
Surveyed the 18th June 1824 by
JAMES SMITH)
Jonathan Wood
JOSEPH NELSON) C.C. Principal
Surveyor of Cocke County

62

JOHN EBBS 160 ACRES

State of Tennessee Cocke County

By virtue of an entry made in the entry takers office for said county at Newport of No 80 dated the 1st of June 1824. Founded on right of occupancy I have surveyed and laid off for JOHN EBBS one hundred and sixty acres of land in said county and state on the waters of Long creek. Beginning at a large White Oak on the side of a hill on a branch of said creek running thence North forty degrees west one hundred and thirteen two tenths poles to a stake thence south fifty deg. west two hundred and twenty six and four tenths poles to three sowerwoods near a dry branch on the West side thereof south forty deg. East one hundred and thirteen and two tenths poles to a stake near the bank of Long Creek thence a direct line to the beginning. Having such form as represented by the next platt in the margin.

Surveyed the 22nd day of June 1824 by

AREN STEADWALL)

Jonathan Wood

JESSE REAVIS) C.C. Principal

Surveyor of Cocke County

WILLIAM MOORE 75 ACRES

State of Tennessee Cocke County

By virtue of an entry made in the entry takers office for the county aforesaid at Newport of No. 72 dated the 24th day of May 1824. Founded on right of Occupancy. I have surveyed for WILLIAM MOORE seventy five acres of land in said county on the North side of French Broad River. Beginning at a beech at CLARKS line near a branch running thence North twenty one and an deg. East forty poles to elm at the foot of a steep hill thence with the same as a boundary North thirty five East sixty four poles and twenty links to a stake North sixty five and an deg. East forty one poles to a Walnut corner to WISE then with a conditional line with dito North thirty west eighty Nine poles to a stake then with MASOUS{MOSOUS} Line south forty Nine west one hundred and thirty three poles to a stake near RAMSY's line thence direct line to the beginning. Having such form as represented by the above platt. Surveyed the 1 day of July 1824 by

JAS. WISE)

Jonathan Wood

*AND. RAMSEY) C.C. Principal

Surveyor of Cocke County

* Could by Aud. Ramsey

63

PETER OTTINGER 50 ACRES

State of Tennessee Cocke County

By virtue of an entry made in the entry takers office for said county at Newport of No 96, dated the 9th day of June 1824. Founded on priority to increase a tract of land containing fifty acres to 100 acres Persuant to the same I have surveyed and lade off for PETER OTTINGER fifty acres of land situate lying and being in the county and state aforesaid on the head waters of Meadow Creek. Beginning at a stake corner to said 50 acre tract running thence with the line thereof North twenty poles to a stake North sixty five deg. East thirty two poles to a stake south seventy Nine deg. East thirty Nine poles to a black oak thence North fifty six poles to a white Oak on a line of ___?___ then with or nearly with dito North eighty seven west seventy eight poles to POTTERS line thence with his line south twenty two and an half West six poles to a White Oak stump south sixteen West one hundred and thirty poles to a stake south seventy two East thirty seven poles to a stake thence a direct line to the beginning. Having such form as represented by the above platt.

Surveyed the 23rd of June 1824 By
HENRY OTTINGER)
Jonathan Wood
NATHANIEL POTTER) C.C. Principal
Surveyor of Cocke County

64
JESSEE REEMS 52 ACRES
State of Tennessee Cocke County
By Virtue of an entry made in the entry takers office for said county at Newport No. 89, dated the 5th day of June 1824. Founded on Priority to increase a deeded tract of land containing 108 acres to 160 acres. I have surveyed and laids off for JESSEE REEMS fifty two acres of land situate lying and being in the county and state aforesaid on the waters of Long Creek. Beginning on a white oak in the line of the aforesaid tract running thence south thirty one East one hundred eleven and an half poles to a stake thence fifty Nine West eighty poles to a stake North thirty one West twenty six and an half poles to a stake on a line of said REEMS deeded land thence with the lines thereof North twenty two East thirty two poles to a spanish oak thence North fifty seven west seventy five poles to a poplar North fifty Nine East Ninety poles to the beginning. Having form as represented by the above platt.
Surveyed the 22nd June 1824 by
ARMSTEAD WALL)
Jonathan Wood
JOHN EBBS) C.C. Principal
Surveyor of Cocke County

M. HICKS 50 ACRES
State of Tennessee Cocke County
By Virtue of an Entry made in the entry takers office for the county aforesaid at Newport dated the 5th day of July 1824. I have surveyed for MOSES HICKS fifty six acres of land situate lying and being in the county and state aforesaid on the waters of English Creek. Beginning at a stake near a post oak corner to THOMAS WILLIAMS running thence South thirty five degrees East thirty five poles crossing the road leading from Newport at thirty poles to a stake on a conditional line with THOMAS ALLEN thence with the same south fifty two degrees West two hundred and eighty poles crossing said road to three white oaks thence north three East Seventy five poles or nearly with said ALLENS conditional line to WILLIAMS' line thence with the same a direct line to the beginning. Having such form as represented by the above platt.
Surveyed the 7th day of July 1824 by
THIMOTHY HICKS)
Jonathan Wood
JAMES WILLIAMS) C.C. Principal
Surveyor of Cocke County

65
JOHN PUCKETT 50 ACRES
State of Tennessee Cocke County
By virtue of an entry made in the entry takers office for the county of Cocke at Newport of No. 121, dated the 28th day of June 1824. Founded on the right of Occupancy. I have surveyed for JOHN PUCKETT 50 acres of land in said county on the south side of the road leading from Clarks ford to Newport at the head of a long hollow. Beginning at a hickory on the East side of said road running thence south six deg. East crossing the road aforesaid at sixty five poles all one hundred and twenty six poles and an half to a post oak and two black Oaks South 84 deg. West sixty three and one fourth poles to a post Oak and a black Oak on the side of a ridge North six degrees West one hundred and twenty six poles and an half to a

hill thence North 84 East crossing the road at forty three poles in sixty threnn [sic] and an fourth poles, to the beginning. Having such form as is represented by the above platt.
Surveyed the 10th day of July 1824 by
FRANCIS PUCKETT)
Jonathan Wood
JAMES PUCKETT) C.C. Principal
Surveyor of Cocke County

<u>JOHN ELLISON 50 ACRES</u>
State of Tennessee Cocke County
By Virtue of an Entry made in the Entry takers office at Newport No 43 dated the 8th of April 1824. Founded on right of Occupancy. I have surveyed for JOHN ELLISON fifty acres of land in said county on the waters of Big Creek. Beginning at a buckeye on the bank of said creek corner to BANDY running thence with his lines South two and an half degreed West sixty seventy poles to a stake thence South forty east eighty three poles to a stake thence with JACOB ELLISON'S line North forty four East Ninety six poles to a beech between two branches then with another of his lines north twenty four east twenty four poles to a white Oak north forty West thirty nine poles to TOBY corner the same course continued with his line forty two poles to the beginning. Having such form as is represented by the above platt.
Surveyed the 13th day of July 1824 by
JACOB ELLISON)
Jonathan Wood
MICHALL ELLISON) C.C. Principal
Surveyor of Cocke County

66
<u>WILLIAM MORGAN 50 ACRES</u>
State of Tennessee Cocke County
By virtue of an Entry made in the Entry takers office at Newport for the county of Cocke at Newport of 44, dated the 18th day of April 1824. Founded on the right of occupancy. I have surveyed to WILLIAM MORGAN fifty acres of land in said county of Cocke on the waters of Big Creek. Beginning at a spruce pine corner to STOCKLEY FAUBION and BANDY running with BANDYS line South thirty eight deg. and forty five Minutes East twenty eight poles to a poplar South two East seventeen and a half poles to a Maple and bush South fifty seven West twenty poles to a red oak North seventy one West Ninety poles to a stake South eighteen poles to a stake then with vacant land West forty two and an half poles to a stake on STOKELY'S line thence with the same North ten West seventy three poles to a dogwood, then a direct line to the beginning. Having such form as is represented by the above platt.
Surveyed the 13th day of August 1824 by
WM RUSSELL)
Jonathan Wood
JOEL BROOKS) C.C. Principal
Surveyor of Cocke County

<u>LEONARD HUFF 50 ACRES</u>
State of Tennessee Cocke County
By virtue of an entry made in the entry takers office at Newport of no. 128 dated the 29th June 1824. Founded on the right of priority to increase a deeded tract of one hundred acres. I have surveyed for LEONARD HUFF fifty acres of land on the south side of French Broad river. Beginning at a white oak and pine corner to the aforesaid tract running with the same South fifty seven and an half east thirty two and an half West 10 poles to a stake on JONATHAN HUFF'S line then with his line thirty two poles to a stake South eighty poles to a pine thence West sixty seven poles to

a stake on the side of a Mountain thence direct line to the beginning. Having such form as represented by the above platt.
Surveyed the 19th day of July 1824 by
JOS. HUFF)
Jonathan Wood
MARTIN DAVIS) C.C. Principal
Surveyor of Cocke County

67
JOSEPH HUFF 50 ACRES

State of Tennessee Cocke County
By virtue of an entry made the entry takers office for the county aforesaid at Newport of No. 106 dated 23rd of June 1824, entered to enlarge deeded tract of seventy acres to a hundred and twenty acres. I have surveyed and laid off for JOSEPH HUFF fifty acres of land situate lying and being in the county and state aforesaid on the south side of French Broad river. Beginning at a dead bush on a line of the above named seventy acre tract running thence with same north fifty seven and an half degrees west sixteen poles to LEONARD HUFF line at the foot of a mountain then with the mountain south fifteen and an half west fourteen and three fourth poles to a white oak JONATHAN HUFF corner then with his line East twenty eight and four tenths poles to a stake his corner then with his lines south fifty six and eight tenth poles to a stake then west sixty eight and four tenths poles to a pine corner to JOHNATHAN HUFF and LEONARD HUFF the same course continued with L. HUFF twenty two poles to a stake at a dry branch South sixty five poles to a black Oak thence last fifty seven poles to a stake on the side of the mountain Then with the same North twenty One East one hundred and sixteen poles to a stake on STEPHEN HUFF'S line then with his lines fifty seven west thirty five poles to a black Oak North fifteen East two and an half poles to a pine stump then with JOSEPH HUFF'S own line North sixty seven degrees west eighteen poles to the beginning. Having such form as represented by the above platt.
Surveyed the 14th of July 1824 by
JONATHAN HUFF)
Jonathan Wood
ABRAHAM HOOPER) C.C. Principal
Surveyor of Cocke County

MOSES FAUBION 60 ACRES

State of Tennessee Cocke County
By Virtue of an entry made in the entry takers office for said county at Newport of No. 16, the 5th day of April 1824. Founded on right of priority to increase deeded land tract of one hundred acres to one hundred and sixty I have surveyed and laid off to MOSES FAUBION sixty acres of land situate lying and being in the county and state aforesaid on the North side of French Broad river. Beginning at a stake between a marked black Oak and hickory said to be on a line of the aforesaid one hundred acre tract running thence North one hundred and thirty eight and an half poles to a stake then East sixty Nine and one third poles to a stake near a large Marked black oak thence south one hundred and thirty eight and an half poles to a stake on said one hundred acre tract thence with the same sixty nine and three tenths poles to the beginning. Having such form as represented by the above platt.
Surveyed the 14th of July 1824 By
HENRY FAUBION)
Jonathan Wood
LEWIS BOYER) C.C. Principal
Surveyor of Cocke County

68
JOSEPH FRANCIS 50 ACRES
State of Tennessee Cocke County
By virtue of an entry Made in the Entry takers office for the county aforesaid at Newport No. 108, dated 3rd of June 1824. Founded on right of occupancy. I have surveyed for JOSEPH FRANCIS fifty acres of land in said county on the south side of French Broad River, Keeney Branch Beginning at a lynn near the Middle branch running north sixty four and an half west seventeen and half poles to a spanish oak at the foot of a steep nob then with the same as a boundary, North sixty one and one half west eight and a half poles to an ash south eighty six and an half west Nine and three fourths poles to a stake south fifty west thirteen poles to a beech North eighty four west twenty and one fourth poles to a stake south fifty eight and half west eight poles to a sugar tree south twenty six and an half west twelve poles to a sugar tree south sixty four west twelve poles to a stake, south fifty five, west 18 poles to a beech North thirty two west thirty one poles to a beech south forty three west twenty one poles to a stake thence north thirty five west sixty one poles to a stake, north thirty two East one hundred and twenty poles to a stake on a line of a tract of land owned by the heirs of JAMES KEENER deceased. Then south said tract south sixteen East seventy Nine poles to a stake, then East forty poles to a large White oak near a branch, North fifty five East thirty two poles to a stake thence south thirty three poles to the beginning. Having such form as represented by the above platt.
Surveyed the 15th of July 1824 by
BIRGESS FRANCIS)
Jonathan Wood
EDWARD FRANCIS) C.C. Principal
Surveyor of Cocke County

69
THOMAS D. ADNY 50 ACRES
State of Tennessee Cocke County
By Virtue of an entry made in the entry takers office for the county aforesaid at Newport of No. 69, dated the 12th day of May 1824. Founded on the right of Occupancy. I have surveyed and laid off for THOMAS D. ADNEY fifty acres of land situate lying and being in the stat aforesaid on the waters of Sinking Creek. Beginning at or near a Marked gum on a line of JAMES PULMAN'S running thence North one hundred and twenty six poles and half to a stake near two white oaks and two hickorys. Thence west sixty three and one fourth poles to a stake south one hundred and twenty six poles and an half to a black oak thence East sixty three and one fourth poles to the beginning. Having such form as represented by the above platt.
Surveyed the twenty day of July 1824
JAS. PUTNAM)
Jonathan Wood
WM. ADNEY) C.C. Principal
Surveyor of Cocke County

69
REUBEN ALLEN SR. 16 [ACRES]
State of Tennessee Cocke County
By virtue of an entry made in the entry takers office for the county of Cocke aforesaid at Newport of No. 239, dated the 21st July 1824. I have surveyed for REUBEN ALLEN SENR. Sixteen acres of land in said county on the waters of Sinking Creek. Beginning at a white Oak the fifth corner of a tract of land belonging to said ALLEN running thence with the same East forty five poles to a stake South 13 degs. West 52 poles with a conditional line between him and JOHN FREE to a dogwood on the side of a hill thence with STRANGES line seventy four degs. West sixty nine poles to a stake on

on the side of a dry branch thence a direct line to the beginning. Having such form as represented by the above platt.
Surveyed the 21st July 1824
REUBEN ALLEN JUNR.) by Jonathan Wood
JOHN FREE) C.C. Principal Surveyor of Cocke County

70
JAMES STRANGE 50 ACRES
State of Tennessee
Cocke County
By virtue of an entry made in the entry takers office for said county aforesaid at Newport of No. 111, dated the 24th day of June 1824. Founded on the right of Occupancy. I have surveyed and laid off for JAMES STRANGE 50 acres of land in the aforesaid County on the waters of Sinking Creek. Beginning at a chestnut running one fourth of a degree East eighty Nine and an half poles to a stake, hickory near a dry branch North 89 3/4 degrees West eighty Nine and an half poles to a stake Marked mouth and eyes with one fourth of a degree West eighty Nine and a half to two sourwoods thence a direct line to the beginning. Having such form as represented by the above platt. Surveyed the 21st July 1824 by
JOSEPH WOOD)
Jonathan Wood
ANTHONY PATE) C.C. Principal
Surveyor of Cocke County

70
NELLY VEAL 16 ACRES
State of Tennessee
Cocke County
By virtue of an entry made in the entry takers office for the county aforesaid No. 129, dated June 29th 1824. Founded on the right of occupancy. I have surveyed and laid off for NELLY VEAL 16 acres of land in said County on the waters of Sinking Creek. Beginning at a White oak on or near JOHN ROGERS line running thence with conditional line with ELY NEWLAND South 26 and an half deg. West seventeen South forty eight deg. East thirty six poles to a white oak, South four, East twelve poles to a pine and black oak North Seventy East forty three poles to a stake North twenty West forty poles to a stake on JOHN ROGERS line thence with same west forty seven poles to the beginning. Having such form as represented by the above platt.
Surveyed the 22 July 1824
ROBIN HOOD) by
Jonathan Wood
WM. CHAMNESS) C.C. Principal
Surveyor of Cocke County

71
JAMES INMAN AND JOHN CORMAN 3 ACRES
State of Tennessee
Cocke County
By virtue of an Entry made in the entry takers office for said County at Newport of No. 207, dated the 6th day of July 1824. I have surveyed for JAMES INMAN and JOHN GORMAN jointly three acres of land the greater part of which is covered with the waters of Big Pigeon river including a small island and a fish trap in said river. Beginning at a stake near an iron wood on JOHN GORMANS line running up the river with ditto south eighty Nine and a half East twenty five poles to a stake thence across the river a conditional line with THOMAS JENNINGS North two and an half west twenty eight poles to a beech on the East bank of the river then with SMITHS line South fifty eight and an half west 29 poles to a beech on the bank of said river then South three and a half East thirteen and a half poles to the

beginning. Having such form as represented by the above platt.
Surveyed the 23rd of July 1824
HUGH SHAWSON) by
Jonathan Wood
JAMES GORMAN)
Principal Surveyor of Cocke County

72
JAMES JENNINGS 40 ACRES
State of Tennessee
Cocke County
By virtue of an entry made in the Entry takers office of Cocke county at Newport of No. 208, dated the 6th July 1824. I have surveyed for JAMES JENNINGS forty acres of land in said County on the West side of Big Pigeon river. Beginning at a stake corner to REUBEN HOOD running with his lines North sixty one poles & an half to a stake west twelve poles to a black Oak South 14 poles to a pine West Ninety eight poles to a stake then with vacant land South forty two poles to a stake East with BOYERS line seventy four poles to a hickory South thirty two poles to a hickory on ROBERT HENRY'S line thence with the same north to a White Oak corner to said HENRY and ROBIN HOOD then with HOOD'S line west eleven poles to the beginning. Having such forma as represented by the above platt.
Surveyed the 23rd July 1824 by
JOHN CORMAN)
Jonathan Wood
HOWELL MORRIS) C.C. Principal
Surveyor of Cocke County

72
JOSEPH WISE 50 ACRES
State of Tennessee
Cocke County
By Virtue of an entry made in entry takers office for the county aforesaid at Newport of No. 78, dated the 25 of May 1824. I have surveyed for JOSEPH WISE fifty acres of land including his occupied claim on the waters of Slate branch. Beginning at a Mulberry in a firld thence south eighty three and an half deg. East one hundred and twelve poles to a stake on his line of a deeded tract thence with the lines of same north fifty six East fifty two poles to a stake south forty seven poles to a stake East fifty one and an half poles to a stake then North sixty three poles to a stake then with the top of a top of a steep precipice as a boundary-west seventy seven poles to a stake south seventy three and an half degrees west thirty four poles to a small black Oak North eighty west ninety seven poles to a stake, south forty four poles to the beginning. Having such form represented by the above platt.
Surveyed the 26th of July 1824.
WILLIAM MOORE) by
Jonathan Wood
PETER WISE) C.C. Principal
Surveyor of Cocke County

JAMES HARRISON 24 ACRES
State of Tennessee
Cocke County
By Virtue of an entry made in the entrytakers office for the county of Cocke aforesaid and at Newport of No 140 dated the 1st of July 1824. I have surveyed for JAMES HARRISON twenty four acres of land on the south side of Nolochucky River in said county. Beginning at a hickory stump near the WILLIAM HARRISON corner running with the lines of WILLIAM HARRISON deceased, north seventy nine degrees west twenty eight poles to two beeches near a branch on a conditional line with JAMES DAVIS then with ditto south eleven west one hundred and thirty two poles and an half to a White oak and dogwood south seventy Nine East twenty Nine poles to Haw bush thence North eleven degrees East one hundred and thirty two and an half poles with WILLIAM HARRISON line to the beginning.

Having such form as represented.
Surveyed the 29th 1824 by
ABNER HARRISON) by
Jonathan Wood
JOHN HARRISON) C.C. Principal
Surveyor of Cocke County

74
JOHN INMAN 100 ACRES
State of Tennessee
Cocke County
By virtue of an entry made in the entry takers office for Cocke county at Newport of No. 102, dated the ninth day of June 1824. Founded on the right of Occupancy. I have surveyed and laid off for JOHN INMAN one hundred acres of land situate lying and being in the county and state aforesaid. Beginning at a beech on the side of a hill near a branch running thence west across the road leading through the narrows at five poles in all ninety six poles to a stake then with conditional lines with JOSEPH WISE, south seventeen west twenty Nine poles to a White Oak west sixteen and a half poles to a stake south six west thirty eight poles to a chesnut, south sixty five poles to a stake East one hundred and twenty seven and half poles to a stake thence a direct line - crossing the aforesaid road to the beginning. Having such form as represented by the above platt. Surveyed the 27th of July 1824.
JOHN SMITH) by
Jonathan Wood
WILLIAM SMITH) C.C. Principal
Surveyor of Cocke County

JOHN HEADRICK 100 ACRES
State of Tennessee
Cocke County
By virtue of an entry made in the entry takers office at Newport of No. 172, dated 5th of July 1824. I have surveyed for JOHN HEADRICK one hundred acres of land in said county on the north side of French Broad River - Beginning at a post oak on the Still house ridge running thence North sixty five East one hundred poles to a stake near two post oaks, North twenty west one hundred and sixty poles to two pines and two post oaks, south sixty five west one hundred poles to a post oak and black oak on a ridge thence south twenty five East one hundred and sixty poles to the beginning. Having such form as represented by the above platt. Surveyed the 6th of July 1824
WM. FAUBION) by
Jonathan Wood
JACOB HUFMAN) C.C. Principal
Surveyor of Cocke County

75
ISAAC ALLEN 50 ACRES
State of Tennessee
Cocke County
By virtue of an entry made in the entry takers office for the county aforesaid at Newport of No. 247 dated the 3rd August 1824. I have surveyed for ISAAC ALLEN 50 acres of land in the aforesaid County on the waters of Sinking Creek. Beginning at two white oaks corner to a tract of land owned by said ALLEN running thence with JOHN NEFFS line North eighty Nine and a half poles to a white Oak on the side of a hill South eighty Nine and an half poles to a stake between two white oaks a dogwood and a black oak- East eighty Nine and an half poles to the beginning. Having such form as represented by the above platt.
Surveyed the 7th July 1824
GEO ALLEN) by
Jonathan Wood
JOSEPH ALLEN) C.C. Principal
Surveyor of Cocke County

REUBEN ALLEN 50 ACRES
State of Tennessee
Cocke County
By Virtue of an entry Made in the Entry takers office for Cocke County at Newport of No. 235, dated the 17th day of July 1824. I have surveyed for REUBEN ALLEN 50 acres of land in said County on the waters of Sinking Creek. Beginning at a stake at a poplar and ash corner to said ALLEN and JNO. FREE running south sixty two and a half west One hundred poles to a gum South twenty seven and a half East twenty three poles to a dogwood at the foot of a Mountain then with the same as a boundary south 75 1/2 East twenty seven poles to a stake South forty to a white oak East (leaving said Mountain) Seventy three and one fourth poles to a stake North sixty six poles to a stake On said ALLENS line thence with his line west fourteen poles toa a bush thence a direct line to the beginning. Having such form as represented by the above platt.
Surveyed the 20th July 1824.
WILLIAM CHAMBERS) by
Jonathan Wood
GEORGE ALLEN) C.C. Principal
Surveyor of Cocke County

76
LAX CASE 50 ACRES
State of Tennessee
Cocke County
By virtue of an entry made in the entry takers office for Cocke County at Newport of No. 87, dated the 3rd of June 1824. I have surveyed for LAX CASE fifty acres of land including his Occupant claims on the waters of English Creek. Beginning at an Elm and poplar running South fifty west eighteen poles to a stake on a conditional line with JEREMIAH HARRISON thence with the same North seventy nine west forty one poles to three black Oaks West with said HARRISONS line One hundred and eighty poles to a stake thence North sixty two and an half to a stake East Eighty Nine poles to a stake on North line then with his lines North four West fourteen poles to a stake South twenty three East forty poles to a stake East forty seven poles to a stake then a direct line to the beginning - Having the same form as represented by the above platt.
Surveyed the 6th July 1824
JAMES WILLILAMS) by
Jonathan Wood
MOSES HICKS) C.C. Principal
Surveyor for Cocke County

E. LEA 50 ACRES
State of Tennessee
Cocke County
By virtue of an Entry made in the Entry takers office for Cocke County at Newport of No. 113, dated the 25 of June 1824. I have surveyed for E. LEA fifty acres of land on the waters of McCOWANS Creek. Beginning at a bush near a small branch running thence North forty Nine and an half deg. West two poles and twenty links to a stake near a beech corner to a said LEA and MURPHY thence with said LEA'S line of a deeded tract North fourteen West one hundred and Nine poles to a stake thence North seventy six East sixty three and one fourth poles to a stake near a large poplar thence South fourteen East One hundred and twenty three poles to a stake thence a direct line to the beginning. Having such form as is represented by the above platt.
Surveyed the 26th July 1824 by
ANDREW RAMSEY)
Jonathan Wood
ABNER HIGHTOWER) C.C. Principal
Surveyor for Cocke County

77
JOHN KELLEY 50 ACRES
State of Tennessee
Cocke County
By Virtue of an entry made in the Entry takers office of Cocke County at Newport of No. 77. Dated the 25th May 1824. I have surveyed for JOHN KELLEY 50 acres of land including his Occupant claim on the waters of McCowans Creek Beginning at a locast in a field running South thirty three and an half deg. East forty six poles to a stake on a conditional line with THOMAS SMITH then with ditto North eighty five East crossing the road leading through the Narrows at eighty six poles in all one hundred and twenty six poles and an half to a stake On the side of a steep hill thence North five west seventy five poles to a stake near a White Oak and a dogwood thence a direct line crossing said road to the beginning. Having such form as represented in the above platt. Surveyed the 35th July 1825.
JOHN SMITH) by
Jonathan Wood
JOSEPH WISE) C.C. Principal
Surveyor of Cocke County

78
JOHN GILES 50 ACRES
State of Tennessee
Cocke County
By Virtue of an entry made in the entry takers office of Cocke County at Newport of No. 46, dated the 8th April 1824. Founded on the right of occupancy. I havesurveyed for JOHN GILES fifty acres of land in said County on the waters of Cosby's Creek. Beginning at a small white oak on the North west corner of a field near the foot of a Mountain thence with the same as a boundary North twenty three West two hundred and forty seven poles to a chestnut and a cucumber, North thirty and One fourth East forty two poles to two branches, then conditional line with SAMUEL McGAHA South fifty six East crossing the Indian Camp fork of Cosbys Creek at 50 poles in all 64 poles to a stake on the __?__ of a mountain, then with ditto south seventeen east one hundred and ten poles to a stake thence a direct line to the beginning Having such form as represented by the above platt.
Surveyed the 8th June 1824.
HOLLOWAY GILES) by
Jonathan Wood
SAMUEL McGAHA) C.C. Principal
Surveyor of Cocke County

78
SAMUEL BOYER 60 ACRES
State of Tenn. Cocke County
By virtue of an Entry made in the Entry takers office for Cocke County at Newport of No. 65 dated the 22nd of April 1824. I have surveyed for SAMUEL BOYER sixty acres of land including his occupant claim upon the West side of Big Pigeon River. Beginning at a pine corner to said BOYER granted land then with Ditto South one hundred and three poles toa a black oak-South thirty one East Ninety six poles with JOHN BOYER'S line to a post Oak on GREGG'S line then with the same North eighty seven deg. East thirty poles to a hickory then with conditional lines with McSWEEN North twenty poles to a stake North forty Nine East Ninety eight poles to a black Oak. North fourteen-East Eighty poles to a hickory on JAMES JENNINGS line then with Ditto a direct line to the beginning. Having such form as represented by the above platt. Surveyed the 22nd July 1824
JOHN BOYER) by
Jonathan Wood
ROBERT HENRY) C.C. Principal
Surveyor of Cocke County

79

<u>JOHN GORMAN 24 ACRES</u>

State of Tenn.
Cocke County
By virtue of an Entry made in the entry takers office for the county aforesaid at Newport of No 110 dated the 24 day of June 1824. I have surveyed for JOHN GORMAN twenty four acres of land including his occupant claim on the West side of Big Pigeon River Beginning at three black oak grubs in a sink hole corner to said GORMAN and JAMES JINNINGS running thence with GORMANS line west ninety five poles to a stake, thence South sixty seven and one forth poles to a stake on JINNINGS line then with his line North sixty and an half deg. East Ninety six poles to a black oak near said GORMAN field thence a direct line to the beginning. Having such form as represented by the above platt - Surveyed the twenty third of July 1824

JAMES JINNINGS)
By Jonathan Wood
HOWEL MORRIS) C.C.
Principal Surveyor of Cocke County

80

<u>THOMAS PHELIN 80 ACRES</u>

State of Tenn. - Cocke County
By virtue of an entry made in the entry takers office for said county at Newport of No 115 the 25th of June 1824. I have surveyed for RHOMAS PHELIN eighty acres of land in said County on the waters of McCowans creek. Beginning at a post oak Corner to AIDEN MASON running thence with his line South thirty and a half deg. East one hundred and twenty poles to a beech and same boundary (crossing said creek several times) South sixty and an deg. West nineteen poles to a stake South sixty and a half - West twenty six poles to an ironwood North seventy five and an half - West twenty three poles to a Lynn North fifteen East fourteen and an half poles to holly corner to a tract of land owned by said PHELIN then with the lines there of North forty poles to a dogwood west eighty three poles to a stake thence North seventy eight poles to a stake then a direct line to the beginning. Having such form as represented by the above platt - Surveyed the 28th of July 1824

AND. RAMSEY)
By Jonathan Wood
EPPY LEA) C.C.
Principal Surveyor of Cocke County

<u>ELIJAH AND JEREMIAH HILL 112 ACRES</u>

State of Tenn. - Cocke County
By virtue of an entry made in the entry takers office for the aforesaid county at Newport of No 192 dated the 5th of July 1824. I have surveyed for ELIJAH HILL and JERAMIAH HILL jointly one hundred and twelve acres of land in said county on the South side of Nolochucky River. Beginning at a forked cedar on the bank of said River above the Mouth of Coal hollow running North forty five East one hundred and two poles to a stake South forty five East one hundred and twenty five poles to a stake South forty five deg. West one hundred and sixty six poles to a stake on WILLIAM GRAHAM line then with his lines North ten poles to a hickory West fifteen poles to a stake in the edge of said River then up the same a direct line to the beginning. Having such form as represented by the above platt. Surveyed the 30th 1824

EPPY LEA)
By Jonathan Wood
ISAAC RODGERS) C.C.
Principal Surveyor of Cocke County

81
HENRY MILLS 100 ACRES

State of Tenn. - Cocke County
By Virtue of an entry made in the Entry Takers office for the aforesaid county at Newport of No 93 dated the 8th of June 1824. I have surveyed for HENRY MILLS one hundred acres oflland in said county on the waters of McCowan creek. Beginning at a hickory on a conditional line between him and SIMON SMITH thence with the same North thirty West one hundred and eighty seven poles to a stake then with conditional lines with LEVI SMITH North sixty East fifty two poles to a stake South Seventy East sixty one poles to a white oak South thirty West eighty eightpoles to a stake on North line then with ditto South seventy poles to a Dogwood two white oaks and a hickory then a direct line to the beginning. Having such form as represented by above platt.
Surveyed July 27th 1824 by
JOHN BRIZINDINE)
Jonathan Wood
LEVI SMITH) C.C. Principal
Surveyor of Cocke County

82
JACOB BOYER 100 ACRES

State of Tenn. Cocke County
By virtue of an entry made in the Entry Takers office for the aforesaid county at Newport of No 71 dated the fifteen of May 1824. Founded on rights of Occupancy. I have surveyed for JACOB BOYER one hundred acres of land situate lying and being in the county and state aforesaid on the waters of Clear Creek on both sides of the road leading from Newport to Greeneville. Beginning at a gum corner to said BOYER running with his lines North eleven and an half poles to a black Oak East Ninety five poles to a stump north three and one fourth to a White Oak East two hundred and twenty poles crossing the road at forty two poles to a stake South fourteen poles to a post Oak on MOSES FORBYS line then with his line West one hundred and thirty seven poles to a stake South sixty three and an half poles to a stake West seventy One poles to a stake South fifty poles to a stake West fifty five poles to a stake on said BOYERS line thence with ditto North crossing said road at twenty poles in all seventy six poles to a black west fifty seven poles to a black Oak thence a direct line to the beginning. Having such form as represented by the above platt. Surveyed the 2nd August 1824
AARON BOYER) By
Jonathan Wood
LEWIS BOYER) C.C. Principal
Surveyor of Cocke County

WM FAUBIAN 148 ACRES

State of Tenn. Cocke County
By Virtue of an entrymade in the Entry Takers office of the aforesaid county at Newport of No. 105 dated the 23rd of June 1824. I have surveyed for WILLIAM FAUBIAN one hundred and forty eight acres of land in said county on the North side of French Broad river including a field called the grass field. Beginning at four post oaks running thence South thirteen East forty four poles to a stake on a line of a tract of land owned by said FAUBIAN thence with the lines thereof West forty two poles poles to a post oak South forty six poles to a stake thence East Seventy three poles to three hickory then with Vacant land South one hundred and fifty poles to a stake West one hundred and twenty poles to

a stake North two hundred and forty poles to a stake thence a direct line to the beginning. Having such form as represented by the above platt
Surveyed the 5th July 1824 by
SPENCER FAUBIAN)
Jonathan Wood
JOHN HEADRICK) C.C. Principal
Surveyor Cocke County

84 83
EDAM KINDRICK 50 ACRES
State of Tenn. Cocke County
By Virtue of an entry made in the Entry Takers office of county aforesaid at Newport of No 159 dated the 3rd of July 1824. Founded on rights of Occupancy. I have surveyed and layed off EDAM KINDRICK 50 acres of land lying and being in the county and state aforesaid on the waters of Clear creek. Beginning at a pine PETER FINE'S corner running thence East crossing the road leading from the mouth of Nolochucky to the Warm springs at eighteen poles the same course continued in all one hundred poles to two hickorys and a black Oak thence North eighty poles to a hickory and black Oak West one hundred poles to a poplar and hickory South eighty poles to the beginning. Having such form as represented by the above platt. Surveyed the 3rd August 1824 by
WILLIAM C. STORY)
Jonathan Wood
WM. ROBINSON) C.C. Principal
Surveyor for Cocke County

83
WM. C. STORY 50 ACRES
State of Tenn. Cocke County
By virtue of an entry made in the entry takers office of the aforesaid County at Newport of No 168 dated the 3rd of June 1824. I have surveyed for WM. C. STORY fifty acres of land in said county on the North side of French Broad River. Beginning at a white oak on EDOM KINDRICKS line of a tract called the dry land plantation running thence North sixty three and one fourth poles to two post oak West one hundred and twenty six poles and an half to two sower woods near some lime stone rocks South sixty three and one fourth poles to a white oak East with the said KINDRICKS line one hundred and twenty six poles and an half to the beginning. Having such form as represented by the above platt.
Surveyed the 3rd April 1824 by
WILLIAM ROBINSON)
Jonathan Wood
EDOM KINDRICK) C.C. Principal
Surveyor Cocke County

84
THOMAS FOWLER 200 ACRES
State of Tenn. Cocke County
By Virtue of an entry made in the entry Takers office for the county aforesaid at Newport of No 179 dated the 5th day of July 1824. I have surveyed for THOMAS FOWLER two hundred acres of land in Cocke County on the South side of Clear Creek. Beginning at a White Oak near two caves running thence with conditional lines between his and MOSES FORBY South forty three poles to a stake South sixteen and an half East thirty four poles to a white oak South forty three deg. East twenty six poles to a pine Southforty five and an half East forty eight poles to a hickory North sixty two and an half East forty two poles to a hickory East to WILLIAM FORBION line forty two and an half poles to a post oak then with conditional lines with JOHN FOWLER North sixty two and an half East one hundred and twenty poles to a stake North fifty four poles to a stake

East one hundred and forty seven poles to a white Oak and black Oak on FORBYS line North sixty seven poles to a stake thence a direct line to the beginning. Having such form as represented by the above plott. Surveyed the 9th day of August 1824

SAMUEL FOWLER) By

Jonathan Wood

ABIJAH FOWLER) C.C. Principal

Surveyor of Cocke County

85

THOMAS FOWLER 50 ACRES

State of Tenn. Cocke County

By virtue of an entry made in the Entry Takers office for the county aforesaid at Newport of No 171 dated the 5th of July 1824. I have surveyed for THOMAS FOWLER fifty acres of land on the waters of Clear Creek in said county. Beginning at a stake corner to a fifty acres tract entered in the name of THOMAS FOWLER then with the same North thirty one East one hundred and ten poles to a stake then with conditional line with JOHN F. FOWLER North four degrees West forty nine poles to a stake on the side of a hill North twelve degrees East sixty poles to a stake West sixty five poles to a stake near a spanish Oak and hickory thence a direct line to the beginning. Having such form as represented by the above platt. Surveyed the 9th of August 1824

SAMUAL FOWLER) By

Jonathan Wood

SAMUEL PARROTT) C.C. Principal

Surveyor of Cocke County

GEORGE PARROTT 100 ACRES

State of Tenn. Cocke County

By virtue of an entry made in the entry takers office for the county aforesaid at Newport of No 170 date the fifth of April 1824. I have surveyed for GEORGE PARROTT in said county on the North side of Clear creek. Beginning at two hickorys the Northward corner of a tract of land belonging to said PARROTT called his lower plantation running thence with conditional lines with THOMAS FOWLER North twenty eight deg. West one hundred and fifty five poles to a stake near two hickorys North sixty one and an deg. East One hundred and three poles and an half to a hickory on the side of a ridge- thence South thirty five- East thirty four poles to a dog wood - South sixty two and an half poles to a white oak on a line of twenty acre tract of said PARROTTS then with the same South seventy five - West twenty four poles to a stake in a deep hollow - South forty poles to a stake on a line of said PARROTTS lower plantation thence with the same a direct course to the beginning - Having such form as represented by the above platt.

Surveyed the 10th of August 1824

SAMUEL PARROTT) By

Jonathan Wood

ABIJAH FOWLER) C.C. Principal

Surveyor of Cocke County

86

GEORGE PARROTT 75 ACRES

State of Tenn. Cocke County

By Virtue of an entry made in the Entry Takers office for the county aforesaid at Newport of No 205 dated the 6th of July 1824. I have surveyed for GEORGE PARROTT seventh five acres of land in the aforesaid county on the waters of Oven Creek. Beginning at a Beech corner to THOMAS FOWLER thence running with his lines North sixty seven West twenty two poles to a dogwood on the west side of the Oven creek road South forty nine west five and three fourth poles to a stake South

forty deg. and twenty three Minutes west fifty four and an half to a gum South eighty west fifty six poles to a White Oak and hickory South thirty five East seventy six poles to an ash and walnut on the East side of the road aforesaid South fifty East forty eight poles to a stake South seventy six and an half East seventeen poles to an Ironwood South thirty East twenty one poles to a stake South eighty seven East forty nine poles to a poplar in the head of a hollow North sixty three East forty eight poles to a stake thence a direct line to the beginning. Having such form as represented by the above platt.
Surveyed the 11th of August 1824

SAMUEL FOWLER) By
Jonathan Wood
ABIJAH FOWLER) C.C. Principal
Surveyor of Cocke County

87
JOHN F. FOWLER 200 ACRES

State of Tenn. Cocke County
By Virtue of an entry made in the entry takers office for the county aforesaid at Newport of No 259 - dated the 10th day of August 1824. I have surveyed for JOHN F. FOWLER two hundred acres of land situate lying and being in the county and state aforesaid on the South side of Clear creek including a part of the grassy woods. Beginning at a white oak near two caves corner to THOMAS FOWLER running thence North thirty two deg. East sixty eight and an half poles to a post Oak stump corner to MOSES FAUBION thence with his line North eighty poles to a stake THOMAS FOWLER corner thence with his line South sixty two deg. East twenty poles to a stake South seven West forty poles to a stake East sixty six poles to a stake South forty poles to a stake - North seventy eight East two hundred poles to a hickory - thence South one hundred and twenty poles to a stake thence direct line to the beginning. Having such form as represented by the above platt. Surveyed the 12th of August 1824

SAMUEL FOWLER) By
Jonathan Wood
ABIJAH FOWLER) C.C. Principal
Surveyor of Cocke County

HUGH STUART 30 ACRES

State of Tenn. Cocke County
By virtue of an entry made in the entry takers office for the County of Cocke at Newport of No 91 dated the 7th day of June 1824, entered to increase an entered tract containing one hundred and thirty acres of land on the waters of sinking creek. Beginning at a white oak on the west side of said tract running thence South sixty deg. West forty nine and two tenths poles to a stake - South thirty - East ninety four an a half poles to a white oak on JOHN EBBS line thence with the same South thirty eight and an half - East four and one forth poles to a white oak North sixty deg. East forty eight poles to a stake - thence a direct line to the beginning.
Having such form as represented by the above platt. Surveyed the 13th day of August 1824

JOHN WINTERS) By
Jonathan Wood
MARTIN JUSTICE) C.C. Principal
Surveyor of Cocke County

88
POLLY JUSTICE 50 ACRES

State of Tenn. Cocke County
By virtue of an entry made in the entry takers office for the County aforesaid at Newport of No 11 dated the 5th of April 1824. Founded on rights of Occupancy. I have surveyed for POLLY JUSTICE fifty acres of land in said county on the waters of Meadow creek. Beginning at a small pine on the west side of said branch running thence thirty five deg. West one hundred poles to a post oak thence North fifty five - East seventy nine and one forth poles to a stake near a black oak - South thirty five - East one hundred and one poles to a stake - thence South fifty five - West seventy nine and one forth poles to the beginning. Having such form as represented by the above platt. Surveyed the 13th of August 1824

MARTIN JUSTICE) By
Jonathan Wood
M. LAKE) C.C. Principal
Surveyor of Cocke County

89
DAVID DRISKILL 100 ACRES

State of Tenn. Cocke County
By virtue of an entry made in the entry takers office of the county aforesaid at Newport of No 86 dated the 5th of June 1824. Founded or entered to increase a larger, a deeded tract of twenty five acres. I have surveyed for DAVID DRISKILL twenty acres of land on the South side of Nolochucky River near Slate creek Beginning at a white oak the second corner of said tract running thence with ARTER DAVIS line North eighty four- West fifty four poles to a sourwood- then with conditional line between him and the said DAVIS South seventy six- West one hundred and sixty four poles to a stake thence South fourteen degrees- East one hundred and fifteen poles to a stake at the foot of a steep Nobb thence with same- North fifty eight and a half deg. East fifty seven poles to a stake North thirty three and a half deg. East fourteen poles and a half to a dogwood North sixty one East twenty two and three fourths poles to a beech- North seventy three and one forth deg. East nine and an half poles to a stake corner to his twenty five acre tract- thence with the same North twenty- West eighty poles to a hickory- North seventy one- East eleven poles to a beech North forty- East thirty two poles to a beech North sixty seven- East fifty two poles to a white oak- North thirty- then East thirty nine poles to the beginning. Having such form as represented by the above platt. Surveyed the 16th of August 1824

LEVI SMITH) By
Jonathan Wood
BARTLETT OVERLY) C.C. Principal
Surveyor of Cocke County

THOMAS L. HALE 150 ACRES

State of Tenn. Cocke County
By Virtue of an entry made in the Entry Takers office of said county at Newport No 112 dated the 24th of June 1824. I have surveyed for THOMAS HALE one hundred and fifty acres of land on the South side of Nolochucky river. Beginning at a white oak and sourwood CONNAYS[?] west corner for WESLY RICES running west seventy poles to HALES corner then with his line North twenty West forty poles to a red oak corner to DEMPSEY MOORE, DAVID MOORE, WILLIAM SMITH (jointly) then with his lines North sixty seven and an half deg. West sixty three and one fourth poles to a stake on the side

of a hill North twenty two and an half deg. East one hundred and twenty six poles and a half crossing SMITH'S ford road to a stake on the bank of Nolochucky thence down the meanders of the same North thirty nine West eighty poles north twenty nine poles North ten poles to a locust on the bank of said river then with conditional lines with NEILSON'S South eighty two West crossing SMITH'S ford road at forty four poles in all one hundred and ten poles to a stake South thirty eight East forty three poles to a gum then with BUCKNER'S line South seventy West one hundred and eighteen poles and an half to a stake South Ninety two poles to a stake East forty two poles to a chestnut and hickory South Nine poles to a stake East with MOORES line sixty poles to a chesnut on CONWAY'S line then with ditto a direct line to the beginning. Having such form as represented by the above platt. Surveyed 17th August 1824 by

JOSEPH HALE)
Jonathan Wood
ALBERT ELLISON) C.C. Principal
Surveyor for Cocke County

90
WILLIAM D. NEILSON 100 ACRES

State of Tenn. Cocke County
By Virtue of an entry made in the Entry Takers office for Cocke County at Newport of No 197 dated the 5th of July 1824. I have surveyed for WILLIAM D. NEILSON one hundred acres of land situate lying and being in the county aforesaid on the South side of Nolochucky River. Beginning at a white oak the beginning corner of WM BUCKNER tract of land running thence with the same North fifty four poles to a stake East fifty five poles to three sourwoods and a white oak on THOS. L. HALES line then with ditto North sixty nine poles to a black gum and dogwood thence with BUCKNER'S line West one hundred and fifty and one fourth poles to a stake South one hundred and twenty three poles to a stake East ninety nine and one fourth polea to the beginning. Having such form as represented by the above platt. Surveyed the 18th August 1824

JOHN BUCKNER) by
Jonathan Wood
EDWARD BUCKNER) C.C. Principal
Surveyor of Cocke County

91
WILLIAM D. NEILSON 65 ACRES

State of Tennessee Cocke County
By Virtue of an entry Made in the entry takers office for Cocke County at Newport of No 175. Dated the 5th July 1824. I have surveyed for WILLIAM D. NEILSON sixty five acres of land situate lying in the County and state aforesaid on the South side of Nola Chucky river Beginning at a stake corner to JAMES BUCKNER and THOS. L. HALES line running then with his lines North seven and one fourth deg. East twelve poles to a gum North thirty eight West fourty three poles to a stake North eighty two deg. East one hundred and ten poles to a locust on the bank of Nola Chuckey river thence down the river North twenty two West forty One poles to a gum on the line of the lines of STEPHEN SMITHS Deed then with the same West one hundred and fifty four poles to a beech Corner to JOHN SMITH thence South eighty deg. East one hundred poles to a stake corner to JAMES BUCKNER then with his line East Seventy poles to the beginning. Having such form as represented by the above platt.

Surveyed the 18th August 1824 by
JAMES BUCKNER) J. Wood
JOHN BRIZENDINE) C.C. Principal
Surveyor for Cocke County

91
DANIEL MOORE 17 ACRES
State of Tennessee Cocke County
By Virtue of an entry Made in the entry takers office for Cocke County at Newport of No. 116 dated the 25th June 1824 founded on the right of Occupancy. I have surveyed for DANIEL MOORE Seventeen acres of [land] situate lying in Cocke County on the waters of Nobb Creek Beginning at a sourwood On CONWAYS line running thence with THOMAS L. HALES line West fifty Nine poles to a stake On WILLIAM BUCKNERS line thence with the same forty six and an half poles to a stake near a large white Oak East with a conditional line between the said DANIEL MOORE and ROBERT MOORE fifty Nine poles to CONWAYS line then with Ditto forty six and an half poles to the beginning. Having such form as represented by the above platt. Surveyed the 9th August 1824 by
WILLIAM RAMSEY)
Jonathan Wood
JONATHAN WOOD) C.C. Principal
Surveyor of Cocke County

92
WILLIAM GRANT 50 ACRES
State of Tenn. Cocke County
By virtue of an entry Made in the entry takers office for the aforesaid county at Newport No. 184 Dated the 5th July 1824. I have surveyed for WILLIAM GRANT fifty acres of land in said county on the waters of sinking Cane Creek Beginning at a hickory of DAVID SHIELDS line running thence with the same East one hundred and eighty five poles to a stake near BROOD HURST'S line thence South sixty Nine poles to a stake on BROOD HURST'S line thence with his line South forty eight West sixty one poles to a post Oak West eleven poles to a white Oak corner to SHIELDS then with his line North seventy five and an half poles to a stake West Ninety poles to a stake then with said GRANTS line to a one hundred and sixty acre tract North fourteen poles to a black Oak West forty poles to a stake North sixteen poles to the beginning. Having such form as represented by the above platt.
Surveyed the 25th August 1824 by
WILLIAM FORBIAN)
Jonathan Wood
JACOB HUFMAN) C.C Principal
Surveyor of Cocke County

93
JACOB FAUBION 50 ACRES
State of Tennessee Cocke County
By Virtue of an entry made in the Entry Takers office of Cocke County aforesaid at Newport of No 23 dated April 5th 1824. I have surveyed for JACOB FAUBION fifty acres of land in said county on the waters of Sinking Cane creek. Beginning at the North East corner of a tract of land where he now lives on a stake running North thirty one and three fourth poles to a stake then with conditional lines with WILLIAM GRANT West twenty eight poles to a hickory bush South eighty five West ten poles to a white Oak South sixty eight West eighty six poles to two pines North seventy five West seventy poles to a post Oak and hickory North twenty one West One hundred and nine poles to a black oak thence with Vacant land West thirty two poles to a stake- South seventy three poles to a stake on WILLIAM FORBIONS line then with ditto South fifty and one half- East seventy seven poles to a pine corner to JACOB FAUBION

then with his line East two hundred poles to the beginning. Having such form as represented by the above platt. Surveyed the 4th of August 1824 by

WILLIAM FORBION) Jonathan Wood

JOSEPH BROADHURST) C.C. Principal Surveyor of Cocke County

94 95

THOMAS FOWLER 119 ACRES

State of Tennessee Cocke County

By virtue of an entry made in the entry takers office for said county at Newport of No. 104 dated the 23rd of June 1824. I have surveyed for THOMAS FOWLER one hundred and nineteen acres of land in said County on the North side of Clear Creek. Beginning at a white Oak on a line of a tract of land of said FOWLERS- thence with the same North sixteen deg. East sixteen poles and an half to a white oak and dogwood on a line of a fifty acre tract of land of said FOWLERS- thence with the same North sixteen deg. East sixteen and one half poles to a white oak and on a line of a fifty acre tract of said FOWLERS thence with Ditto North twenty four and an half- East sixteen poles to a stake- North sixty eight deg. West sixty poles to a dogwood- South eighty five- West crossing the road to Oven Creek at 26 poles in all 90 1/2 poles to a stake North with another tract of said FOWLERS land one hundred and thirty and an half poles to two gums thence with Ditto West sixty three and three tenth poles to a stake- South three and an half poles to an ash then with conditional lines with BRIANT West six poles to a stake North ten West Ninety two poles to a stake with conditional line with JOHN F. FOWLER- South seventy East one hundred and thirty five poles to a sourwood near a dry branch- South fifty seven- East twenty one and three forths poles to a black Oak South twenty two and one half- East eleven poles and an half to a hickory- South sixty one East twenty two and an half poles to a white oak- North seventy five East thirty three and an half poles to a stake near the Morgin of the aforesaid road then with conditional lines with PARROTT South fourty four deg. and twenty three Minutes- West fifty four and an half poles to a gum- South thirty five- East seventy six poles to an ash and walnut by the side of said then with conditional lines with JOHN F. FOWLER, South five West twenty two poles to a poplar South forty and an half- East eight and an half poles to a white oak- North eighty seven East six poles to a post oak stump South seventy eight East twenty two poles to a post oak stump South seventy eight East twenty two poles to a post oak- North thirty two poles to a post oak- East fifteen and an half poles to PARROTT line, then with his lines South thirty East two poles to a stake- South eighty seven- East eighteen poles to a stake then with JOHN F. FOWLERS conditional lines South thirty two and an half- East fifty three poles to a white oak South five West thirteen and an half poles to a chesnut oak- South seven East forty four to a spanish oak the conditional line with PARROTT- South sixty six- West twelve poles to a locust North forty six- West twenty nine poles to the beginning. Having such form as represented by the above platt- Surveyed the 11th day of August 1824 by

ABIJAH FOWLER) Jonathan Wood

SAMUEL PARROTT) C.C. Principal Surveyor of Cocke County

95
WILLIAM SOLOMON 50 ACRES

State of Tennessee Cocke County
By virtue of an entry made in the entry takers office for said county at Newport of No 62 dated the 11th of June 1824- Founded on right of occupancy. I have surveyed and laid off fifty acres of land for WILLIAM SOLOMON, situate lying in said county of Neeleys creek, waters of Nolochuckey river. Beginning at a white oak corner to SOLOMONS deeded land thence with HARLE line South eighty- East twenty poles to a stake then with conditional line with said HARLE- South six- East forty poles to a stake- South forty six- East one hundred poles to a stake on the side of a steep hill thence one and one half- East eighty two poles to a stake thence with vacant- North thirty six- East eighty five poles to a stake thence with JARNAGAN'S line North- Sixty eight and an half West thirty one poles to a dogwood- North twelve and an half East fourteen poles to a beech- North twenty and one fourth - East nine and an half poles to a sourwood- North seventy one and an half- East twenty poles to a stake on the line of a 150 acre tract belonging to said SOLOMON- thence with the same- a direct line to the beginning. Having such form as represented by the above platt.
Surveyed the 17th day of June 1824 by
WM BRAGG)
Jonathan Wood
JAMES SOLOMON) C.C.
Principal Surveyor of Cocke County

96
THOMAS CHRISTIAN 60 ACRES

State of Tenn. Cocke County
By virtue of an entry made in the entry takers office for Cocke County at Newport of No. 14 dated the 5th day of April 1824. Founded on the right of occupancy. I have surveyed for THOMAS CHRISTIAN sixty acres of land in said county on the waters of Clay creek. Beginning at a ash corner to said CHRISTIAN running thence with his lines North fifteen- East twenty eight poles to a black oak- North fifty four West eighty eight poles to a gum- North forty seven and one half- East eighty poles to a white oak- North sixty five- East sixty poles to a stake- North eighty eight and an half- West one hundred and four poles to a black oak and a dogwood near a road South fourteen and one fourth- West sixty nine poles to a black oak- South seventy one and an half- West forty six poles to a white oak- South thirty seven- West forty poles to a white oak- East seventy three poles to a hickory- South forty Nine- East forty five poles to a stake- East twenty two poles to the beginning- Having such form as represented by the above platt- Surveyed the 12th of April 1824
JOHN HALE)
Jonathan Wood
JAMES CHRISTIAN) C.C. Principal
Surveyor of Cocke County

97
ELIZABETH LAX 96 ACRES

State of Tenn. Cocke County
By virtue of an entry made in the entry takes office for said county at Newport of No. 82 dated the 3rd of June 1824. I have surveyed for ELIZABETH LAX ninety six acres of land including her Occupant claim on the waters of BOGARD creek. Beginning on an ash, dogwood and hickory near a branch running thence South three and a half- East ninety one poles crossing a steep hill to a stake- East forty one poles to two white oaks, then

with conditional with BUTLER North forty deg. East twenty two and an half poles to a hickory North seventy six and one fourth- East twenty five poles to a chesnut- North eighty three and an half- East eighty three poles to a stake on a line of BUTLERS surveyed land then with the same North fifty seven and an half- East fifteen poles to a poplar- North thirty- West ninety six poles to a stake- West forty one poles- South thirty one and an half poles to a black oak and white oak North seventy and an half- West forty four poles to a white oak- North seventy and an half West forty four poles to a white oak North seventy and an half- West twenty poles to a stake North seventy West seventeen poles South one and an [half] poles to the beginning- Having such form as represented by the above platt- Surveyed the 7th July 1824

JAMES WILLIAMS) By
Jonathan Wood
MOSES HICKS) C.C. Principal
Surveyor of Cocke County

98

THOMAS E. CHRISTIAN 50 ACRES

State of Tenn. Cocke County
By virtue of an entry made in the entry takers office for the said county at Newport of No 41 dated the 8th of April 1824. I have surveyed for THOMAS E. CHRISTIAN fifty acres of land including his occupant claim on the waters of Clay Creek. Beginning at a white oak corner to a tract of land where on he now lives running thence with conditional lines with THOMAS CHRISTIAN SENR. South eighty two and an half deg. West eighty eight poles to a stake South sixteen and an half deg. East seventy five poles to a stake on ANTHONY CHRISTIONS line then with the same East eighty two poles to some hickory bushes on the said THOMAS E. CHRISTIANS od a seven acre tract then North the lines of the same North ten poles to a white oak East seventy four poles to a stake on the top of a ridge thence with vacant land North twenty seven and an half poles to a stake on BRIANTS line then with his line West three and a half poles to a white oak North forty six poles to a stake then with vacant land West twenty two and a half poles to a stake on or near said CHRISTIANS line with his line South forty poles to a stake South five West twelve and an half poles to a hickory South sixty eight West twenty two poles to a sugar tree North thirty six West fourteen poles to an ironwood thence a direct line to the beginning- Having such form as represented by the above platt. Surveyed the 9th of June 1824

JOHN LOVELL) By
Jonathan Wood
JOHN HALL) C.C. Principal
Surveyor of Cocke County

JOHN HOOD 60 ACRES

State of Tenn. Cocke County
By virtue of an entry made in the Entry Taker's office for Cocke County at Newport of No 95 dated the eight day of June 1824. I have surveyed for JOHN HOOD sixty acres of land including his occupant claim on the waters of Cosby's Creek. Beginning at a stake near a large black Oak marked mouth and eyes on the West side of a field running thence North twenty three deg. East one hundred and eighteen poles to a white Oak South sixty seven East eighty nine poles to a black oak South seventy three West ninety seven poles to a stake on or near said HOOD line of a tract of land where on he now lives thence a direct line to the beginning. Having such form as represented by the above platt. Surveyed the 21st of September 1824

ABRAHAM DENTON) By
Jonathan Wood
JAS. CARTER) C.C. Principal
Surveyor of Cocke County

99
JOHN LANE 100 ACRES

State of Tenn. Cocke County
By virtue of an entry made in the Entry Takers office for said county at Newport of No 150 dated the 3rd of July 1824. I have surveyed for JOHN LANE one hundred acres of land including his occupant claim on the waters of English Creek. Beginning at a stake on a conditional line between his and JOHN HOOD North fourteen deg. East one hundred and three poles to a stake on a line of a tract where on he now lives thence with the line thereof West thirty poles to a walnut stump in a field North Ninety two poles to a post Oak East twenty poles to a hickory North twenty two poles to a stake thence six and an half poles to a black Oak then with conditional lines with BRUDON South forty six West seventeen poles to a hickory South fifty seven poles to a white Oak South fifty two and an half deg. West twenty one poles to a black Oak then with vacant land South one hundred and three poles to a stake East Ninety poles to the beginning. Having such form as represented by the above platt. Surveyed the 31st day of September 1824
JOHN HOOD)
By Jonathan Wood
WM LANE) C.C.
Principal Surveyor of Cocke County

100
WILLIAM LOUIS 50 ACRES

State of Tenn. Cocke County
By virtue of an entry made in the Entry Taker's office for said county at Newport of No 153 dated the 3rd day of July 1824. I have surveyed for WILLIAM LOUIS fifty acres of land including his occupant of the waters of Bogard Creek. Beginning at a white oak near the bank of said creek running thence North twenty eight and an half deg. West sixty three and 1/4 poles to a chesnut and chesnut Oak near a dry branch thence South sixty one and an half West one hundred and twenty six and an half poles to two persimmons bushes near a large poplar South twenty eight and an half deg. East sixty three and one fourth poles to crossing said creek to a stake, thence North sixty and an half poles crossing said creek to the beginning. Having such form as is represented by the above platt. Surveyed the 22nd day of September 1824 by
WM GREGORY) Jonathan Wood
ARCHIBALD GREGORY) C.C. Principal Surveyor of Cocke County

WILLIAM VINSON 50 ACRES

State of Tenn. Cocke County
By Virtue of an entry made in the entry takers office for said county at Newport of No 180 dated the 5th of July 1824. I have surveyed for WILLIAM VINSON fifty acres of land on the East side of Big Pigeon River. Beginning at a white oak on a line of said VINSON near the falling branch running thence South thirty five and an half Deg. East eighty four poles to a spanish oak thence South fifty four and an half west one hundred and seven poles to a stake thence North thirty five and an half deg. West sixty six poles and an half poles to a stake on said VINSONS line- then with Ditto a direct line to the beginning. Having such form as is represented by the above platt.
Surveyed the 24th of September 1824
ANDERSON VINSON) By Jonathan Wood
JOHN VINSON) C.C. Principal Surveyor of Cocke County

101
SAMUEL BROYLES 25 ACRES [75 acres]
State of Tenn. Cocke County
By Virtue of an entry made in the entry takers office for said county at Newport of No 118 dated the 26th of June 1824. I have surveyed for SAMUEL BRPYLES seventy five acres of land lying on both sides of Cosbys Creek. Beginning at a post Oak SAMUEL BROYLES corner to a tract of land whereon he now lives, running thence with Ditto North thirty West fifty three poles to a locust stump in Cosby's creek road North thirty Nine East eighteen and three fourths poles to a dogwood in the Margin of said road corner to WEAVER, then with his lines South seventy six- West forty two poles to a dogwood North twenty five West sixty eight poles crossing Cosby's creek to a white oak thence South sixty five West sixty one poles to a stake then with GILES lines South ten and an half deg. East twelve poles crossing said creek to a white oak South seventeen East eighty eight poles to a sourwood near a steep clift thence with Ditto South fifty East fifty three and an half poles to a hickory of GILLILANDS line then with Ditto East thirty two poles to a stake thence a direct line to the beginning- Having such form as is represented by the above platt- Surveyed the 23rd of September 1824.
JAMES GILLILAND) By
Jonathan Wood
ABRAHAM LILLARD) C.C. Principal
Surveyor of Cocke County

102
PHILLIP JENKINS 50 ACRES

State of Tennessee Cocke County
By virtue of an entry made in the entry takers office for said county at Newport of No 252 dated the 5th of August 1824. I have surveyed for PHILLIP JENKINS fifty acres of land on Ground hog creek. Beginning at a beech near the head of a branch called the falling branch running thence South twenty five deg. East sixty three and one fourth poles to a stake thence South fifty five West one hundred poles to two dogwoods near the foot of a mountain thence with the same North fifty five and an half degrees West forty four poles and one fourth to a beech corner to a tract of land of said JENKINS then with the same North sixty four degrees West seven poles to a stake North twenty five West twenty nine poles to a stake thence a direct line to the beginning. Having such form as represented by the above platt.
Surveyed the 22nd of September 1824.
JESSE JENKINS) By
Jonathan Wood
JOEL JENKINS) C.C. Principal
Surveyor of Cocke County

PHILLIP JENKINS 50 ACRES

State of Tenn. Cocke County
By virtue of an entry made in the Entry Takers office at Newport of No 101 dated the 19th June 1824. I have surveyed for PHILLIP JENKINS fifty acres of land including his Occupant claim on Ground Hog creek. Beginning at a buch [bush] near a field thence down the creek by a mountain North sixty Nine and an half deg. West one hundred and four poles to a buch South eighty seven and an half West eleven poles and an half to a buch South fifty five West twelve poles to a spruce pine thence South twelve deg. West fifty six poles to a large bunch of laurel at the foot of a mountain thence South seventy three and an half East one hundred and twenty four poles to a stake thence a direct line to the beginning. Having represented such form as represented by the above platt.
JESSE JENKINS) By
Jonathan Wood
JOEL JENKINS) C.C. Principal
Surveyor of Cocke County

103
WILLIAM GRANT 50 ACRES

State of Tenn. Cocke County
By Virtue of an entry made in the Entry Takers office for said county at Newport of No 123 and dated the 28th of June 1824. I have surveyed for WILLIAM GRANT fifty two acres of land in said county on the waters of Meadow creek a branch of the Nolochucky river. Beginning at a chesnut tree mark W.W. standing on a line of a twenty acre tract of said GRANTS running thence North one hundred and thirty poles to a stake between a spanish oak and chesnut and sourwood thence last [East] sixty five poles to a chesnut thence South one hundred and thirty poles to a sourwood thence West sixty five poles to the beginning. Having such form as represented by the above platt.
Surveyed the 27th day of September 1824
AMOS FORESTER) By Jonathan Wood
JERIMIAH HONSLEY?) C.C. Principal Surveyor of Cocke County

WM C STORY 50 ACRES

State of Tenn. Cocke County
By virtue of an entry made in the entry takers office for the county aforesaid at Newport of No 125 dated the 29th of June 1824. I have surveyed for WILLIAM C. STORY fifty acres of land including his improvement on the North side of French Broad river. Beginning at a pine on the top of a high clift of rocks corner to EDOM KINDRICKS dry land plantation running thence along said clift. South seventy Nine East fifteen poles and an half to a spanish oak- thence with a conditional line with MOSES FAUBION North twenty Nine deg. East crossing the road leading from Newport of Greeneville one hundred and eighty two poles to a white oak on the North side of a hill thence West Ninety two and three fourths poles to a sourwood stump thence with KINDRICKS line direct line crossing said road to the beginning. Having such form as represented by the above platt. Surveyed the 29th of September 1824 By -
ISAAC TILLERY) Jonathan Wood
WM ROBINSON) C.C. Principal Surveyor of Cocke County

104
WM HUFF 100 ACRES

State of Tennessee Cocke County
By virtue of an entry made in the entry takers office for the County aforesaid at Newport of No 58 dated the 9th of April 1824. I have surveyed for WILLIAM HUFF one hundred acres of land including his improvement or occupant claim on the North side of French Broad river. Beginning at a poplar and sugar tree corner to a seven acre tract of said HUFF running West one hundred and twelve poles to a stake - South nine deg. East with NOBBS one hundred and an half poles to a stake on a line of said HUFF deeded land then with Ditto South seventy three - East one hundred and fourteen poles to a stake near a black Oak - South sixty three poles to a stake corner to JAMES STEPHENS old survey then with Ditto East eighty two poles to a stake corner to a twenty five acre tract of said HUFF - then with the same North sixty two and an half - West sixty poles to a beech - North fifty - West 18 poles to a stake - North fifty two poles to a stake North thirty three poles to a stake - South forty seven - East ten poles to a stake - North sixty poles to a stake - thence a direct line to the beginning. Having such form as

represented by the above platt. Surveyed the 15th of April 1824
JOHN LENNING) By
Jonathan Wood
JAMES ROBBS) C.C. Principal
Surveyor of Cocke County

105
<u>SUSANAH CLARK 8 ACRES</u>

State of Tennessee Cocke County
By virtue of an entry made in the entry takers office for the aforesaid county at Newport of No 246 dated the 2nd day of August 1824. I have surveyed for SUSANAH CLARK eight acres of land covered with the water of French Broad river including a fish trap. Beginning at a stake on the North side of Said river on ANDREW RAMSEYS line at the bluff running thence up the river. South forty one deg. East thirty two poles to an ironwood on the bank of the river thence forty Nine deg. West forty poles to a rock in said river thence down said river North forty one West thirty two poles to a rock in said river thence North forty Nine East forty poles to the beginning- Having such form as represented by the above platt. Surveyed the 10th of October 1824
JOHN CLARK) By
Jonathan Wood
CHARLES TALLEY) C.C. Principal
Surveyor of Cocke County

<u>JOSEPH SELVESTER 50 ACRES</u>

State of Tenn. Cocke County
By virtue of an entry made in the entry takers office of said county at Newport of No 124 dated the 29th of June 1824. I have surveyed for JOSEPH SELVESTER fifty acres of land including his imprivement on the waters of Indian Creek. Beginning at a stake near a dogwood on the North side of the Sevierville Road running thence North fifty four and an half deg. East crossing said road at the poles and Ditto at thirty poles the same course contained in all sixty three and one fourth poles to a white oak North thirty five and an half deg. West one hundred and twenty six and an half poles to a black oak and spanish oak South fifty four and an half deg. West sixty three and an half poles to a hickory and dogwood on the west side of a branch- thence a direct line to the beginning. Having such form as represented by the above platt - Surveyed the 11th of October 1824
REUBEN ALLEN) By
Jonathan Wood
JOHN ELLIS) C.C. Principal
Surveyor of Cocke County

106
<u>ROBIN HOOD 40 ACRES</u>

Stae of Tenn. Cocke County
By virtue of an entry made in the Entry Takers office for the aforesaid county at Newport of No 92 dated the 8th of June 1824. I have surveyed for ROBIN HOOD forty acres of land on the West side of Big Pigeon River. Beginning at a stake on MARY FINIS line corner to JOHN GORMAN running with said GORMAN'S line North seventy one and an half poles to a stake then with JOHN NEFF'S line West eighty seven and three fourths poles to a stake near a white oak on the side of a hill South seventy four and an half poles to a stake on said HOOD'S line then with the same East forty four and one fourths poles to a pine thence North with MARY FINIS line three poles to a hickory East forty three poles to the beginning. Having such form as represented by the above Platt. Surveyed the 12th day of

October 1824 by
ISAAC NEFF)
Jonathan Wood
JOHN NEFF) C.C.
Principal Surveyor of Cocke County

107
JOHN WORTH 32 ACRES

State of Tennessee Cocke County
By Virtue of an entry made in the Entry Takers office for said county at Newport of No. 94 dated the 8th of June Founded on rights of priority to increase a deed tract. I have surveyed for JOHN WORTH thirty acres of land on the waters of Slate Creek. Beginning at a white Oak on said WORTH'S line running thence with same South sixty poles to INMAN'S line the same courses continues therewith in all from the beginning eighty six poles to a stake near a beech East sixty poles to a stake North eighty six poles to a stake on said WORTH'S line then with the same West sixty poles to the beginning. Having such form as is represented by the above platt. Surveyed the 22nd day of October 1824, by
HENRY MILLS)
Jonathan Wood
ABEL LOFTY) C.C. Principal
Surveyor of Cocke County

POLLY DAVIS 50 ACRES

State of Tennessee Cocke County
By Virtue of an entry made in the Entry Takers office for the aforesaid county at Newport of No. 163 dated the 3rd of July 1824. I have surveyed for POLLY DAVIS fifty acres of land including his [sic] occupant claim on the middle fork of Cosbys Creek. Beginning at a white Oak corner to JOSEPH DUMIS running thence North thirty deg. West one hundred and seven poles to a black Oak on the top of a ridge North 53 East seventy five poles to a dogwood South thirty seven East one hundred and seven poles to a stake then South fifty West seventy five poles to the beginning. Having such form as represented by the above platt. Surveyed the 14th February 1825 by
JOHN BRIANT)
Jonathan Wood
THOMAS BRIANT) C.C. Principal
Surveyor of Cocke County

WM REYNOLDS, MERRYMAN PAYNE AND GEORGE T. GILLESPIE 50 ACRES

State of Tennessee Cocke County
By Virtue of an entry made in the entry takers office of said county at Newport of No. 224 dated the 10th day of July 1824. I have surveyed for WILLIAM REYNOLDS, MERRYMAN PAYNE and GEORGE T. GILLESPIE fifty acres of land on the waters of Wolf creek above the big falls of said creek on the West side there of on the East side of the Brushey Mountains including two Ore banks supposed to be lead. Beginning at a rock Marked W running thence North eighty Nine and a half poles to a stake on the side of a Mountain Near a chestnut, dogwood and hickory Marked as pointers and a rock Marked R. thence East eighty Nine and an half poles to two bushes of laurel thence south eighty nine and a half poles to a spruce pine on the bank of a small branch thence West eighty Nine and a half poles to the beginning. Having such form as represented by the above platt - Surveyed the 3rd of November 1824
THOMAS REYNOLDS) By
Jonathan Wood
JAMES RUSSEL) C.C. Principal
Surveyor of Cocke County

JOHN EISENHOUR 50 ACRES

State of Tennessee Cocke County
By virtue of an entry made in the entry takers office for the aforesaid county at Newport of No 186 dated the 5th day of July 1824. I have surveyed for JOHN EISENHOUR fifty acres of land on the waters of Clear Creek. Beginning at a post Oak on said EISENHOURS line running thence North five and an half deg. East one hundred and twenty six poles and an half to a white oak and Maple North eighty four and a half - West sixty three and one fourth poles to a stake in a hollow thence South five and an half deg. West one hundred and twenty six poles and an half to a stake on or near said EISENHOURS line then with or nearly with the same a direct line to the beginning. Having such form as represented by the above platt. Surveyed the 27th of December 1824

DANIL BLAZER) By
Jonathan Wood
PETER EISENHOUR) C.C. Principal
Surveyor of Cocke County

109
JONATHAN DENTON 50 ACRES

State of Tennessee Cocke County
By virtue of an entry made in the entry takers office for the aforesaid county at Newport of No 147 dated the 2nd of July 1824. I have surveyed for JONATHAN DENTON fifty acres of land on the waters of Cosby's Creek. Beginning on a hickory corner to said DENTON running thence with HUFF'S line North thirty three West four poles to a hickory South thirty eight and an half West ninety and an half poles to ablack oak - North fifty two and an half west eleven poles to a stake on THOMAS DENTON'S line then with Ditto North four East crossing the Cocby's Creek road at fifty poles the same course continued in all one hundred and forty one to a stake South eighty six - East thirty one poles to a stake then south twenty nine East thirty one poles crossing the aforesaid road to a post oak corner to JOHN ALLEN then with his line South sixty three last sixty two poles to two black oak corner to said DENTON then with his line South fifty six - West forty two poles to the beginning. Having such form as is represented by the above platt.
Surveyed the 16th of November 1824

SAMUEL DENTON) By
Jonathan Wood
JOHN ROBERTS) C.C. Principal
Surveyor of Cocke County

110
STEPHEN LEA 50 ACRES

State of Tennessee Cocke County
By virtue of an entry made in the entry takers office for the aforesaid county at Newport of No 33 dated the 5th of April 1824. I have surveyed for STEPHEN LEA fifty acres of land on the North side of Big Pigeon River. Beginning at a black oak on WILLIAM VINSONS line running thence with the same South seventy eight poles to a white oak, black oak and walnut at the foot of a rocky ridge then with the same South seventy five degrees East one hundred poles to two chesnuts North one hundred and three poles to a stake - West ninety six poles to the beginning. Having such form as represented by the above platt.
Surveyed the 17th of February 1825

PEASANT LOYD) By
Jonathan Wood
JAMES LEA) C.C. Principal
Surveyor of Cocke County

ABRAHAM LILLARD 50 ACRES

State of Tennessee Cocke County
By Virtue of an entry made in the entry takers office for the aforesaid county at Newport of No 276 dated the 27th day of August 1824. I have surveyed for ABRAHAM LILLARD fifty acres of land lying on the waters of Cosby's creek. Beginning at a sour wood on the WILLIAM WILLHEIGHT line running thence with the same South seventy three deg. West seventy poles to a leaning poplar thence South seventeen deg. East one hundred and eight poles to a walnut on the side of Neddy's Mountain thence North seventy three degrees East seventy four and an half poles to a hickory thence North seventy two deg. West one hundred and eighty poles to a stake - South seventy three West four and an half poles to the beginning, including a place called the grape vine thicket - Having such form as represented by the above Plott   Surveyed the 15th day of February 1825

ROBERT GILLILAND) By
Jonathan Wood
JOHN WOOD) C.C. Prin. Sur.
of Cocke County

111

CLEMENT HOOPER 50 ACRES

State of Tennessee Cocke County
By virtue of an entry made in the entry takers office for the aforesaid county at Newport of No 137 dated the 30th of June 1824. I have surveyed for CLEMENT HOOPER fifty acres of land including his occupant on the main fork of Wolf creek. Beginning at a White pine near the bank of said creek running thence up the same and with Mountain South twenty two degrees West one hundred and fourteen poles to a large spruce pine South seven and a half degrees - West thirty eight to a poplar South twenty two and an half - West ten poles to a spruce pine and black gum thence South sixty eight deg. East fifty poles to a stake on the side of a Mountain - thence along the same North ten deg. East one hundred and seventy poles to a stake - thence a direct line to the beginning - Having such form as is represented by the above plott - Surveyed the 2nd of November 1824

THOMAS REYNOLDS) By
Jonathan Wood
WM. REYNOLDS) C.C. Prin. Sur.
of Cocke County

F. J. CARTER 84 ACRES

State of Tennessee Cocke County
By virtue of an entry made in the entry takers office for the aforesaid County at Newport of No 165 dated 3rd day of July 1824. I have surveyed for FRANCIS J. CARTER eighty four acres of land on the South side of French Broad river on the waters of Kenny's branch. Beginning at a dog wood in a hollow the North East corner of a tract of land granted by the state of Tennessee to WILLIAM WOOD running thence North one hundred and sixty poles to a hickory West eighty two poles to a dog wood and sweet gum thence south one hundred and sixty seven poles to a stake on the line aforesaid tract of WOODS then with the same a direct line to the beginning - Having such form as is represented by the above platt - Surveyed the 11th of February 1825

SHEPPY PUCKETT) By
Jonathan Wood
FRANCIS PUCKETT) C.C. Principal
Surveyor of Cocke County

112
CLEMENT HOOPER 50 ACRES

State of Tennessee - Cocke County
By Virtue of an Entry Made in the Entry Takers office for the aforesaid county at Newport of No. 136 dated the 30th June 1824. I have surveyed for CLEMENT HOOPER fifty acres of land including the improvement of the dry fork of Wolf Creek. Beginning at a beech on the South side of said Creek running thence South sixty Eight deg. East one hundred and twenty six and one half poles to a stake Near two locusts and a chesnut tree, thence South Twenty two deg. West sixty three and one fourth poles to two white Oaks on the side of a Ridge thence North sixty Eight deg. West one Hundred and twenty six and one half poles to a white pine North twenty two deg. - East sixty three and one fourth poles to the beginning - Having such form as represented by the above platt. Surveyed the 3rd November 1825

WILLIAM REYNOLDS) By
Jonathan Wood
THOMAS REYNOLDS) C.C. Principal
Surveyor for Cocke County

113
JESSE SMITH 12 ACRES

State of Tennessee Cocke County
By Virtue of an entry made in the Entry takers office for the aforesaid county of Cocke at Newport of No. 304 dated the 14th day of December 1824. I have surveyed for JESSEE SMITH twelve acres of land on the waters of Neeleys creek - Beginning at a sweet gum sapling on or near his line running thence with or nearly with *TSPRIPS[?] line South eighty nine and one half West seventy one poles to a stake near two horn beams and a hickory thence North one half a deg. West forty poles to a stake on the side of a hill North eighty nine and one half East forty Eight poles to a stake on said SMITHS line thence with the same South thirty poles to a large Oak stump East twenty five poles to a stake thence a direct line to the beginning. Having such form as is represented by the above platt - Surveyed 27th day of January 1825 by

*NATHAN TRPREP[?]) Jonathan
Wood
JAMES MASON) C.C.

*The longhand copy is giving the typist trouble. It is certain that the name is not as it looks, possible some ss's misread for p's.

BEGIMA [sic] DAVIS 50 ACRES

State of Tennessee Cocke County
By Virtue of an Entry made in the Entry takers office for the above said county at Newport of No 283 dated the 11th day of October 1824 I have surveyed for BEGIMON DAVIS fifty acres of land on the waters of Big creek Beginning on a white Oak corner to JAMES NICHOLS and JOHN STOKELY lines running thence with said STOKELY line South forty Eight degrees and thirty Minutes East one hundred and thirty six poles and one half to a stake in a hollow thence forty one deg. and thirty Minutes East sixty three and one fourth poles to a pine North forty Eight deg. and thirty Minutes West one hundred and twenty six poles and one half to a post Oak on the top of the ridge Thence a direct line to the beginning. Having such form as is represented by the above platt. Surveyed the 30th day of November 1824

ROYAL STOKELY) By
Jonathan Wood
JAMES NICHOLS) C.C. Principal
Surveyor of Cocke County

114

EPPY LEA 50 ACRES

State of Tennessee Cocke County
By Virtue of an entry made in the entry takers office for the aforesaid county at Newport of No 245 dated the 29th day of July 1824. I have surveyed for EPPY LEA fifty acres of land on the south side of Nolychucky river near the Mouth there of. Beginning at a stake near a beech on a line of a tract of land belonging to said LEA running thence North seventy six deg. East thirty four poles to a hickory on the side of a steep hill North fourteen West seventy six poles to a stake eight poles from a Marked Iron wood South seventy six West one hundred and twenty two poles to a stake eight poles above a Spanish Oak on the side of a steep bluff of Nolachucky river south fourteen deg. East sixty three poles to a stake on LEAS line thence with ditto North seventy six East eighty eight poles to a post oak south fourteen East thirteen poles to the beginning. Having such form as represented by the above platt. Surveyed the 9th of October A.D. 1824
LEVI DANIEL) By
Jonathan Wood
CETH MOORE) C.C. P. S. of C.
C.

BENGIMAN BRYANT 8 ACRES

State of Tennessee Cocke County
By Virtue of an entry made in the entry takers office for the aforesaid county at Newport of No. 203 dated the fifth day of July 1824. I have surveyed for BENGIMON BRYANT eight acres of land on the waters of Clay Creek Beginning at a White Oak corner to said BRYANT and T. E. CHRISTIAN Running thence with said CHRISTIAN line south Eighty East three and three fourths poles to a hickory South twelve East thirty Nine poles to a stake and White Oak on SHELDS line then with the same East thirty one poles to a stake on or near said BRYANTS line North thirty eight poles to a stake on said BRYANTS line then with ditto West thirty six poles to the beginning. Having such form as represented by the above platt. Surveyed the 26th of October 1824.
WM. BRYANT) By
Jonathan Wood
WM. COMOCH[?]) C.C. Principal
Surveyor of Cocke County

115

JAMES TALLEY 50 ACRES

State of Tennessee Cocke County
By Virtue of an entry made in the entry takers office for the aforesaid county at Newport of No 242 dated the 27th of July 1824. I have surveyed for JAMES TALLEY fifty acres of land on the waters of Nobb Creek. Beginning at Beech tree Marked with three Notches standing near a small branch running thence North thirty six and one half deg. West thirty eight poles to a stake on a line of a tract of land belonging to said TALLEY thence with the line thereof thirteen poles to a stake North thirty two poles to a stake south sixty two deg. West one hundred and twenty six poles to a stake near a hickory White Oak and ash thence south twenty eight East sixty four poles to a stake then a direct line to the beginning Having such form as represented by the above platt. Surveyed the 21st day of October 1824
JOEL MASON) By
Jonathan Wood
WM. ROBERTS) C.C. Principal
Surveyor of Cocke County

116

AMOS DAWSON 50 ACRES

State of Tennessee Cocke County
By virtue of an entry made in the entry takers office for the aforesaid county at Newport of No114 dated the 25th of June 1824 I have surveyed for AMOS DAWSON fifty acres of land including his occupant claim on the North side of French Broad River on the waters of the Middle fork of Clay creek Beginning on a white Oak running thence North seventy five deg. East one hundred and twenty six poles and one half to a stake North fifteen degrees West thirty poles to a stake on JOHN GREENE line then with his lines south sixty four degrees west thirty six poles to a stake on JOHN GREENS line then with his line sixty four degrees south thirty six poles to a stake North Twenty six deg. West seven and an half poles to a stake thence South seventy five deg. West Eighty Eight poles to two White Oaks then south fifteen East sixty four poles to the beginning. Having such form as represented by the above platt. Surveyed the 27th of October 1824

JOHN GREENE) By
Jonathan Wood
ISAAC FOWLER) C.C. Principal
Surveyor of Cocke County

JOHN LAIN 50 ACRES

State of Tennessee Cocke County
By virtue of an Entry takers[sic] for the aforesaid county at Newport of No 37 dated the 17th of July 1824 I have surveyed for JOHN LAIN fifty acres of land on the waters of sinking creek Beginning at a Spanish Oak corner to JOB COCKRANS running thence south twenty six deg. west ninety four poles to a dogwood and poplar and JAMES STRANGES line then with ditto South thirty three poles to a birch south sixty four deg. East fifty six poles to a stake North twenty six deg. East Eighty four poles to Chesnut Oak then with steep[?] Nobbs North fifty six poles to a gum on COCKRANS line then with the same a direct line to the beginning Having such form as represented by the above platt
Surveyed the 9th of November 1824

EDMOND VAN   ) By
Jonathan Wood
JAMES STRANGE) C.C. Principal
Surveyor of Cocke County

117

JOHN GREEN 50 ACRES

State of Tennessee Cocke County
By Virtue of an Entry made in the entry takers office for the aforesaid county at Newport of No. 141 dated the 1st of July 1824. I have surveyed for JOHN GREEN including his improvement on the waters of Oven Creek Near the head of Slate branch Beginning at a White Oak running thence South sixty four degrees West sixty six poles to a White Oak South twenty six degrees East Twenty one poles and one half North sixty four deg. East sixty poles to a small White Oak in a hollow then a direct line to the beginning Having such form as represented by the above Platt. Surveyed the twenty seven of October 1824

AMOS DAWSON) By
Jonathan Wood
ISAAC FOWLER) C.C. Principal
Surveyor of Cocke County
This record void and recorded Heretofore

118

WILLIAM RUSSELL 50 ACRES

State of Tennessee Cocke County

By virtue of an Entry Made in the entry takers office for the aforesaid county at Newport of No. 258 I have surveyed for WILLIAM RUSSELL dated the 9th August 1824 fifty acres of land on the Middle fork of Wolf Creek Beginning at pine on CLEMENT HOOPERS line running thence with the same North Twenty two deg. East eighty Nine and one half poles to a stake near a poplar North sixty Eight deg. West eighty Nine and a half deg. to a birch and horn beam on the south side of the dry fork of said creek thence south twenty two deg. West Eighty Nine and one half poles to a dogwood red Oak and hickory bushes on the side of a rocky ridge then a direct line to the beginning Having such form as is represented by the above platt.

Surveyed the 3rd day of November 1824.

WILLIAM REYNOLDS) By

Jonathan Wood

THOMAS REYNOLDS) C.C. Principal

Surveyor of Cocke County

A. MASON 50 ACRES

State of Tennessee Cocke County

By Virtue of an entry made in the Entry takers office for the aforesaid county at Newport No. 227 dated the 12th day of July 1824. I have surveyed for AIDEN MASON fifty acres of land on the waters of McCowans Creek Beginning at a White Oak near a branch running thence South sixty seven and one half deg. East eighty nine and one half poles to a spanish Oak and dogwood North Twenty two and one half West Eighty Nine and one half poles to a stake South sixty seven and one half West eighty nine and one half poles to a hickory on the side of a ridge then a direct line to the beginning Having such form as is represented by the above platt. Surveyed the 25th day of January 1825 By

JAMES MASON)

Jonathan Wood

ANDREW RAMSEY) C.C. Principal

Surveyor of Cocke County

119

GEO. NEAS 25 ACRES

State of Tennessee Cocke County

By Virtue of an entry made in the entry makers office for the aforesaid county at Newport of No. 181 dated the 5th day of July 1824 I have surveyed for GEO. NEAS twenty five acres of land on the waters of Clear Creek. Beginning at a chesnut grub corner to a fifty acre tract of said NEAS running thence with same North fifty Eight West one hundred and seventy two poles to a stake on the line of a four hundred acre tract of said NEAS then with the same south fifty one West three and one half East sixty Eight poles to a stake thence a direct line to the beginning. Having such form as is represented by the above platt. Surveyed the 22nd day of December 1824

HENRY OTTINGER) By

Jonathan Wood

SAMUEL NEAS   ) C.C. Principal

Surveyor of Cocke County

JOHN HENDERSON 24 ACRES

State of Tennessee Cocke County

By Virtue of an Entry made in the entry takers office for the aforesaid county at Newport of No. 250 dated 5th day of August 1824 I have surveyed FOR JOHN HENDERSON Twenty five acres of land on the waters of Clear Creek Beginning at a stake corner to JAMES POTTER near the south side of the Road leading from Newport to Comp[Camp] Creek Iron works running thence with said HENDERSONS line crossing said road North eighteen West fourteen

and one half poles to a post Oak West Eighty nine poles to a black Oak North eighty poles to a stake in a field West thirty three poles to a black Oak and a black Jack South eighty seven and one half poles to a black Oak on POTTERS line then with the same a direct line to the beginning Having such form as is represented by the above platt.
Surveyed the 23rd day of December 1824 by
JOHN HENDERSON)
Jonathan Wood
JOSEPH HENDERSON) C.C. Principal
Surveyor of Cocke County

120

D. BLAZER 50 ACRES

State of Tennessee Cocke County
By Virtue of an entry made in the entry takers office at Newport of No. 97 dated the 11th day of June 1824 I have surveyed for DANIEL BLAZER fifty acres of land on the waters of Clear Creek Beginning at a post Oak corner to said BLAZER running thence with his line North sixty poles to a post Oak North seventy West fifty Nine poles to a stake corner to JAMES MALAY[MALOY] then with his lines south 22 1/2 West seventy three poles to a poplar south seventeen East fifty seven poles to a stake East eighty poles to a stake on the line of a forty acre tract of said BLAZER then with the same a direct line to the beginning Having such form as is represented by the above platt.
Surveyed the 21st January 1825 by
JAMES BLAZER) Jonathan Wood
CHRISTOPHER BLAZER) C.C. Principal Surveyor of Cocke County

JOHN AND THOMAS BRIANT 50 ACRES

State of Tennessee Cocke County
By Virtue of an entry made in the Entry takers office for the above said county at Newport of No. 79 dated the 31st day of May 1824. I have surveyed for JOHN and THOMAS BRIANT 50 acres of land on the waters of Coslings [Caslings?] Creek Beginning at a white Oak on JOSEPH DENNIS line running thence down the creek North sixty seven deg. East thirty six poles to a beech at the foot of a steep Nobb then down the same at [?] a hundred deg. North eighty four East thirty four poles to a Spanish Oak North sixty seven East sixty poles to a stake near a white Oak on the south side of the creek thence North twenty three deg. West sixty four poles to a stake south sixty seven West one hundred and twenty six poles to a stake thence a direct line to the beginning Having such form as is represented by the above platt Surveyed the 12th day of February 1825 by
JOSEPH DENNIS)
Jonathan Wood
THOS DENNIS) C.C. Principal
Surveyor of Cocke County

121

HENRY OTTINGER 25 ACRES

State of Tennessee Cocke County
By Virtue of entry made in the entry takers office for the above said county at Newport of No 182 dated the 5th of July 1824 I have surveyed for HENRY OTTINGER twenty acres of land on the waters of Clear creek Beginning at a stake at the end of a line of a two hundred acre tract of land Granted by the state of Tennessee to GEO NEAS running thence with COOKS line-running-thence last eight poles to a stake near a black Oak on HENDERSON'S line then with Ditto South forty eight poles to a stake West eighty four poles to a stake on GEORGE NEAS line then with the same forty eight poles to the beginning Having such form as is represented by the

above platt Surveyed the 22nd day of December 1824 by
GEORGE NEAS)
Jonathan Wood
SAMUEL NEAS) C.C. Principal
Surveyor of Cocke County

ISAAC JESTER 16 ACRES

State of Tennessee Cocke County

By Virtue of an entry made in the entry takers office for the aforesaid county at Newport of No. 308 dated the 24th December 1824 I have surveyed for ISAAC JESTER sixteen acres of land on the waters of Neely's Creek Beginning at a beech said to be on or near NATHAN TYRYS [?] line running with or nearly with Ditto North eighty seven and one half West sixty four poles to a dogwood Thence North two and one half east forty poles to a stake near SMITHS line at the foot of a hill South seventy seven and one half deg. East fifty six poles to a stake on JESSE SMITHS line then with his line south 28 poles to a large stump then east eighteen poles to a stake thence South fifteen poles to a stake on the side of a steep hill then a direct line to the beginning Having such form as is represented by the above platt.
Surveyed the 27th day of January 1825 by
JAMES TURNER)
Jonathan Wood
NATHAN TYRY) C.C. Principal
Surveyor of Cocke County

122
GEORGE LAREW 4 ACRES

State of Tennessee County of Cocke

By Virtue of an entry made in the entry takers office for the aforesaid county at Newport of No. 265 dated the 23rd of August 1824 I have surveyed for GEORGE LAREW four acres of land partly covered with the waters of French broad River including a fish trap in said river Beginning at a willow on the south side of said river just below a part of a shoal running thence with conditional line with JAMES CLARK North seventy Nine and a half deg. West twenty two poles to a stake in the river North Ten and a half East thirty four poles to a stake south seventy nine and a half deg. East thirteen poles to a papaw and sycamore then down the meanders of the river with his own lines South twelve and an half thirteen poles to a beech south ten poles to a sycamore south one and an half deg. East six poles to a stake south eleven and a half West eleven poles to the beginning. Having such form as represented by the above platt. Surveyed the 12th day of October 1824 By
WM. LAREW)
Jonathan Wood
JAMES PUCKETT) C.C. Principal
Surveyor of Cocke County

123
JAMES NICHOLS 15 ACRES

State of Tennessee Cocke County

By Virtue of an entry Made in the entry takers office for said county at Newport No. 295 dated the 5th day of November 1824 I have surveyed for JAMES NICHOLS fifteen acres of land on the waters of Big Creek bounded as Viz Beginning at a post Oak near JAMES NICHOLS and JOHN STOKELY HEIRS corner running thence with conditional lines with BENGIMON DAVIS North sixty five poles to a chesnut west thirty eight poles to a stake a the foot of a Mountain then along ditto south twenty East twenty two poles to a spanish Oak south forty five West eight poles to a stake on said NICHOLS line then with the same a direct line to the beginning. Having such form as represented by the above platt. Surveyed the 29th day of November 1824.
ISAAC HOOPER) By
Jonathan Wood
BENJIMON DAVIS) C.C. Principal
Surveyor of Cocke County

CHARELES NICHOLS 50 ACRES

State of Tennessee Cocke County
By Virtue of an entry made in the entry takers office for the aforesaid county Cocke at Newport of No. 211 dated the seven day of July 1824 I have surveyed for CHARLES NICHOLS fifty acres of land on the North side of French broad river. Beginning at a white Oak in the fork of a branch running thence south sixty eight poles to an ash on the said NICHOLS line then with the same south eighty nine deg. west one hundred and seventy poles to a post Oak on the side of a Mountain and along ditto East one hundred and forty two poles to a stake East twenty eight to the beginning. Having such form as represented of the above platt. Surveyed the 2nd day of November 1824

JAMES NICHOLS) By
Jonathan Wood
MICAJAH ESTRIDGE) C.C. Principal
Surveyor of Cocke County

124
BEGIMON BRYANT 25 ACRES

State of Tennessee Cocke County
By Virtue of an entry made in the entry takers office for the aforesaid county at Newport of No. 193 dated the 13th day of July 1824 I have surveyed for BENGIMAN BRYANT twenty five acres of land Beginning at a stake by a beech on a line of a tract of land belonging to said BRYANT thence along a steep Nobbs North sixty nine deg. East seventy one poles to a chesnut and hickory North twenty one West fifty six poles and an half to a stake near a dogwood then south sixty nine deg. West seventy one poles to a stake south twenty one East fifty six and a half poles to the Beginning the above platt is a true representation of the above described land Surveyed the 26th of October 1824

WM BRYANT) By
Jonathan Wood
JNO HAMPTON) C.C. Principal
Surveyor of Cocke County

JERAMIAH HILL 74 ACRES

State of Tennessee Cocke County
By Virtue of an entry made in the entry takers office for the aforesaid county at Newport of No. 244 dated the 29th day of July 1824. I have surveyed for JERIMIAH HILL seventy four acres of land on the south side of Nola Chucky river Beginning at a forked cedar above the Mouth of the Cool hollow on the bank of said river runing up ditto North twenty one West sixty poles to a sycamore supposed to be a corner of JAMES HILL then with said HILLS line along the foot of a steep hill North twenty four and two thirds poles to a stake near a Elm North thirty East sixteen poles to a papaw North forty six East seventeen poles to a buckeye North four poles to a stake near a beech North twenty and an half East twenty one and an half East twenty one and an half poles to a beech thence along steep Nobb North forty five East forty poles to a stake south forty five East eighty two poles to a stake south forty five West fifty five poles to a stake on E and I line then with ditto North forty five West six poles stake then a direct line to the beginning. Having such form as is represented by the above Platt. Surveyed the 9th day of October 1824.

ELIJAH HILL) By
Jonathan Wood
WILLIAM HARRISON) C.C. P.S.C.C.

125
GEORGE HOLT 5 ACRES
State of Tennessee Cocke County
By Virtue of an entry made in the entry takers office for aforesaid county Newport of No. 99 dated the 4th day of June A.D. 1824 I have surveyed for GEORGE HOLT five acres of land including his improvements of the waters of Clay creek on the south side thereof. Beginning at a stake on the North side of an branch by or near a sugar tree on his own line running thence North seventy nine deg. West thirty seven poles to a stake at the foot of a steep hill then along ditto South eighty two West twenty nine poles to a sugar tree then with a conditional line with BENGIMON BRYANT North eleven west nineteen poles to a Ironwood then with a conditional line with JOHN HAMPTON south eighty three East sixty nine poles to said HOLTS line then with ditto south fourteen poles to the beginning. Having such form as represented by the above Platt. Surveyed the 27th October 1824. By
G. HOLT)
Jonathan Wood
I. HOLT) C.C.
Principal Surveyor of Cocke County

126
JOHN WOOD 16 ACRES
State of Tennessee Cocke County
By Virtue of an entry made in the entry takers office for the aforesaid count at Newport of No. 305 dated the 18th day of December 1824 I have surveyed for JOHN WOOD sixteen acres of land on the waters of Clay creek Beginning at a poplar and sugar tree corner to WILLIAM HUFF thence with his line south fifteen East twenty six poles to a stake south eighty seven deg. xxxx poles to a black Oak then with a conditional line with the same South twenty East fifty three poles to a stake corner to DAVID WOOD then with his line North fourteen poles to a stake West thirty eight poles to a stake North thirty one and one half poles to a stake on a line of a tract of land whereon DAVID WOOD now lives Then with Ditto West seventeen poles to a Mulberry North thirty West twenty two poles to a stake then a direct line to the beginning. Having such form ad is represented by the above platt. Surveyed the 31st day of January 1825.
WM. HUFF)
By Jonathan Wood
DAVID WOOD) C.C. P. S.
of C.C.

JOHN BORDEN 24 ACRES
State of Tennessee Cocke County
By Virtue of an Entry made in the entry takers office for the aforesaid county at Newport of 293 dated the 27th of October 1824. I have surveyed for JOHN BORDEN twenty four acres of land on the waters of Clear Creek. Beginning at a black Oak on or near his own line running with KILBREATHS line south fifty six East forty six poles to two post Oaks North Eighty seven and an half deg. East forty one poles to a stake North one hundred and sixty two poles to a stake on or near GORDENS line of his big survey West thirty eight poles to a stake on BORDENS line then with his line south ten West forty poles to a stake thence South forty nine and an half poles to a post Oak then a direct line to the beginning. Having such form as is represented by the above platt. Surveyed the 28th day of December 1824 By
GEORGE BLAZER)
Jonathan Wood
ELISHA BORDEN) C.C. Principal
Surveyor of Cocke County

127
JOSEPH DENNIS 40 ACRES
State of Tennessee Cocke County
By Virtue of an entry made in the Entry takers office for the aforesaid county at Newport of No. 138 dated the 30th day of June 1824. I have surveyed for JOSEPH DENNIS forty acres of land on the waters of Cosbys creek Beginning at a buckeye on the south side of said creek running thence with BRYANTS line North Eighteen and one half West, forty six poles to a stake then with a conditional line with JOHN DEAVERS south seventy seven West forty eight poles to a black Oak North seventy six and one half West thirty poles to a sour wood North thirty four and one half West nineteen and an half poles to a White Oak on POLLEY DEAVERS line then with same south seventy seven and an half West twenty eight poles to a White Oak south eleven and an half West thirty seven and an half poles to a stake on HAMBYS line then with the same south eight East thirty two poles to a stake on the side of a steep hill then along ditto a direct line to the beginning Having such form as represented by the above platt. Surveyed the 14th of February 1825.

JOHN BRYANT) By
Jonathan Wood
THOMAS BRYANT) C.C. Principal
Surveyor of Cocke County

128
JOHN ALLEN 50 ACRES
State of Tennessee Cocke County
By Virtue of an entry made in the Entry takers office for the aforesaid county at Newport of 271 dated the 23rd of August 1824 I have surveyed for JOHN ALLEN (Bricklayer) fifty acres of land part of which is covered with the waters of Pigeon. Beginning at a stake near a white Oak on the west bank of said river below his sawmill running thence across ditto South forty five East thirty poles to a beech on the East side of said river then up the meanders of South twenty nine East sixty three poles to a sycamore South thirty five East ninety five poles to a stake south nine west crossing P. river forty seven poles to a poplar on a clift of rocks south sixty eight and an half deg. West seventy poles to a stake then with the line of a one hundred and ten are tract of said ALLEN North twenty one deg. West ninety two poles to a stake on LILLARDS old line then with gis line xxxxxxxx two poles to a stake North fifty seven East twenty poles south fifty seven East fort [sic] poles to a beech North seventy five East ten poles to a beech on the west bank of P. River and then down to meanders thereof and with said LILLARDS lines then [?] to the beginning including ALLENS saw Mill. Having such form as represented by the above Platt. Surveyed the 19th of November 1824

JOHN LILLARD) By
Jonathan Wood
ABRAHAM DENTON) C.C. Principal
Surveyor of Cocke County

JOHN OTTINGER SR. 23 3/4 ACRES
State of Tennessee Cocke County
By Virtue of an entry made in the entry takers office for the aforesaid county at Newport of No. 201 dated the 5th day of July 1824 for twenty five acres I have surveyed for JOHN OTTINGER SR. twenty three and three fourths acres of land it being all the Vacant land that could be had with the limits of the entry. Beginning at a stake near the corner of GEORGE GORDENS Northwardly line running thence with BORDENS line south eighty eight and an half West thirty three poles and an half to a white Oak STINES [STINER?] corner then with his line North eighty three poles to a post Oak on a conditional line between said JOHN OTTINGER SR. and

JOHN OTTINGER JUNR. then with the same North twenty nine deg. East seventy poles to a stake near a marked pine on or near said OTTINGERS line then with the same south one hundred and forty five poles to the beginning Having such form as represented by the above platt. Surveyed the 27th day of December 1824.

PETER OTTINGER) By
Jonathan Wood
JOHN OTTINGER) C.C. Principal
Surveyor of Cocke County

129

ABRAHAM LILLARD 13 ACRES

State of Tennessee Cocke County

By Virtue of an entry made in the entry takers office for the aforesaid county at Newport for fifty acres of No 277 dated the 27th day of August 1824 I have surveyed for ABRAHAM LILLARD thirteen acres of land on the waters of Cosby Creek it being all xxxxxxxxxxxx[sic] bounded as follows viz Beginning at a white Oak his own corner to WILLHIGHTS line running thence with his line North fifty two and an half degrees East twenty eight poles to a walnut stump corner to ISAAC O,DELL then with his line North forty four degrees East fifty eight poles to a white Oak on JENNINGS line then with the same south fifteen degrees West Ninety four poles to a black Oak on WILLHIGHTS line then with the same a direct line to the beginning Having such form as represented by the above platt. Surveyed the 15th day of February 1825. by

THORNTON WOOD)
Jonathan Wood
JOHN WOOD   ) C.C. P. S. C. C.

JOHN WOOD 50 ACRES

State of Tennessee Cocke County

By Virtue of an entry made in the entry takers office of said county at Newport of No. 261 dated the 16th of August 1824 I have surveyed for JOHN WOOD fifty acres of land on the waters of Cosbys Creek. Beginning at a beech on the south side of said branch running thence North ten West eighty poles to a stake on WILLIAM WILLHIGHTS line then with the same South seventy East ninety four poles to a large White Oak on a ridge then along Nobbs south ten East one hundred and eleven poles to a stake on the side of Neddys Mountain thence a direct line along ditto to the beginning. Having such form as represented by the above platt. Surveyed the 13th day of February 1825. by

THORTON WOOD)
Jonathan Wood
ABE LILLARD) C.C. Principal
Surveyor of Cocke County

130

WILLIAM FOX 15 ACRES

State of Tennessee Cocke County

By Virtue of an entry made in the entry takers office for the aforesaid county of Cocke at Newport of No. 134 dated the 30th day of June 1824. Founded on the Right of occupancy I have surveyed to WILLIAM FOX fifteen acres of land on the south side of French Broad river Beginning at a gum on said FOXES own land running thence along the top of a clift along said river south thirty three deg. West forty six poles to a stake south forty five West seven poles to a xxxxxxxx[sic] and an half deg. West sixteen poles to a stake near a pine stump corner to BENJIMAN O,DELL then with said O,DELLLS line west fourteen poles to a stake North forty eight West three and three fourths poles to a walnut North sixty one and an half

deg. East three and an half poles to a willow North thirty four west Eleven poles to a white Oak North fifty five west Eighty poles to a stake south eighty four west sixteen poles to a stake North twenty one poles to a stake on his own line then with the same a direct line to the beginning. Having such form as represented by the above platt. Surveyed the 9th day of Dec. 1824 by
GEORGE GANN)
Jonathan Wood
LEVI FOX) C.C. Principal
Surveyor of Cocke County

131
A. DENTON 60 ACRES

State of Tennessee Cocke County
By Virtue of an entry made in the entry takers office for the aforesaid county of Cocke at Newport of No. 190 dated the 5th day of July 1824 I have surveyed for ABRAHAM DENTON sixty acres of land on the waters of Cosbys creek Beginning at a stake on JOSEPH HUFFS line near a small branch and corner to JOHN ALLEN running thence with said HUFFS lines west twenty one poles to a black Oak south fifty Nine West twenty five and an half poles to a pine North sixty West forty three poles to a large poplar corner to LILLARDS then with his line south one East forty seven poles to a beech South 19 East 15 poles to an elm south fifty three West four poles to a hickory South thirty seven east twenty one poles to a black Oak south seven East forty nine poles to a dogwood south sixty one east fifty poles to a stake corner to JOHN ALLEN then with his line a direct course to the beginning. Having such form as is represented by the above paltt. Surveyed the 18th day of November 1824 by
JOHN LILLARD)
Jonathan Wood
DAVID HICKS) C.C. Principal
Surveyor of Cocke County

132
ELIJAH MURPHY 50 ACRES

State of Tennessee Cocke County
By Virtue of an entry made in the entry takers office for the aforesaid county at Newport of No. 255 dated the 7th day of August 1824 I have surveyed for ELIJAH MURPHY fifty acres of land on the North side of French Broad river Beginning at a stake on the bank of McCowans Creek near a sugar tree running thence with THOMAS PHELMS[?] line North forty poles to a stake West five and an half poles to a stake North one hundred and Ninety poles to a stake East fifty two poles to a stake on the top of a ridge North twenty poles to an elm on or near MASONS line then with his line West twenty five poles to a stake North eighty poles to a stake then West forty six poles to a stake then with LEAS lines south fourteen degrees east eighty two poles to a hickory south seventy six West thirty four poles to a beech south fourteen deg. East one hundred and nine poles and an half to a stake then with MURPHYS line south twenty two West one hundred poles to a stake on the side of a steep Nobb then with the same a direct line to the beginning. Having such form as represented by the above platt Surveyed the 25th day of January 1825 by
AND. RAMSEY)
Jonathan Wood
ROBT. ROGERS) C.C. Principal
Surveyor of Cocke County

JOHN ALLEN 110 ACRES

State of Tennessee Cocke County
By Virtue of an entry made in the entry takers office for the aforesaid county at Newport of No. 270 dated the 23rd day of August 1824 I have surveyed for JOHN ALLEN (Bricklayer) one hundred and ten acres of land on the west side of Big Pigeon Beginning at a black Oak corner to said ALLEN running thence south twenty one deg. East one hundred and ninety two poles to a sourwood at the foot of a steep hill then along ditto south fifty eight East forty four and one half poles to White Oak and black Oak xxxxxx [sic] East thirty eight poles to a poplar North sixty Eight and a half East fifty two poles to a stake then with said ALLEN fifty acre tract North twenty one West seventy two poles to a stake on said ALLENS line with his old line North thirty five west seventy nine and a half to a stake south eighty two west thirty five poles to a black Oak west fifty three poles to the beginning. Having such form as represented by the above platt. Surveyed the 19th of November 1824
ABRAHAM DENTON) By
Jonathan Wood
JOHN LILLARD) C.C. P. S. of
C.C.

133
JOHN COOPER 50 ACRES

State of Tennessee Cocke County
By Virtue of an entry made in the entry takers office for the aforesaid county at Newport of No. 221 dated the 10th of July 1824 I have surveyed for JOHN COOPER fifty acres of land agreeable to the calls of said entry the same lying on the waters of long creek Beginning at a stake corner to ROBERT COOPER on the East side of his BIGHAM tract running thence with same south forty eight west one hundred and fifty poles to a large chesnut thence South forty two East fifty three and one half poles to a red Oak spanish Oak and hickory thence North forty eight east one hundred and fifty poles to a stake one and one fourths poles from a Marked Locust North forty two West fifty three and an half poles to the Beginning Having such form as represented by the above Platt. surveyed the twenty eighth of January 1824 By
JAMES COOPER)
Jonathan Wood
WM. KELLY) C.C. Surveyor of
C. C.

134
LUNA CHAPMAN 75 ACRES

State of Tennessee Cocke County
By Virtue of an entry made in the entry takers office for the aforesaid county at Newport of No. 264 dated the 21st day of August 1824 I have surveyed for LUNA CHAPMAN seventy five acres of land between the waters of Clear creek and sinking caine [cave?] Beginning at a stake at ROBERT SMITH west line running thence with same south twenty three deg. West one hundred and forty poles to a black Oak stump in the field corner to JOHN FAUBIAN then with his lines North seventy West eighty four poles to a stake North fifteen West twenty eight Poles to a stake near or in the edge of a field North eighty seven deg. West thirty eight poles to two black Oak on or near SWAGERTYS line then North seventeen and an half East thirty poles to a stake near two hickorys thence a direct line the Beginning Having such form as represented by the above platt. Surveyed the 20th day of January 1825 By
HENRY JONES)
Jonathan Wood
WM. GRANT) C.C. Surveyor of
Cocke County

WM. HUFF 32 ACRES
State of Tennessee Cocke County
By Virtue of an entry made in the entry takers office for the aforesaid county at Newport of 318 dated the 18th day of January 1825 I have surveyed for HUFF thirty two acres of land on the North side of French Broad River and on the North side of Clay Creek Beginning at a black Oak on the south side of a hill running thence with JOHN WOODS line North eighty seven West eleven poles to a stake corner to an one hundred acre tract of said HUFF then with the same south sixty poles to a white Oak black Oak and stake on the line of a twenty five acre tract of said HUFFS then with the same forty nine and one fourth two poles to a black Oak and sourwood corner to ANTHONY CHRISTIAN then with his line North thirty four poles to a small poplar then with conditional line with JOHN WOOD North forty five west one hundred xxx to a small pine west Eleven poles to stake North twenty west fifty three poles to the beginning. Having such form as represented by the above platt. Surveyed the 30th of January 1825 by
JOHN WOOD)
Jonathan Wood
DAVID WOOD) C.C.
Surveyor of Cocke County

135
NATHANIEL POTTER 50 ACRES

State of Tennessee Cocke County
By virtue of an entry made in the entry takers office for the aforesaid county at Newport of No. 131 dated the 13th day of January 1824 I have surveyed for NATHANIEL POTTER fifty acres of land between the head waters of Clear creek and long creek. Beginning at a stake on NEAS line near a white Oak on the south side of a 400 acre tract of said NEAS running thence with ditto fifty eight and an half East sixteen poles to a Spanish Oak south seventy five East thirty one and an half poles to a chesnut POTTERS corner then with his line south sixty two and an half deg. West twenty eight poles to a stake south ten West twenty one poles to a red Oak south eighty East one hundred poles to a white Oak south 15 West fifty two poles ro a black Oak thence North eighty West Ninety six poles to a stake on HICKEYS line thence with his line North five West Nine poles to a white Oak West twelve poles to a white Oak south Nine poles to a sycamore North eighty west twenty poles to a stake then a direct line to the beginning Having such form as is represented by the above platt surveyed the 21st day of January 1825 by
BENTLY POTTER)
Jonathan Wood
SAMUEL POTTER) C.C. Surveyor of
Cocke County

136
WILLIAM VINSON 18 ACRES
State of Tennessee Cocke County
By Virtue of an entry made in the entry takers office for the aforesaid county at Newport of 292 Dated the 23rd day of October 1824 I have [surveyed] for WILLIAM VINSON eighteen acres of land on the east side of Big Pigeon river. Beginning at a black Oak on his own line running thence with the line of a fifty acre tract of said VINSON south fifty deg. East sixty two and an half poles to a stake thence south 40° west forty poles to a stake on the side of a hill thence North fifty deg. West seventy poles to a stake xxxxxx and where on the said VINSON now lives then with the same a dorect line to the beginning having such form as represented by the above platt. surveyed the 18th day of Feby. 1825 by
ENOCH NETHERTON)
Jonathan Wood
PRESTON LOYD   ) C.C. Surveyor of
Cocke County

ANTHONY CHRISTIAN 50 ACRES
State of Tennessee Cocke County
By Virtue of an entry made in the entry takers office at Newport for the aforesaid county of No. 303 dated the 8th day of December 1824. I have surveyed for ANTHONY CHRISTIAN fifty acres of land on the North side of French Broad river and on the south side of Clay creek Beginning at a stake corner to a fifty acre tract of said CHRISTIAN running thence south with the same one hundred and two poles and an half ro a black Oak and sourwood corner to WILLIAM HUFFS twenty five acre tract thence with the same North fifty nine deg. West one hundred and fifty four poles to a stake corner to said HUFF tract then with the same north thirty one poles to a stake thence East eighteen and one fourth poles to a stake on JOHN WOODS line then with his line south twenty one deg. East thirty poles to a stake East sixty two poles to a chesnut then with DAVID WOODS line North fourteen poles to a stake East sixty poles to a stake thence south twenty five poles to a stake supposed to be on a line of said CHRISTIANS then with the same a direct line to the beginning. Having such form as is represented by the above platt. Surveyed the 17th day of March 1825

THOMAS GILLETT) By Jonathan Wood
ANTHONY CHRISTIAN) C.C. Surveyor of Cocke County

137
GEO. & BAPTIST McNABB 75 ACRES
State of Tennessee Cocke County
By Virtue of an entry made in the entry takers office for the aforesaid county at Newport of No. 311 the 6th day of January 1825 I have surveyed for GEO. McNABB and BAPTIST McNABB jointly seventy five acres of land on the East side of Big Pigeon river Beginning at the stake corner to WILLIAM VINSON running thence with said VINSONS line of a fifty acre tract south fifty deg. East sixty three and and one fourth poles to his corner the same course continued in all all one hundred and thirty poles to a dogwood then south forty degrees West sixty poles to a stake on the side of a ridge thence west with or nearly with ditto one hundred and eight poles to a stake on VINSONS line then with his line North ninety seven poles to a large Spanish Oak North fifty deg. East fifty nine poles to the beginning. Having such form as is represented by the above platt.
N. B. this entry on which this survey is founded calls adjoining the lands of GEO. McNABB as well as VINSON when in fact it does not join said McNABBS land. Surveyed the 7th day of January 1825 by

JOHN McNABB)
Jonathan Wood
ROBERT PHILLIPS) C.C. Principal
Surveyor of Cocke County

138
B. BRYANT 130 ACRES
State of Tennessee Cocke County
By Virtue of an entry made in the entry takers office for the aforesaid county at Newport of No. 162 dated the 3rd day of July 1824 I have surveyed for BENGIMAN BRYANT one hundred and thirty acres of land on the North side of Clear creek Beginning xxxxx corner of thirty acres tract of said BRYANTS line thence south fifty two west thirty one poles to a stake then with a conditional line with GEORGE PARROTT North twenty one west Two Hundred and ten poles to a stake North fifty nine East one hundred poles to a stake North twenty seven East Two Hundred and seventy five poles to a stake corner to PARROTT on said BRYANT own line then with his line

North eighty five West forty poles to a stake West thirty three poles to the beginning. Having such form as represented by the above Platt, surveyed the 28th day of October 1824. By

WILLIAM BRYANT)
Jonathan Wood
Only one given) c.c. P. S. C. C.

JOHN ALLEN (CONSTABLE) 70 ACRES

State of Tennessee Cocke County

by Virtue of an entry made in the entry takers office for the aforesaid county at Newport of No. 272 dated the 24 day of August 1824 I have surveyed for JOHN ALLEN CONSTABLE seventy acres of land including improvement made by JOHN JENKINS on the waters of Cosby creek Beginning at a white Oak on the bank of a branch running thence south twenty seven and one deg. west one hundred and twenty nine poles to a stake on said ALLEN line then with the same south three East nine poles to a pine near the foot of a hill then along ditto East seventeen poles to a stake thence south fifty two and one half East sixty six poles to a chesnut Oak North thirty seven and one half East one hundred and twenty six poles to a stake North fiftytwo and an half West eighty six and an half poles to the beginning Having such form as represented by the above platt. Surveyed the 21st day of March 1825. By

JOEL BROOKS)
Jonathan Wood
SAMUEL ELLINGTON) C.C. Surveyor of
Cocke County

139

THORTON WOOD 100 ACRES

State of Tennessee Cocke County

By Virtue of an entry made in the entry takers office for the aforesaid county at Newport of No. 67 dated the 24th day of April 1824 I have surveyed for THORTON WOOD one hundred acres of land including an improvement transfered to him by WILLIAM WILLHIGHT on the waters of Cosbys creek Beginning at a chesnut tree said to be a corner to JOHN WEAVER running thence with said WEAVERS lines south forty five West forty poles to a white Oak south sixty two west thirty poles to a locust corner SAMUEL BROYLS then with his lines south fifty West sixty nine poles to a hickory south eighty East twenty one poles to a dogwood then East along Denneys Mountain one hundred and eight five poles to a white Oak and dogwood then North one hundred and twenty five poles to a stake on WILLHIGHTS line then with his lines North sixty eight west six poles to a dogwood North seventy seven and one half West Eighty poles to a black Oak then a direct line to the Beginning. Having such form as represented by the above Platt. Surveyed the 22nd day of March 1825.

A. LILLARD) By
Jonathan Wood
THOS BRIANT) C.C. Surveyor of
Cocke County

140

WILLIAM GILLILAND 12 ACRES

State of Tennessee Cocke County

By Virtue of an entry made in the entry takers office for the aforesaid county of Cocke of No. 251 dated the fifth day of August 1824 I have surveyed for WILLIAM GILLILAND twelve acres of land on the water of little fork of Cosby Creek Beginning at a white walnut on the bank of the creek corner to ROBERT GILLILAND thence with his line south seventy five and one fourth east twenty two poles to Iron Wood stump corner to JOHN DENTONS old survey then with the same north four East thirty seven poles to an elm North seventy two Eat thirty nine poles to a buckeye stump North seventy

West crossing the creek twelve poles to a sycamore xxxxxx West twenty poles to a stake then south sixty one and a half West forty seven poles to a stake on or near DEVERS[?] line then with or nearly with ditto a direct line to the beginning. Having such form as represented by the above Platt. Surveyed 16th day of November 1824

JAMES LILLARD) By
Jonathan Wood
DAVID LEWIS) C.C. Surveyor of
Cocke County

JOHN SUTTON 50 ACRES

State of Tennessee Cocke County

By Virtue of an entry made in the entry takers office for the aforesaid county at Newport of No. 139 dated the thirtith day of June 1824 I have surveyed for JOHN SUTTON fifty acres of land including occupants claim on both side of Cosbys creek Beginning at a poplar on the east side of said creek running thence up ditto south forty one and a half East forty seven poles to a spruce pine then along ditto south sixty two East one hundred and two poles to a stake thence North thirty four East forty five poles to a stake at the foot of a mountain then along the same North forty eight West one hundred and fifty seven poles to a dogwood thence south thirty four deg. West sixty three and one fourth poles to the beginning Having such form as represented by the above Platt. Surveyed the 23rd day of March 1825

JAMES PHILLIPS) By
Jonathan Wood
JOHN RAINS) C.C. Surveyor of
Cocke County

141

ROYAL STOKELY 24 ACRES

State of Tennessee Cocke County

By Virtue of an entry made in the entry takers office for the aforesaid count at Newport of No. 300 dated the twenty seventh of November 1824. I have surveyed for ROYAL STOKELY twenty four acres of land on the waters of Big creek Beginning at a chesnut near WM FAUBIAN line running thence with conditional lines with ELLISONS south fifty three deg. East seventy three poles to a white Oak xxxxxx half East thirty nine poles to a sourwood North fifty one East twenty six poles to a stake on a clift of big creek south eighty two and an half East crossing said creek twenty six poles to a Maple on JAMES NICHOLS line then with ditto North twenty one and an half West sixty four poles to a stake corner to said STOKELY then with his line a direct line to the beginning. Having such form as is represented by the above Platt. Surveyed the thirtith of November 1824 By

BENGIMON DAVIS)
Jonathan Woos
JOHN SHARP) C.C. Surveyor of
Cocke County

142

JONAS PHILLIPS 50 ACRES

State of Tennessee Cocke County

By Virtue of an entry made in the entry takers office for the aforesaid county at Newport of No. 155 dated the 3rd day of July 1824 I have surveyed for JONAS PHILLIPS fifty acres of land on Cosbys creek Beginning at a white walnut on the south side of said creek running down the same seventy four and an half deg. West one hundred and fifty seven poles to a stake sixteen poles below a beech Marked with three notches thence North thirty five and an half deg. West forty poles to a stake on the top of a ridge then with a conditional [line] with WILLIAM HOOPER south fifty six East one hundred and fifty three poles to a Maple then north

thirty one and an half deg. East sixty three and one fourth poles to the Beginning. Having such form as represented by the above platt. Surveyed the 23rd of March 1825. By
WM SMITH)
Jonathan Wood
WM HARPER?) C.C. Surveyor of
Cocke County

B. BUCKNER 35 ACRES
State of Tennessee Cocke County
By Virtue of an entry made in the entry takers office for the aforesaid county at Newport of No. 196 dated 5th day of July 1824 I have surveyed for BORROW BUCKNER thirty five acres of land on the waters of English creek. Beginning at a stake on JOHN LEWIS line and on or near North corner running thence with North line North forty three and one fourth West twenty eight poles to a white Oak on said BUCKNERS line then with ditto south sixty nine West forty nine poles to a stake in the edge of the co---? Road south fifty two West crossing said road eighty poles to a stake south forty four poles to a stake East thirty nine poles to a stake on LEWIS line then with his lines North forty five poles to a hickory stump North sixty four East one hundred and three poles to the beginning Having such form as represented by the above Platt. Surveyed the 16th of February 1825
TARLTON BRYANT) By Jonathan
Wood
SAND[?] LEWIS) C.C. Surveyor of Cocke County

143
WILLIAM COLEMAN 100 ACRES
State of Tennessee Cocke County
By Virtue of an entry made in the entry takers office for the aforesaid county at Newport of No. 169 dated the 5th day of July 1825 I have surveyed for WILLIAM COLEMAN one hundred acres of land on the West side of Pigeon river Beginning at a hickory on a ridge corner between said COLEMAN and WELCH South forty five and a half degrees west Ninety eight poles to a white Oak on the side of a ridge south forty four and an half East two hundred poles to three chesnuts and one hickory on a ridge thence North forty five and an half East sixty three and an half poles to a stake on said COLEMANS line of a tract of land where on he now lives thence with the same North four and one half west xxxxxx the Beginning Having such form as represented By the Platt. Surveyed the 18th day of April 1825
COUNSELLOR I. COLEMAN) By Jonathan
Wood
JOSEPH RUTHEFORD) C.C. Surveyor of Cocke County

BENGIMONN O.DELL 50 ACRES
State of Tennessee Cocke County
By Virtue of an entry made in the Entry takers office for the county aforesaid at Newport of No. 178 dated the 5th day of July 1824 I have surveyed for BENGIMON O.DELL fifty acres of land in the county and state aforesaid between the rivers of French Broad and Big Pigeon. Beginning at a locust corner to said O.DELL thence South with one hundred and twenty six poles and forty hundredths of a pole to a stake near two lege poplars Thence west sixty three poles and twenty three hundreths of a pole to a stake in a flat thence north one hundred and twenty six poles and forty six hundreths of a pole to a stake thence East sixty three poles twenty three hundreths of a pole to the beginning. Having such form as represented by the above platt. Surveyed the 25th day of April 1825
ABRAHAM McCAY[COY]) By Jonathan
Wood
LEWIS O.DELL) C.C. Principal Surveyor of Cocke County

JOSEPH BLACK 50 ACRES

State of Tennessee Cocke County
By Virtue of an entry made in the entry takers office for the aforesaid county at Newport of No. 122 dated the 8th June 1824 I have surveyed for JOSEPH BLACK fifty acres of land on the waters of long creek. Beginning at a loge? poplar not far from a spring and on the North side of the road leading from Newport of HOLLANDS ferry runing thence south twenty deg. West eighty nine and a half poles crossing the aforesaid road to a stake thence south sixty seven deg. East eighty nine and a half poles to a stake near a Marked chesnut thence xxxxxxxxxx crossing said road at sixty six poles the same course continued in all Eighty nine and a half poles to a stake in a hollow thence a direct line to the beginning Having such form as is represented by the above platt. Surveyed the 1st day of June 1825 by
JACOB HUFFMON)
Jonathan Wood
JAMES M. BENSON) C.C. Principal
Surveyor of Cocke County

JACOB SMITH 75 ACRES

State of Tennessee Cocke County
By Virtue of an entry made in the entry takers office for the aforesaid county at Newport of No. 301. Dated the 4th day of December 1824 I have surveyed for JACOB SMITH seventy Five acres of land in said county on the waters of Long creek Beginning at a white Oak running thence North fifty Nine deg. East sixty eight poles to a post Oak and a pine on JESSE RUVIS[?] line then with his lines south thirty three East fifty six poles to a chesnut stump North thirty Nine east eighty poles to a black gum south sixty East sixty one poles to a black Oak south thirty West one hundred and forty to two white Oaks thence a direct line to the beginning Having such form as is represented by the above platt. Surveyed the 5th day of May 1825 By
HENRY NETHERTON)
Jonathan Wood
RICHARD COOPER) C.C. Surveyor of
Cocke County

145
DAVID ESLINGER 50 ACRES

State of Tennessee Cocke County
By Virtue of an entry made in the entry takers office for Cocke County at Newport of No 200 dated the 5th day of July 1824 I have surveyed for DAVID ESLINGER fifty acres of land in said county on the waters of Oven creek. Beginning at a white Walnut near the mouth of a branch corner to said ESLINGER running thence with a conditional line xxxxxx xxxxxxxx south fifty two deg. West sixty three and one fourth poles to a black Oak grub on the side of a ridge North thirty Eight deg. east one hundred twenty six and an half poles to a white Oak on the top of a high ridge thence south fifty two degrees east sixty three and one fourth poles to a stake on the line of a tract of land whereon the said ESLINGER now lives thence with the same south thirty Eight west one hundred twenty six and a half poles to the beginning having such form as is represented by the above platt. surveyed the 11th day of May 1825 By
IVY GAMMON)
Jonathan Wood
JOHN NEAS) C.C.
Surveyor of Cocke County

JOHN HUFF 16 ACRES

State of Tennessee Cocke County
By Virtue of an entry made in the entry takes office of aforesaid county at Newport of No. 310 dated 4th of January 1825. I have surveyed for JOHN HUFF sixteen acres of land on the waters of big creek Beginning at a poplar near a small branch by the foot of a steep Nobb running thence a long the foot of said Nobb North eighty one deg. East forty nine poles to a stake on said HUFF line near two large poplars then with said line North forty four poles to a sour wood on the line of the heirs of JOHN STOKELY Dec., then with ditto west sixty poles to a black Oak on the side of a hill a direct line to the Beginning. Having such form as is represented by the above Platt. surveyed the 3rd day of May 1825.

NICHOLAS WOODY) By Jonathan Wood
JETHU[RE?] GESTER) C.C. Surveyor of Cocke County

JOHN HUFF 16 ACRES

State of Tennessee Cocke County
By Virtue of an entry made in the entry takers office for said county at Newport of No. 310. dated 4th of January 1825. I have surveyed for JOHN HUFF sixteen acres of land on the waters of big creek Beginning at a poplar Near a small branch by the foot of a steep Nobb running thence along the foot of said Nobb North Eighty one deg. East forty Nine poles to a stake on said HUFF line near two large poplars then with said line North forty four poles to a sourwood on the line of the heirs of JOHN STOKELY DEC. then with ditto West sixty poles to black Oak on the side of a steep hill then a direct line to the Beginning. Having such form as is represented by the above Platt. Surveyed the 3rd day of May 1825.

NICHOLAS WOODY) By Jonathan Wood
JETHU[?] JESTER) C.C. Surveyor of Cocke County

Note: It is likely that the person who copied in long hand from the original survey book has copied this one twice, there being such a long space between page numbers.

146
WILERY WYNFREE[WynFree] 120 ACRES

State of Tennessee Cocke County
By Virtue of an Entry made in the entry takers office for the aforesaid county at Newport of No. 90 dated the 5th day of June 1825 I have surveyed for WHYLY WINFREE[WinFree] one hundred and twenty acres of land on the North side of French Broad river Beginning at a hickory corner to said WynFree fifteen acre tract running thence xxxxx sixty west fifteen poles to a white Oak North thirty Nine west sixty eight poles to a black gum the original corner of a 400 acre tract thence west seventy eight poles to a white Oak on McROYS line then with the same south thirty Two West forty poles to Two black Oaks bushes south fifty five poles to a stake near a Marked post Oak East one hundred and eighty seven poles to a hickory North One hundred poles to the Beginning. Having such form as is represented by the above platt. Surveyed the 28th day of May 1825 By

ABRAHAM McCAY[COY]) Jonathan Wood
JEREMIAH McCAY[COY]) C.C. Surveyor of Cocke County

HENRY NETHERTON 50 ACRES
State of Tennessee Cocke County
By Virtue of an entry made in the entry takers office for the aforesaid county at Newport of No 290 dated 16th of October 1824 I have surveyed for HENRY NETHERTON fifty acres of land on both sides of long creek. Beginning at on Ash on the line FRUSHIAS ev all[?] deed running thence North seventy one East one hundred and twenty four poles to a dogwood and hickory on the side of a ridge then south Nineteen East crossing long creek at Nineteen poles the same course continued in all seventy four poles to a stake on the side of the Mountain ten poles from a Marked chesnut Oak thence south seventy one West Ninety two poles to a stake on the line of FRUTHIAS dec. then with the same North forty three west crossing said creek at thirteen poles the same course continued Sixty Eight poles to the Beginning Having such form as represented by the above platt. Surveyed the 5th day of May 1825
JACOB SMITH   )   By Jonathan Wood
ABRAHAM HOOPER) C.C.   Surveyor of Cocke County

147
B. O,DELL 50 ACRES

State of Tennessee Cocke County
By Virtue of an entry made in the Entry takers office for the aforesaid county of No. 144 dated the 2nd of July 1824 I have surveyed for BENGIMON O,DELL fifty acres of land on the waters of French broad between big Pigeon and French broad. Beginning at a willow running with conditional lines with WM. FOX North Twenty four West seven poles to a white Oak north fifty five West eight poles to a stake South eighty four West Twenty four poles to a stake North thirty five West Nineteen poles to a white Oak on said FOXES old line then with his line south sixty six west twenty three poles to a stake North eighty eight West fifty six poles to a black Oak thence south eighteen poles to a stake on Said O,DELLS lines of a tract whereon he now lives then with the same East one hundred twenty one and a half poles to a stake then with FOXES lines north forty eight west six poles to a walnut north sixty one and a half East three and one half to the beginning. Having such form as is represented by the above platt. Surveyed the 25th of April 1825.
ABRAHAM McCOR[CAY])   By Jonathan Wood
LEWIS O,DELL   ) C.C.   surveyor of Cocke County

148
JOHN ELLISON SR. 50 ACRES

State of Tennessee Cocke County
By Virtue of an entry made in the entry takers office for the aforesaid county at Newport of No. 325 - Dated 1st day of March 1825. I have surveyed for JOHN ELLISON SR. fifty acres of land on the waters of Big Creek Beginning at a dogwood corner to said ELLISON running thence with his lines south forty six deg. West fifty six poles to a white Oak at the foot of the ugly ridge North sixty one west twenty six poles to a branch the same course continued in all eighty poles to a cucumber on the side of a mountain then along do- North thirteen deg. east twenty two poles to a chesnut on JOHN ELLISON SR. line then with ditto North thirty one east twenty two poles to beech North forty four xxxxxxxx to a buck Eye then along a Nobb and branch south thirty six and one half east seventy five poles to a stake Near a white Oak and sourwood in a hollow thence south thirty six and one half East forty five poles to a sorvis and Birch then a direct line to the Beginning Having such form as is represented by the above Platt.

surveyed the 5th of May 1825 By
MOTTIE[MATTIE] ELLISON) Jonathan Wood
JACOB ELLISON) C.C.surveyor of Cocke County.

JAMES HUFFMON 50 ACRES
State of Tennessee Cocke County
By Virtue of an entry made in the entry takers office for the aforesaid county at Newport of No. 182 dated the 5th day of October 1824. I have surveyed for JACOB HUFFMAN [sic] fifty acres of land on the North side of French Broad river. Beginning at a stake on the line of a hundred and twenty five acre tract of WYLY WINFREE near a black Oak bark[?] thence south thirty two deg. West one hundred and twenty seven poles to a stake near McCOYS [McCAYS] line South fifty Eight East eighty Eight and one half poles to three pines. North thirty two East Ninety two poles to a stake on WINFREE [written Winfree] line then with his lines West fiftyfive poles to a stake North Eighty five poles to the beginning. Having such form as represented by the above Platt. surveyed the 31st day of May 1825 By
WYLY WINFREE)
Jonathan Wood
JOHN HUFFMAN) C.C. surveyor of Cocke County

149
WILLIAM GIBSON 50 ACRES
State of Tennessee Cocke County
By Virtue of an entry made in the entry takers office for the aforesaid county at Newport of No. 315 dated the 13th January 1825 I have surveyed for WILLIAM GIBSON fifty acres of land on both sides of sinking creek Beginning at a stake twenty poles from the south side of said creek near a double chesnut Marked Mouth and Eyes, running thence south thirty eight West Eighty four poles to a black Oak North fifty two West crossing sinking creek twenty three poles to a beech in ELLIOT SIMS line thence with ditto North twenty seven and one half poles to two white Oaks Thence West sixty four poles to a stake corner to SIMS North crossing Severeville road at sixteen poles in all seventy poles to a stake then a direct line to the beginning. Having such form as represented by the above Platt. surveyed the 14th day of June 1825. By
JOHN HAND)
Jonathan Wood
CHARLES GIBSON) C.C. surveyor of Cocke County

150
JOHN HUFF 100 ACRES
State of Tennessee Cocke County
By Virtue of an entry made in the entry takers office for the aforesaid county at Newport of No. 75. Dated the 24th od May 1824 I have surveyed for JOHN HUFF one hundred acres of land on the waters of big creek. Beginning at a chesnut near a Mountain on the East side of a branch running thence North forty five West five poles to a stake and North forty five East eighty poles to a hollow chesnut then along a Mountain - North thirty one poles to a Lynn North sixteen East thirty five poles to a large Maple South seventy four East nine and a half poles to a clift of rocks then along ditto and a branch south twenty six and a half East sixty six poles to a chesnut south seventy three East thirty six poles to a poplar south thirty five East Eighty five poles to a stake on the side of a Mountain thence a direct line to the beginning. Having such form as is represented by the above platt. surveyed the xxxxx 1825 By
DAVID HUFF)
Jonathan Wood
JOHN MASON) C.C.
SURVEYOR OF Cocke County

THOMAS MANTOOTH 100 ACRES

State of Tennessee Cocke County
By Virtue of an Entry made in the entry takes office for the aforesaid County at Newport of No. 228 dated 12th day of Jany 1824 I have surveyed for THOMAS MANTOOTH one hundred acres of land on the East side of Big Pigeon River Beginning on a White Oak near a small branch at the foot of a ridge running thence North Eighty Nine and an half poles two hickorys and a black Oak near GAMES[?] big surveys line thence west one hundred and forty one poles to a large spanish Oak south one hundred and fourteen poles to a dead locust. thence East one hundred and forty one poles to a stake on the side of a ridge thence North Twenty Having such form as represented By the above Platt. surveyed the 24th day of June 1825. By
STEPH LEA)
Jonathan Wood
JOHN FOX) C.C.
surveyor of Cocke County

151
NANCY HICKS 50 ACRES

By Virtue of an Entry made in the Entry takers office for the aforesaid county at Newport of No. 199 dated the 5th day of July 1824. I have surveyed for NANCY HICKS fifty acres of land on bogard creek Beginning at a stake near a hickory fer corner running thence south crossing said creek thirteen poles to a buckeye at the foot shortass Mountain thence along Ditto North seventy one West thirty six poles to a stake north thirty Nine west forty poles to an Ironwood North fifty five poles west fortytwo poles to a White Oak then With MORRISONS line North seventeen East ten poles to a hickory North thirty Two and one half. East sixty eight poles to a White Oak corner to ALLENS then with his line south seventy three East twelve poles to a White Oak North thirty five East twelve poles to a stake Eighty East thirty five poles to a pine on his line thence with same a direct line to the beginning Having such form as is represented by the above platt. surveyed the 5th day of September 1825 By
WM GREGORY)
Jonathan Wood
THOMAS ALLEN) C.C Surveyor of
Cocke County

PHILIP NEAS 50 ACRES

State of Tennessee Cocke County
By Virtue of an entry made in the Entry Takers office for the aforesaid county at Newport of No. 229 dated 13th July 1824 I have surveyed for PHILIP NEAS fifty acres of land on the waters of Clear Creek Beginning on at a black Oak corner to JOHN OTTINGERS on said NEAS line running with thence with said lines North seventy six poles to a white Oak East forty eight poles to a pine North twenty Eight East twenty poles to a black Oak and post Oak North sixty poles to a stake on SMELCERS[?] line then with same West one hundred and ten poles to a hickory South sixty eight poles to a white Oak and poplar near a cove seventeen poles to a Walnut south six poles to a stake near OTTINGERS line thence a direct line to the beginning Having such from as is represented by the above platt. surveyed the 29th day of August 1825 By
JOSIAH REN[RIN, RICE?]) Jonathan
Wood
FREDRICK SMELSER) C.C. surveyor of Cocke County

152

SAMUEL STUART 50 ACRES

By Virtue of an Entry made in the Entry takers office for the said County at Newport of No 342 dated the 23rd day of August 1824 I have surveyed for SAMUEL STUART fifty acres of land on the waters of long Creek Beginning at a White Oak corner to said STUART and GEORGE NEAS running thence South one fourth of a degree East one hundred and twelve poles to two White Oaks corner to HUGH STUART near three springs thence with said HUGH STUARTS line North fifty four East thirty four poles to Two White Oaks and a poplar East thirty eight poles to a red Oak North fifteen East ninety eight poles to a black Oak then a direct line to the beginning. Having such form as represented By the above platt. surveyed the 30th of August 1825

WM McROY) By
Jonathan Wood
SAMUEL STUART) C.C. surveyor of
Cocke County

JOSEPH WILLIAMS 7 ACRES 3 RODS & 5 POLES

By Virtue of an entry Made in the Entry takers office for the aforesaid county at Newport of No 330 dated 1st day of April 1825 for eight acres I have surveyed for JOSEPH WILLIAMS seven acres three rods and five poles it being all the Vacant land that could be had for adjoining lands. Beginning at a stake on MALOYS[?] line Corner to JOHN EISENHOURS on the south side of Clear Creek running thence with said EISENHOURS line south Eighty three poles to a post Oak on MALOYS[?] line then with said MALOYS line North thirty three deg. East fifty four poles to a dead post Oak thence a direct line to the beginning. Having such form as is represented By the above platt surveyed the 30th August 1825 By

JAMES MALOY)
Jonathan Wood
JOHN EISENHOUR) C.C. surveyor of
Cocke County

153

JESSE SMITH 50 ACRES

By Virtue of an Entry Made in the entry takers office for the aforesaid County of No. 289 dated the 16th of October 1824 I have surveyed for JESSE SMITH fifty acres of land on the waters of Neelys Creek Beginning at a White Oak on ISAAC JESTUS line Near said SMITHS old corner running thence East eighty Nine and a half poles to a hickory south eighty Nine and a half poles to a White Oak West eighty Nine and a half poles to a stake North eighty Nine and a half Poles to the beginning Having such form as is represented by the above platt, surveyed the 21st of July 1825. By

JOHN SMITH)
Jonathan Wood
WM TYRY) C.C.
surveyor of Cocke County

JOSEPH SUTTON 20 ACRES

State of Tennessee Cocke County

By Virtue of an entry Made in the entry takers office for the aforesaid county at Newport of No. 156 dated the 3rd day of July 1824. I have surveyed for JOSEPH SUTTON twenty acres of land on Chools? creek. Beginning at a persimmon at the foot of English Mountain Near the West side of said Creek running thence along said Mountain South Nine deg. West eighty poles to a large poplar and dogwood thence south eighty one deg. East forty poles crosing said creek to a sourwood, North Nine East eighty poles to Treeble [or trubble] dogwood thence North eighty one West forty poles to the Beginning Having such form as is represented by the above platt. Surveyed the 6th day of September 1825 - By

SOLOMON STEPHENS)
Jonathan Wood
GEORGE RUNIONS) C.C. Surveyor of
Cocke County

154
<u>THOMAS D. ADNEY & JAMES PUTMON 20 ACRES</u>

By Virtue of an entry Made in the entry takers office for the aforesaid county at Newport of No 297 dated the 18th day of March 1824 I have surveyed for THOMAS D. ADNEY and JAS. PUTMON twenty acres of land on the waters of sinking creek Beginning at a beech corner to WILLIAM TOADMAN on the West side of said creek running with said ROADMAN line West fifty poles and an half poles to a dogwood thence North fifty seven poles to a stake on EILLIOT SIMS line thence with the same East fifty seven and an half poles crossing the aforesaid creek to a Spanish Oak and beech thence South fifty six poles to the Beginning-Having such form as represented by the above Platt. Surveyed 29th day of July 1825

JOHN SIMS)
Jonathan Wood
WILLIAM SMITH) C.C. Surveyor of
Cocke County

<u>WM W. BIBEE 5 ACRES</u>

State of Tennessee Cocke County
By Virtue of an entry Made in the entry takers office for the aforesaid county at Newport of No 154 dated the 3rd of July 1824 I have surveyed for WILLIAM W. BIBEE fifty acres of land including his improvement on the waters of the dry fork of Clay Creek. Beginning on a White Oak Near a large hickory on ALEXANDER DRISKILL line running thence with the same south thirty six and an half East fifty four and three fourths poles to a White Oak south forty Eight and a half West forty poles to White Oak then with conditional line with ALEXANDER DRISKILL North eighty eight West six poles to a gum south fifty four West forty four and an half poles to a hickory south Eighty Nine West Nineteen poles to a stake on GILLETTS line then with the same North twenty Eight East Nineteen poles to a dogwood West twenty poles to a stake South Ninety poles to a stake then a direct line to the beginning Having such form as represented by the above platt surveyed the 20th of July 1825.

JNO. EDWARDS)
Jonathan Wood
THOS. GILLETT) C.C. surveyor of
Cocke County

155
<u>MARTHA DENTON 10 ACRES AND 64 POLES</u>

State of Tennessee Cocke County
By Virtue of an entry Made in the entry takers office for the aforesaid county at Newport of No. 306 dated the 20th day of December 1824 I have surveyed for MARTHA DENTON ten acres and sixty four poles of land it being all the Vacant land that could be had for interfearing lines. Beginning at a stake on the waters of Cosbys Creek Near a post Oak on JOSEPH HUFF line running thence with the same south twenty eight East twenty six poles to a black Oak south twenty four West eighty one poles to a black Oak corner xxxxxxxxxx [sic] thence With his line Nine xxx[sic] East seventeen poles to a post Oak North Nineteen Eat seventeen poles to a post Oak North thirty three and on poles [sic] to a stake corner to JONATHAN DENTON then with his lines south fifty two and a half East Eleven poles to a large black Oak then a direct line to the Beginning Having such form as represented By the above platt. Surveyed the 22nd day of June 1825

JAMES FULLER) Jonathan
Wood
JOS. POGITT[PAGETT?]) C.C. surveyor of Cocke County

156
THOMAS GANN 50 ACRES

State of Tennessee Cocke County
By virtue of an entry made in the Entry takers office for the aforesaid county at Newport of No. 286, dated the 12th day of October 1824 I have surveyed for THOMAS GANN fifty acres of land on the waters of Bognard? Creek. Beginning at a white Oak corner BITSY LOX running thence with her lines south fifty three East twenty two poles and an half to a hickory North seventy six and an half East twenty five poles crossing the cave[cove] road to a chesnut North eighty three and an half East eighty three poles to a stake on Butlers [or Bullers] line then with his lines South fifty six poles to Two Black Oakes south sixty West one hundred and fifty three poles crossing said road to a stake North seventy six poles to a pine on a ridge then a direct line with E. LOSES to the beginning. Having such form as represented by the above platt. Surveyed 22nd day of June 1825.
JOHN HENRY   )
Jonathan Wood
WILLIAM MURRELL) C.C. surveyor of
Cocke County

POLLY COOPER 8 ACRES

State of Tennessee Cocke County
By Virtue of an entry made in the Entry takers office for the aforesaid County at Newport of No 324, dated 28th of February 1825. I have surveyed for POLLY COOPER Eight acres of land on the waters of Boguard Creek Beginning at a gum and poplar corner to MOSES HICKES thence running with or nearly with his line East twenty five and one fourth Poles to a White Oak crossing the public road then along a rocky ridge south eleven poles to a sasafras south twenty six and an half West ten poles to a white Oak south thirty poles to a beech south twenty five East twenty and an half poles to a red Oak south eighteen poles to a sassafras stump then with BUTLERS lines north twenty six west seventy Eighty poles to a White Oak then a direct line to the beginning. Having such form as is represented by the above platt. Surveyed the 22nd day of June 1825.
JOB MERRELL)
Jonathan Wood
JOHN BULLEN) C.C. surveyor of
Cocke County
[Butler is written more like Butter while the John at bottom is plainly written Bullen.]

157
WILLIAM FOX 50 ACRES

State of Tennessee Cocke County
By Virtue of an entry made in the entry takers office of the county aforesaid at Newport of No. 132 dated the 30th June 1824 I have surveyed for WILLIAM FOX fifty acres of land on the South West side of French Broad river. Beginning at an Ash on the bank of said river a corner to said FOX running thence down the same North sixteen west fifty three poles to a sycamore tree then with conditional lines with KINDRICK west thirty one poles to a black Oak South Twenty Eight poles to a white Oak corner to said KINDRICK then with his line south fifty four west sixty poles to Two dogwoods and a white Oak south forty poles to a stake on or near said FOXES line then with the same one xxxxx stake north twenty East fifty six poles xx East twenty one poles to the beginning Having such form as represented by the above platt. Surveyed the 12th day of September 1825.
ABRAHAM FOX)
Jonathan Wood
LEVI FOX   ) C.C. surveyor of
Cocke County

ALEXANDER E. SMITH 500 ACRES

State of Tennessee Cocke County
By Virtue of an entry made in the entry takers office for the aforesaid county at Newport No 189 Dated the 5th day of July 1824. I have surveyed for ALEXANDER E. SMITH Five hundred acres of land in Cocke County on the west side of Big Pigeon river Bounded as follows Viz Beginning at a white Oak on the spur of a ridge between two branches about 30 poles from the junction thereof running thence north seventy deg. West one hundred and nineteen poles to a stake on SAMUEL JACKS line then with the dame north fifty nine deg. East thirty poles to a chestnut on a ridge corner to HENRY JACK then with his line north twelve East One hundred and thirty poles to a white Oak North sisty four and one half East thirty three poles to a white Oak and gum corner to WM COLEMAN then with his line North thirty four and an half west Twenty five poles to a stake then with conditional line with said COLEMAN North fifty four west nineteen poles to a stake North Eighty Nine and a half west twelve poles to a stake south sixty six and an half west fourteen poles to a black oak north fifty four west sixteen and a half poles to a white Oak then with COLEMANS new survey south forty five and a half west twenty sic poles to three chestnuts Oaks and a hickory on a ridge north forty four and a half west two hundred poles and a half west Two hundred poles to a white Oak thence with vacant land south forty five and an half two hundred and four poles to a sugar tree near a branch not far from FRANCIS J. CORXXXXXXXXXXXXXXXXXXXXXXXXXXXX [sic]
[Evidently there was a part missing or not legible, where these x's are in this handwritten copy.]

WILLIAM FOX 50 ACRES

State of Tennessee Cocke County
By Virtue of an entry made in the Entry takers office for the aforesaid county at Newport of No. 133 dated the 30th of June 1824 I have surveyed for WILLIAM FOX fifty acres of land on the south west side of French Broad river Beginning at a black oak and dogwood corner to JOSEPH CAMERON on what is called Bald ridges Big survey running thence with said CAMERONS line East ninety three poles to a stake in the puvlic road thence with said FOXES line south forty west forty eight poles to a stake south twelve West one hundred and five poles to a red Oak and hickory west forty poles to a sourwood and two chesnuts near a clift of rock on the west side of a steep hollow then north one hundred and forty poles to the beginning Having such form as is represented by the above platt. surveyed the 12th day of September 1825.
ABRAHAM FOX)
Jonathan Wood
LEVI FOX) C.C. Surveyor of
Cocke County

SHADRICK WILLIAMS 150 ACRES

State of Tennessee Cocke County
By Virtue of an entry made in the entry takers office for the aforesaid county at Newport of no 142 dated the 1st of July 1824 I have surveyed for SHADRICK WILLIAMS one hundred and fifty acres of land on the waters of Wileys Creek Beginning on a dead white Oak on JESTUS line in a field running thence East one hundred and sixty poles to stake in a hollow North one hundred and sixty poles to Two hickorys on JOHN TURNER'S line then with his line south three and one half west thirty poles to a white Oak south forty eight west thirty poles to a stake on or near JAMES TURNERS line then a direct line with TURNER'S line and ISAAC JESTUS to the beginning. Having such form as is represented by the above platt Surveyed the 22nd day of April 1825 by
JAMES TURNER & WM WILLIAMS C.C.Jonathan Wood surveyor of Cocke County

GEORGE LARUE 50 ACRES

State of Tennessee Cocke County
By Virtue of an entry made in the entry takers office for the aforesaid county of No. 331 dated 13th day of July 1824 I have surveyed for GEORGE LARUE fifty acres of land on the south side of French Broad River beginning a a white Oak on said LARUES line in a hollow running thence north sixty East sixty three and one fourth poles to a take on the side of a hill north four and an half west forty six and a half poles to a spanish oak on the top of a ridge north twenty five west Eighty poles to a stake sixteen poles from a marked beech twenty two poles to a white Oak corner to said LARUE and JAMES CLARK then with his own lines south ten west ninty seven poles to a white oak stump north seventy two East Two and an half poles to a hickory south seventy two East sixty one poles to the Beginning Having such form as is represented by the above platt. Surveyed the 13th of October 1824 By
JAMES PUCKET)
Jonathan Wood
WM LARUE) C.C. Surveyor of
Cocke County

160
ABRAHAM FINE SR. 16 ACRES

State of Tennessee Cocke County
By Virtue of an entry made in the entry takers office for the aforesaid county at Newport of No. 161 dated the third day of July 1824. I have surveyed for ABRAHAM FINE SR. sisteen acres of land on the waters of English Creek Beginning at a White Oak corner to JAMES GRAY running thence with his line north forty four and an half deg. East crossing Cosbys creek road at Ninety eight poles to a stake near a marked black Oak north forty five and an half west twenty seven poles to a stake on ROMNER? line then with the same south forty four west one hundred and thirteen and an half poles to a stake on HENRY JONES line then a long the same south fifty and an half East twenty seven and an half poles to the Beginning Having such form as represented by the above platt. Surveyed the 21st day of September 1825 By
ABRAHAM FINE)
Jonathan Wood
GEORGE GRAY) C.C. Surveyor of
Cocke County

161
W. C. STORY 50 ACRES

State of Tennessee Cocke County
By Virtue of an entry made in the entry takers office for the said county at Newport of No. 274 dated the 25th day of August 1824. I have surveyed for WILLIAM C. STORY fifty acres of land on the north side of French Broad river. Beginning at a white Oak the south west corner of STORYS new survey of fifty acres running thence south twenty three west one hundred and seven poles to a black oak corner to EDOM KINDRICK then with his line west nineteen poles to a stake and black Oak on PETER FINES? line then with the same south twenty poles to a stake thence East one hundred poles to a stake then north with KINDRICKS line one hundred and twenty poles to a post Oak stump on said STORYS line then with the same west thirty nine poles to the beginning. Having such form as is represented By the above platt. Surveyed the 28th day of July 1825.
JACOB FAUBION)
Jonathan Wood
THOMSON BROYELS) C.C. surveyor of
Cocke County

ESTHER O'DELL 50 ACRES

State of Tennessee Cocke County
By Virtue of an entry made in the entry takers office for said county at Newport of No. 209 dated the 6th day of July 1824 I have surveyed for ESTHER O'DELL fifty acres of land including her improvement on the waters of Boguard Creek Beginning at a poplar on the north side of said creek running thence with LEWIS lines north twenty two and an half East thirty five poles to a stake in the creek north five west six poles to a beech then with MARTHA DENTONS lines north thirteen West seven poles to a stake North eighty Two East ten poles to a pine North six East fifty poles to a stake North forty three West six poles to a black Oak North twenty six West sixty poles to two black Oakes and a white Oak south fifty one west one hundred poles to a white oak then a direct line to the beginning. Having such form as represented by the above platt. Surveyed the 7th day of September 1825
TIMOTHY HICKS)
Jonathan Wood
ABRAHAM DENTON) C.C. Surveyor of
Cocke County

162
THOMAS ALLEN 50 ACRES

By Virtue of an entry made in the Entry Takers office for the aforesaid county at Newport of No. 198 dated the 5th day of August 1824 I have surveyed for THOMAS ALLEN fifty acres of land on the waters of Cosbys Creek. Beginning on a stake near a poplar running North sixty East one hundred and twenty poles to a stake in a sink hole thence south thirty East eighty poles to a stake then south sixty West thirty six poles to Two poplars on said ALLENS line then with the same North sixty five West sixty poles to a locast south fifty poles to two hickorys south sixty west Twenty five poles to a post Oak and stake then a direct line to the Beginning. Having such form as is represented by the above platt. surveyed the 5th day of September 1825
WILLIAM GREGORY)
Jonathan Wood
WILLIAM HICKS) C.C. surveyor of
Cocke County

163
THOMAS FOWLER 75 ACRES

State of Tennessee Cocke County
By Virtue of an entry made in the Entrytakers office for the aforesaid county of Newport of No. 266 dated 23rd August 1824 I have surveyed for THOMAS FOWLER seventy five acres of land on the North side of Clear Creek. Beginning an a black [oak] supposed to be on or near said FOWLERS line running thence south eighty three and a half East twenty eight poles to a white Oak corner to JOHN SWAGERTY then with his line East one hundred and seven poles to a stake in a hollow North twenty poles to a dead white Oak then conditional line North forty west fifty one poles to a black Oak West thirty nine poles to a white Oak North thirty two West One hundred and eight poles to a stake on a ridge West forty four and a half poles to a stake south thirty six and a half East one hundred poles to a sassafras South sixty two west fifty five poles to a post Oak then a direct line to the beginning. Having such form as is represented by the above platt. surveyed the 20th of June 1825
A FOWLER)
Jonathan Wood
L. FOWLER) C.C.
surveyor of Cocke County

MURDOCK McSWIEN 75 ACRES

State of Tennessee Cocke County
By Virtue of an entry made in the entry takers office for the aforesaid county at Newport of No. 158 Dated the 3rd day of July 1824. I have surveyed for MURDOCK McSWIEN seventy five acres of land including his improvements on the south side of Big Pigeon river Beginning at a black Oak bush near a large pine on a conditional line between him and ADAM GANN running thence with ditto south forty three and a half East one hundred and fourteen poles to a stake on JOHN RUTHERFORDS line thence along ditto South thirty poles to a stake supposed to be not far from McKAYS line then South seventy five West eighty five poles to two black Walnuts on the side of a rocky hill North thirteen East sixteen poles to a poplar corner to ABRAHAM FINE thence with his line North Eighty five poles to a white Oak stump North sixty five and an half West thirty nine poles to a pine corner to said McSWIEN then with his line East forty eight poles to a hickory and white Oak on HENRY'S line south forty eight East forty five poles to a post Oak south thirty Nine West twenty Nine poles to the beginning. Having such form as is represented by the above platt. surveyed the 20th of September 1825 -
ABE FINE   )
Jonathan Wood
GEORGE GRAY) C.C.   surveyor of
Cocke County

164
ABRAHAM McKAY JR. 31 ACRES & 40 POLES

State of Tennessee Cocke County
By Virtue of an entry made in the entry takers office for said county at Newport of No. 337 dated the 25th day of May 1825 for fifty acres of land surveyed for ABRAHAM McKAY JUNR. thirty one acres and forty poles of land it being all that could be had for interfearing lines nonral[normal?] boundaries. Beginning at two black oaks corner to WYLY WINFREE on McKAYS linerunning thence with JACOB HUFFMANS south thirty two West one hundred and twenty poles to a stake south fifty eight east eighty eight poles to three pines corner to JAMES JENNINGS then with his line south thirty two West twelve poles to two pines on the North bank of French Broad of French Broad [sic] river thence down the dame and with a steep cliff of rocks north seventy one west fourteen poles to a pine South sixty five west twenty six poles to a black Oak south seventy seven west eighty poles to two white Walnuts and Hickory North two West twelve poles to a white Oak then with ABRAHAM McKAYS own line North thirty two East Two hundred and seven poles to the beginning, having such form as is represented by the above platt, surveyed the 9th day of September 1825.
LEWIS O.DELL   )
Jonathan Wood
MODER NETHERTON) C.C.   surveyor of
Cocke County

165
ALIZABETH CARUTHUS 75 ACRES

State of Tennessee Cocke County
By Virtue of an entry made in the entry takers office for the county aforesaid at Newport No. 309 dated 29th December 1824 I have surveyed for ELIZABETH CARUTHUS seventy five acres of land on the north side of French Broad river Beginning at a post Oak corner to JOHN HEADRICK running thence south forty seven degrees West sixty poles to a stake on WILLIAM FAUBIONS line then with same North twenty seven and a half West five poles to a pine south wighty west one hundred poles to a white Oak on the side of a rocky ridge Northten West eighty six poles to a stake six poles from a marked post OakNorth eighty east one hundred and thirty five poles to a stake on JOHN HEADRICKS line then with the same a direct line to the beginning. Having

such form as is represented by the above platt. surveyed the 2nd day of June 1825
JOHN HEADRICK)
Jonathan Wood
JAMES WILLIAMS) C.C. surveyor of
Cocke County

JACOB EASTERLY 25 ACRES

State of Tennessee Cocke County
By Virtue of an Entry made in the entry takers office for the aforesaid county at Newport of No. 226 dated the 12th day of July 1824. I have surveyed for JACOB EASTERLY twenty five acres of land on the waters of Oven[?] creek. Beginning at a white Oak on the county line and on his own line thence with the same south twenty three West eighty eight and an half poles to a stake on his line of a tract where on he now lives then with the same South eighty six and a half West twenty one and a half poles to a2post Oak on a fifty acre tract then with the same North forty poles to a post Oak West thirty Nine poles to a dogwood south thirty five East thirty five poles to a hickory south four west twenty four poles to a black Oak and a dogwood North fifty seven West seventeen and an half poles to a hickory North twenty West twenty two poles to a stake thence North fifty five East three poles to a stake on the countylline thence with the same a direct line to the beginning. Having such form a2s is represented by the above platt. surveyed the 11th May 1825
CHRISTOPHER ESLINGER) Jonathan
Wood
JAMES CALLIHER[GALLIHER]) C.C.SURVEYOR OF Cocke County

166
ISAAC A. MASSEY 50 ACRES

State of Tennessee Cocke County
By Virtue of an Entry made in the Entry takers office for said county at Newport of No. 74 dated the twenty fourth day of May 1824 I have surveyed for ISAAC A. MASSEY fifty acres of land including his improvements on the waters of INDIAN Creek Beginning at a stake near a marked ash in the mouth of a hollow on the south side of the public road leading from Newport of Severvill[sic] running thence across said road North thirty six and a half West One hundred poles to a dogwood and one hickory then North fifty three and a half East eighty poles to a pine on the side of a hill thence south thirty six and an half East one hundred poles to a stake thence a direct line crossing said road to the beginning. Having such form as represented by the above platt. surveyed the 6th day of October 1825
DANIEL THORTON)
Jonathan Wood
ALLEN GARRETT) C.C. surveyor of
Cocke County

167
GEORGE LAREW 50 ACRES
State of Tennessee Cocke County
By Virtue of an entry made in the entry takers office for said county at Newport of No. 307 dated the 1st of December 1824. I have surveyed for GEORGE LAREW fifty acres of land on the south side of French Broad River on Bunys [Burrys] Branch including the place where THOMAS DAFFREN [Doffren] now lives. Beginning at a white oak on the East side of a branch at the hill running thence along do south thirty West crossing said branch several times to a beech south six west sixty poles to a small poplar and birch North fifty four west fifty one to a large poplar near THOMAS MARTINS line thence North six East one hundred and forty poles to a stake then a cross north a direct line to the beginning. Having such form as represented by the above platt. surveyed the 8th day of January 1826
WILLIAM LAREW)
Jonathan Wood
JOHN LAREW) C.C. surveyor of
Cocke County

ABRAHAM DENTON 12 ACRES

State of Tennessee Cocke County
By Virtue of an entry made in the entry takers office for said county at Newport of No. 185, dated the 5th day of July 1824, for 25 acres I have surveyed for ABRAHAM DENTON twelve acres of land it being all the vacant land that could be had for older tract Beginning at a stake on JOSEPH HUFFS line near the bank of Cosby creek running thence with his line North Nine East four poles North thirty seven East Eighteen poles North fifteen East fourteen poles North sixteen West twenty poles to a large sycamore North forty Eight and an half East twenty poles to a sugar tree North thirty four and an half East thirty four poles to a sugar tree North forty eight and an half East ten poles to an Ash on the bank of said creek thence crossing the same North forty six West sixteen poles and seven links to a pine stake corner to LILLARD MEADOWS [?] tract then with the same south thirty five West twenty four poles North fifty three West two poles and three fourths corner to MARTHA DENTON then with her line south forty one an a half West thirty two poles south sixteen and an half west fifty poles south fourteen East eleven poles thence a direct line to the beginning Having such form as represented by the above platt surveyed the 17th day of Nov. 1824.

WM DENTON)
Jonathan Wood
THOS. JENKINS) C.C. surveyor of
Cocke County

168
JOHN FRESHOUR [?] 50 ACRES

State of Tennessee Cocke County
By Virtue of an entry made in the Entry takers office for said county at Newport of No. 127 dated 29th of June 1824 I have surveyed of JOHN FRESHOUR fifty acres of land including his improvements on the waters of shots creek Beginning at a white Oak running thence south forty East sixty eight poles to a spanish oak on JOHN WORTHS line thence with his line East Eight Poles to a spanish Oak south fourteen corner THOMAS DRISKELL thence North fifty East one hundred and twelve poles to a hickory North forty West seventy two poles to a sassafras bush on the side of a Ridge thence a direct line to the beginning Having such form as represented by the above platt. surveyed the second day of Nov. 1825.

JAMES TALLEY)
Jonathan Wood
ASA HOLT) C.C.

169
WM PRUITT 100 ACRES

State of Tennessee Cocke County
By Virtue of an entry made in the entry takers office for said county at Newport of No. 241 dated the 24th day of July 1824 I have surveyed for WM PRUITT one hundred acres of land on the waters of sinking creek beginning at a stake between a spanish oak and Gum said to be where JAMES ELLIS land joins REUBIN ALLEN running thence south fifty degrees west crossing public road one hundred and sixty five poles to a large poplar and chesnut thence south forty East fifty poles to some gum bush on JOHN LANE line then with the same North Eighty four East twenty three poles to a gum thence south forty East forty poles to a hickory on the side of a hedge then North fifty degrees East one hundred and forty four poles to a leaning black Oak thence a direct line to the beginning. Having such form as represented by the above platt. surveyed the 19th of October 1825

SAM PRUITT)
Jonathan Wood
HENRY GARRETT) C.C. Surveyor of
Cocke County

ALLEN SURRATT 50 ACRES

State of Tennessee Cocke County
By Virtue of an entry made in the entry takers office for said county at Newport of No. 151 dated the 3rd day of July 1824 I have surveyed for ALLEN SURRETT fifty acres of land on the waters of Indian Creek including the place where on said SURRETT Now lives Beginning at a stake running thence North twenty West one hundred and Twenty six and an half poles to a stake on the East side of a branch between a marked chesnut spanish Oak and two sour woods thence south seventy West sixty three and one fourth poles to a hickory on the side of a steep hill then with Nobb south twenty East one hundred and twenty six and a half poles to a poplar and sourwood then North seventy East sixty three and one fourth poles to the beginning. Having such form as represented by the above Platt. surveyed the 6th day of October 1825.
ISAAC NEFF
Jonathan Wood
SAML SIMMERILL[?]
surveyor of Cocke County

170
JONATHAN WOOD 50 ACRES

State of Tennessee Cocke County
By Virtue of an entry Made in the entry takers office of the aforesaid county for said county at Newport of No. 173 dated the 5th day of July 1824 I have surveyed for JONATHAN WOOD fifty acres of land adjoining the lands formerly owned by JAMES WOOD in the Dutch Bottoms Beginning at a stake on the East side of the land formerly owned by JAMES WOOD on his line Near a beech tree running thence south Eighty five East forty five poles to a sugar tree on the top of a steep precipice then along said precipice south fifty East forty two poles to a white Oak thence south twenty five deg. West one hundred and fifty poles to a stake thence North sixty five deg. West sixty six poles to a beech corner to the aforesaid tract then with the lines of the same North forty East fifty four poles to two sugar trees then North seven and three fourths West sixty six poles to beginning. Having such form as is represented by the above Platt. surveyed the 16th day of February 1826.
WM. RUVES[REEVES?]) Jonathan Wood
ISAAC BAKER) C.C. surveyor of Cocke County

171
*THOMAS MARTIN 50 ACRES

State of Tennessee Cocke County
By Virtue of an entry made in the Entry takers office for said county of No. 166 dated the 3rd day of July 1824 I have surveyed for THOMAS MARTIN fifty acres of land on the south side of French Broad river on the side of the road leading from Newport to Dandridge including the place whereon HENRY CAMERON now lives Beginning at a black Oak on the East side of a small branch Running thence North twenty five and an half deg. West one hundred and twenty one poles to a stake on JOSEPH CAMMERNS Line North seventy three West ten poles to a stake and black Oak and white Oak thence south sixty four and one half West crossing the public road fifty poles to a white Oak South seventy five and an half East one hundred and twenty six poles and an half to two pines North sixty four and an half East five poles to the beginning. Having such form as is represented by the above Platt. surveyed the 22nd day of October 1825.
HENRY CAMMERON)
Jonathan Wood
HAWKINS MORTIN) C.C. surveyor of Cocke County

*The handwriting has all a's and o's just the same, could be Mortin or Martin.

GEORGE MADDOX 25 ACRES

State of Tennessee Cocke County
By Virtue of an entry made in the Entry takers office for said county No. 157 dated the 3rd of July 1824. I have surveyed for GEORGE MADDOX twenty five acres of land on the waters of Groundhog[?] Creek. Beginning at a Maple running thence south thirty East thirty eight poles to a cucumber on the bank of said creek then along ditto south twenty one West forty six poles to a stake at the foot of a mountain then across a spur of said mountain North 66 West seventy five poles to a stake Near a leaning poplar thence North twelve West thirty five poles to a stake thence a direct line to the beginning. Having such form as is represented by the above Platt. surveyed the 26th day of Oct. 1825
WILLIAM WHITSON)
Jonathan Wood
JAMES BAXTER) C.C. surveyor of
Cocke County

172
ANDERSON NORTH 50 ACRES

State of Tennessee Cocke County
By Virtue of an Entry m4ade in the Entry takers office for said county at Newport of No. 183 dated the 5th day of July 1824 I have surveyed for ANDERSON NORTH fifty acres of land in said county on the waters of English Creek on the West side of Big Pigeon river beginning at a Mor [?] Red locust said to be over near JOHN GRIGSBYS line running thence South sixty nine East fifty four crossing Cosbys Creek road to a black Oak South thirty four west one hundred seven and a half poles to a black Oak and hickory on JONATHAN DENTONS line then North Eighty three west with his line Ninety six poles to a hickory sapling supposed to be on THOMAS DENTONS line then with ditto North two and an half west four poles to a stake then with or nearly with NORTHS line to the beginning Having such form as is represented by the above Platt. surveyed the 4th day of January 1826.
HIRAM ALLEN)
Jonathan Wood
WM FILKER) C.C. Surveyor of
Cocke County

173
JAMES CLARK 50 ACRES

State of Tennessee Cocke County
By Virtue of an Entry made in the Entry takers office for said county at Newport of No. 298 dated the 19th day of November 1824 I have surveyed for JAMES CLARK fifty acres of land in the said county on the south side of French Broad river on the waters of Irish Branch Beginning at a double dogwood on a ridge near the road leading from the dutch Bottoms to the JAMES CLARKS Mill running thence south seven deg. East eighty Nine and a half poles to an elm ash and locust thence south eighty three west eighty Nine and an half three west eighty nine and an half thence to a chestnut thence North seven deg. West eighty nine and an half poles to a black Oak thence North eighty three East eighty nine and an half poles to the beginning. Having such form as is represented by the above Platt. Surveyed the 24th day of January 1826.
JAMES WOOD)
Jonathan Wood
JOHN LAREW) C.C.
surveyor of Cocke County

HARRIS & NANCY DEWITT 86 ACRES

State of Tennessee Cocke County
By Virtue of an entry made in the Entry takers office for the said county at Newport of No. 103 dated 21st day of June 1824 I have surveyed for HARRIS nad NANCY DEWITT eighty six acres of land on the East side of Cosbys creek Beginning on a white oak on a line of a 73 1/4 acre tract of said HARRIS and NANCY DEWITT running thence with the same south eighty three East seventy five and a half poles to a large spanish Oak corner to LILLARD then with his lines North one East forty two poles to a white Oak North seventy two East fifty nine East thirty seven poles to a hickory south thirty nine East thirty five poles to a stake a sourwood north seven East seventy two and an half poles to a white Oak North Eighty three west one hundred and sixty one poles to a poplar and black Oak in the head of a steep howwow then a direct line to the beginning. Having such form as is represented by the above Platt. Surveyed the 24th day of October 1824.
DOCTOR JENNINGS) By
Jonathan Wood
JESSEE JENNINGS) C.C. Principal
surveyor of Cocke County

174
ARTHUR DAVIS 50 ACRES

State of Tennessee Cocke County
By Virtue of an entry made in the Entry takers office for said county at Newport of No. 260 dated the 12th day of August 1824 I have surveyed for ARTHUR DAVIS fifty acres of land on the waters of Slate Creek. Beginning at a red Oak on the corner of his six acre tract running thence North eighty five East one hundred and four poles to a chestnut North five West sixty seven to a dogwood thence south eighty five west one hundred and thirty seven poles to a white Oak thence south five East thirty four poles to a stake near a ash corner to the aforesaid then with the same East thirty four poles to a stake south thirty two poles to the beginning. Having such form as represented by the above Platt. Surveyed the 2nd day of November 1825.
BEN DAVIS)
Jonathan Wood
WM DAVIS) C.C.
surveyor of Cocke County

175
JOHN WALCH 100 ACRES

State of Tennessee Cocke County
By Virtue of an entry made in the Entry takers office for said county at Newport of No. 260 dated twenty of August 1824 I have surveyed for JOHN WALCH one hundred acres of land on the west side of Big Pigeon River. Beginning at a double beech the south west corner of a fifty acre tract of said WALCH running thence with same North sixty deg. East one hundred and fourteen to a hickory corner to a tract of land whereon the said WALCH now lives then with the same south one hundred and sixty eight poles to a chesnut Oak and a hickory on a ridge thence west one hundred and eight poles to a dogwood in the head of a steep hollow then North one hundred and thirty poles to the beginning. Having such form as represented by the above Platt. surveyed 23rd day of February 1826.
ABSOLOM ABBOTT)
Jonathan Wood
WM LANE[LOVE]) C.C. surveyor of
Cocke County

JACOB McDANIEL 80 ACRES

State of Tennessee Cocke County
By Virtue of an entry Made in the Entry Takers office for said County at Newport of No. 229 dated the 21st day of March 1825 I have surveyed for JACOB McDANIEL Eighty acres of land on the waters sinking cr up on both sides of the road leading from Newport to Dandridge. Beginning at a stake on the North side of said road on ELLI'S (or ELLIS) line running thence North sixty two and an half West one hundred and thirty six poles to a black Oak & post Oak on the side of a ridge south Twenty seven and an half West thirty eight poles to a stake on the top of a precifice then along Ditto and with a conditional line with ADAM GANN south thirty five and an three fourths poles to a black Oak south seventy and three fourth poles crossing said road to a stake thence East one hundred and twenty poles to a stake on JAMES ELLIS line thence with same north seventy and an fourth poles to the beginning. Having such form as is represented By the above Platt. Surveyed the 5th day of October 1825
JAMES ELLIS)
Jonathan Wood
JOHN G. GILBERT) Surveyor of
Cocke County

176
JAMES CLARK 10 ACRES

State of Tennessee Cocke County

By Virtue of an Entry Made in the Entry Takers office for the said County at Newport of No. 297 dated the 19th day of November 1824 I have surveyed for JAMES CLARK 10 a. of land on the south side of French Broad River. Beginning at a White Oak corner to said CLARK and GEORGE LAREW running thence with said CLARKS line North Twenty Two West thirty Eight poles to Two small Ashes a hickory and sugar tree then with conditional line With GEORGE LAREW East forty eight poles to a stake Near a elm, post Oak and forked dogwood then south thirty five poles to a stake then West with said LAREWS line of a 50 acre entry thirty eight poles to the beginning. Having such form as represented by the Above Platt. Surveyed the 24th day of January 1826.
JOHN LAREW)
Jonathan Wood
JAMES CLARK)
Surveyor of Cocke County

177
JOHN WALSH 50 ACRES

State of Tennessee Cocke County
By Virtue of an Entry Made in the Entry Takers office for said County at Newport of No. 232 dated the Thirteenth day of July 1824. I have surveyed for JOHN WALSH fifty acres ofland in said county on the west side of Pigeon River. Beginning at a hickory corner to said WALSH and JOHN WORD (WARD) running thence North twenty West seventy poles to a large chestnut on a high Nobb thence south twenty west One hundred and fourteen and three tenths poles to a large chinkapin in the head of a steep hollow then south twenty deg. East seventy poles to a double beech in a hollow thence North seventy East one hundred fourteen and three tenths poles to the Beginning. Having such form as is represented by the above Platt. Surveyed the 22nd day of February 1826.
ABSOLON ABBOTT, SOR) Jonathan
Wood
ABSOLON ABBOTT, JR.) Surveyor of
Cocke County

MARTIN PHILLIPS 100 ACRES

State of Tennessee Cocke County
By Virtue of an Entry Made in the Entry Takers office for said county at Newport of No. 475. dated 14th day of February 1826 I have surveyed for MARTIN PHILLIPS one hundred acres of land in said county on the south side of French Broad River. Beginning at a black oak the south East corner of a fifty acre tract entered in the name of WILLIAM SORTEN in the entry takers office for said county running thence East fifty eight poles to a chestnut on FRANCES G. CARTER [looks line Froncereg?] line on the North West side of a ridge Near a chesnut Marked with three Notches then with said CARTERS line North Eighty Eight poles to a Gum corner to said CARTER same course continued forty eight and fourth poles further to a black oak dogwood and sour wood then west one hundred and fifty five poles to a Spanish Oak then south fifty four poles to a Ironwood corner to the aforesaid SORTON then with his line south fifty three East One hundred and twenty six and one half poles to the Beginning. Having such form as is represented by the above Platt. Surveyed the 15th day of February 1826
GEORGE BOOKER)
Jonathan Wood
ISAAC BOOKER) C.C. surveyor of
Cocke County

178
JAMES BAXTER 16 ACRES

State of Tennessee County of Cocke
By Virtue of an Entry Made in the Entry Takers office of said county at Newport of No. 202 dated 5th day of July 1824. I have surveyed for JAMES BAXTER sixteen acres of land on the Canys fork of Cosbys creek. Beginning at chesntu corner to said BAXTER and ISAAC GILES running North Nineteen East sixty four poles to a black Oak south seventy one East sixty one poles to a stake near a Marked double dogwood at the foot of a steep Nobb then along the same South forty seven West seventy one poles to a stake in the line of said BAXTERS aforesaid tract, then with the same North seventy one West twenty six poles to the beginning. Having such form as is represented by the above Platt. Surveyed 27th day of October 1825.
JESSE GILES)
Jonathan Wood
WM VALENTINE) C.C. surveyor of
Cocke County

179
GEORGE McNABB 50 ACRES

State of Tennessee Cocke County
By Virtue of an Entry Made in the Entry Takers office for the said county at Newport of No. 282 dated the 10th day of October 1824 I have surveyed for GEORGE McNABB fifty Acres of land in said county on the West side of Big Pigeon River in TURMONS Bottom including the place where on THOMAS LEATHERWOOD Now lives. Beginning at a hollow poplar on the Bank of said river running thence down the meanders there of south thirty Two West forty four poles to a spruce pine south fifty west twenty four poles to a beech south thirty six west twenty six poles south sixty west fifty poles south sixty nine west One hundred poles to a small sourwood thence North twenty one West fifteen poles to a stake at the foot of Mountain thence along ditto North fifty four East Two hundred and twenty four poles to a black Oak south fifty six East thirty poles to the beginning. Having such form as is represented by the above Platt. Surveyed the 25th October 1825.
REUBEN HARRISON   ) Jonathan
Wood
DANIEL LEATHERWOOD) C.C. Surveyor of Cocke County

JACOB HUFFMAN FIFTY ACRES

State of Tennessee Cocke County
By Virtue of an Entry Made in the Entry Takers office for said county at Newport of No. 257 dated the 9th day of August 1824 I have surveyed for JACOB HUFFMAN fifty acres of land on the North side of French Broad river Beginning at a pine corner to JOHN HEADRICK running thence North forty three and a half degrees East One hundred and twenty two poles to a stake on WILLIAM FORBIANS line then with same South one hundred and forty six poles to a stake Near a Marked White Oak thence South sixty five West fifty four poles to a stake on JOHN HEADRICKS line then With same a direct line to the beginning.
Having such form as is represented by the above Platt. Surveyed the 31st day of May 1825.
JOHN HEADRICK)
Jonathan Wood
ROBT. HELTON)
surveyor of Cocke County

180
REUBEN HARRISON 50 ACRES

State of Tennessee Cocke County
By Virtue of an Entry Made the Entry Takers office of said county aforesaid at Newport of No. 216 dated 7th day of July 1824. I have surveyed for REUBEN HARRISON fifty acres of land including an Island and the place whereon he now lives in Firmons Bottom Beginning at a spruce pine in said Island running thence with the same North Eighteen West Twenty Two poles North sixty three and an [half] West four poles to a spruce pine then crossing the sluice North forty five West twenty poles to a stake at the Mouth of the Mill Creek, then of the same North twenty two East Twenty Two poles to a poplar North forty five East thirty six poles passing through to a stake in the Middle of a branch then across a Mountain West fifty six poles to a beech North Eighty West thirty six poles to a poplar south Eighty Eight west sixty poles to a post Oak south Twenty Nine poles to a sourwood on the river thence North twelve poles South fifty seven East seventy One East eighty poles to a stake on the corner End of the aforesaid Island then with the meanders of said river including said Island to the Beginning.
Having such form as is represented by the above Platt.
Surveyed the 26th of October 1826.
JAMES BAXTER)
Jonathan Wood
GEORGE MATTOX) C.C. surveyor of
Cocke County

181
REBECCA DOUGHTYS 150 ACRES

State of Tennessee Cocke County
By Virtue of an Entry Made in the Entry Takers office of said county at Newport of No. 451 dated the 24th day of January 1826 I have surveyed for REBECCA DOUGHTY One hundred and fifty acres of land on Nellys [Nollys] Creek beginning at a stake Near a white Oak on BENJAMON DOUGHTYS line near a White Oak said to be his corner running south Eighty One East Nine poles crossing creek to a stake at the foot of a steep Nobb then along the same as a conditional boundary North forty two and an half East twenty six poles to a buckeye North twenty one East six poles Norththirty two East forty six poles to a spanish oak North thirteen East twenty nine poles to an elm North thirty three East thirty poles to a gum North forty four East twenty six poles to a stake North twenty three East seventeen poles to a beech thence North Eight West eight poles crossing said creek to a white

Oak corner to JOHN MARTIN then with his lines North forty nine West twenty poles to a spanish Oak North fifteen West Nineteen poles to a ash North twenty one hundred and nineteen poles to a stake Near a white Oak thence south Ninty two West two hundred poles to a stake twelve poles from a Marked gum and two dogwoods then with BENJAMON DOUGHTYS line south twenty six and a half east one hundred and thirty poles to the beginning. Having such form as is represented by the above platt. Surveyed the 26th day of January 1826 by

WM BROWN)
Jonathan Wood
JAMES MILLER) C.C. surveyor of Cocke County

182
THOMAS CHRISTIAN 5 ACRES

State of Tennessee Cocke County
By Virtue of an Entry made in the entry takers office for said county at Newport of No. 177 dated the 5th day of July 1824 I have surveyed for THOMAS CHRISTIAN five acres of land on the waters of Clay Creek Beginning gum tree corner to said CHRISTIAN WM BYBEE running thence with BIBEE line North thirty two deg. West sixty poles to WM KELLEYS corner the same course continued with his line forty 8 poles futher to a chestnut then with another of his lines North fourteen degrees East twenty and a half poles to two sweet gums then with CHRISTIAN line south twenty five degrees and ten Minutes East One hundred and twenty five poles to the beginning. Having such form as represented by the above platt. Surveyed 21st day of March 1826

THOS E. CHRISTIAN) Jonathan Wood
THOS. STORY) C.C. surveyor of Cocke County

183
JAMES SWAGERTY 50 ACRES

State of Tennessee Cocke County
By Virtue of an entry made in the entry takers office for said county at Newport of No. 119 dated the 26th day of June 1824 I have surveyed for JAMES SWAGERTY fifty acres of land on Oven Creek. Beginning at a dogwood on or near his Uper corner of a twelve acre tract running thence with Nobbs south twenty one East fifty six poles to a small ash Near the foot of a steep Nobb then with conditional line with JOB PARROTT south sixty eight and a half East crossing the public road twenty five poles and Oven Creek at 27 poles in all thirty one poles to a dogwood North fifty seven East twenty three poles to an Ironwood North sixty and an half East Ninety two poles to a White Oak North fifty Nine West sixty six poles to a stake then a direct line crossing said road and Creek to the beginning. Having such form as represented by the above platt. Surveyed the 16th day of Marh 1826

SIMMION H. SWAGERTY) Jonathan Wood
ABRAHAM SWAGERTY) C.C. Surveyor of Cocke County

JOB PARROTT 50 ACRES

State of Tennessee Cocke County
By Virtue of an entry Made in the entry takers office for said county at Newport of No. X dated the XX day of XXX 1826.[sic] I have surveyed for JOB PARROTT fifty acres of land on a branch of Clear Creek. Beginning at the North West corner of the tract of land Whereon he now

lives on JOHN SWAGERTY line running with said SWAGERTYS line south twenty two and an half West thirty six poles to his corner the same continued in all sixty three poles to a stake on JAMES SWAGERTYS line then with his line south three and an half West One hundred and eighteen poles to a stake thence East sixty seven poles to a stake on said PARROTTS line then with the same North one hundred and thirty Nine poles to the beginning. Having such form as is represented by the above platt.
Surveyed the 16th day of March 1826.
S. H. SWAGERTY)
Jonathan Wood
W. R. SWAGERTY) C.C. surveyor of Cocke County

SAMUEL JENNINGS AND GRAY GARRETT 100 ACRES

State of Tennessee Cocke County
By Virtue of an entry made in the entry takers office for said county at Newport of No. 223 dated the 10th day of July 1824. I have surveyed for SAMUEL JENNINGS and GRAY GARRETT One hundred acres of land on the Waters of Indian [Creek], on both sides of the road leading from Newport to Dandridge. Beginning at a stake in the forks of the road that leads to the Yellow Springs known by the name of Dunns Old road running thence across said Newport road North fifty two east forty six poles crossing a small branch to a white Oak black Oak and pine thence forty eight West Ninety four poles to a black Oak forty two West crossing said road at forty eight poles in all One hundred and seventy one and one fourth poles to a poplar in the head of a steep hollow thence south forty eight East Ninety four poles to a Maple White Oak and pine on a ridge thence North forty two East One hundred and twenty four poles and one fourth to the beginning. Having such form as is represented by the above platt. Surveyed the 5th day of October 1825
JAMES ELLIS) Jonathan Wood
JOHN [JOE]McDANNEL) C.C. surveyor of Cocke County

185
WM SORTEN 50 ACRES

State of Tennessee Cocke County
By Virtue of an entry Made in the entry takers office for said county at Newport of No. 313 dated 11th day of January 1825. I have surveyed for WM SORTEN fifty acres of land on the south side of French Broad river including the house and improvements where said SORTEN now lives. Beginning at a White Oak just above Where FRANCES J. CARTER land [lives] Near a small branch at the foot of a steep hill running thence North fifty three West One hundred and twenty poles and an half to a beech on the West side of a hill thence North thirty seven East sixty three and one fourth poles to a small Ironwood Near a branch thence south fifty three East One hundred and twenty six and an half poles to a black Oak on a ridge thence south thirty seven and a half West sixty three and one fourth poles to the beginning. Having such form as is represented by the above platt. Surveyed the 15th day of February 1826.
ISAAC BOOKER)
Jonathan Wood
GEORGE BOOKER) C.C. surveyor for Cocke County

186
WM T ELLIS 100 ACRES

State of Tennessee Cocke County
By Virtue of an entry Made in the entry takers office for said county at Newport of No. 410 dated the 7th day of January 1826. I have surveyed of WM T ELLIS one hundred acres of land on the waters of Indian Creek. Beginning at a locust and pine on the side of a hill running south forty six poles to a stake thence East one hundred and fifty five poles to a stake thence North one hundred and three and one third poles to a forked black Oak thence west one hundred and fifty five poles to a stake Near pine black Oak Marked Mouth & Eyes thence south fifty seven and one third poles to the beginning, including an improvement Made by JOHN MITCHEL. Having such form as is represented by the above platt. Surveyed the 4th day of April 1826.
S. P. POTTER) Jonathan Wood
ASARIAH LANN [LANE]) C.C. surveyor of Cocke County

187
WM T. ELLIS 50 ACRES

State of Tennessee Cocke County
By Virtue of an entry made in the entry takers office for said county at Newport of NO. 409 dated the 7th day of January 1826. I have surveyed for WM T. ELLIS fifty acres of land on the waters of sinking creek beginning at three White Oaks south East corner of a tract of land containing eighty six acres belong to said ELLIS running thence North forty four East twenty four poles to two black Oaks Near JOHN ROGERS line thence south forty six East sixty nine poles and sixith D with to three white Oaks then south forty four West one hundred and fifty poles to a white Oak in a hollow Not far JONES [?] field thence North forty six west Nine poles and sixteenth to a stake on the point of a ridge on said ELLIS line of said eighty six acres tract then with the same North forty six East Ninety one poles to the beginning. Having such form as is represented by the above platt. Surveyed the 5th day of April 1826.
NATHANIEL POTTER)
Jonathan Wood
MOSES LANE) C.C. Surveyor of Cocke County

SETH MOORE 10 ACRES

State of Tennessee Cocke County
By Virtue of an entry Made in the entry takers office for said county at Newport No. 331 - dated the 8th day of April 1825 I have surveyed for SETH MOORE ten acres of land partly covered with the Waters of French broad river. Beginning at a stake on ISAAC RODGERS line on the south side of French broad river Near to a sycamore opposit of the uper end of small Island running thence across said river North sixty one East fifty poles to a box elder on the North side of said river on MOORES line then down the Meanders of said river thirty three poles to a stake four poles above a Marked elm then across said river south sixty one west fifty poles to a stake four poles above three Marked sycamores on said ISAAC W. RODGERS then up the river with the same south twenty four East Nineteen poles to a stake south thirty East fourteen poles to the beginning including a small strip[?] landard[?]. Having such form as is represented By the above Platt. Surveyed the 23rd day of February 1826.
SHETTOR[?] CLARK)
Jonathan Wood
BENJAMON RAYTON) C.C. surveyor of Cocke County

188
SAMUEL HARNED 200 ACRES

State of Tennessee Cocke County
By Virtue of an entry made in the entry takers office for said county at Newport of No. 187 dated 5th day of July 1824 I have surveyed for SAMUEL HARNED Two hundred acres of land on the waters of Oven Creek. Beginning at a White Oak the south East corner of a tract of land of said HARNED containing one hundred and fifty acres running thence across the Nobb North thirty Nine East three hundred and thirty poles to a stake thence West two hundred and thirty four poles chinquapin Oak and black Walnut among some limestone rocks thence south forty eight and an half West one hundred and twenty four poles to a stake on his old line corner to his hundred and fifty acre tract aforesaid then with the same East one hundred and thirteen poles to a stake south one hundred and eighty poles to the beginning, including a place called the Cloves [?] hill, Having such form as is represented by the above Platt. Surveyed 17th day of March 1826
DAVID HARNED)
Jonathan Wood
W S N FONCHIR[?]) C.C. surveyor of
Cocke County

189
WM W. BIBEE 16 ACRES

State of Tennessee Cocke County
By Virtue of an entry Made in the entry takers office for said county at Newport of No. 299 dated 25th of November 1824 I have surveyed for WM W. BIBEE sixteen acres of land on the Waters of Clay Creek. Beginning at a stake on JOHN WOODS line corner to said BYBEES hundred acre tract running thence With his own line North forty Nine poles to a small White Oak bush on THOMAS CHRISTIANS line then with his line south fifty three East fifty poles a long black Oak East sixteen poles to a dogwood North three poles to a stake corner JOHN LOVEL then with his line south sixty eight east thirty two poles to a stake thence south two west thirty poles to a stake then east eighty seven poles to the Beginning. Having such form as is represented by the above Platt. Surveyed 28th day of March 1826.
BARTHEW OURREY[ONRREY]) Jonathan
Wood
WASHINGTON ONEAL) C.C. surveyor of Cocke County

RACHEL ODELL 72 ACRES

State of Tennessee Cocke County
By Virtue of an entry made in the entry takers office for said county at Newport of No. 344 dated the 22nd day of September 1825 I have surveyed for RACHEL ODELL seventy two acres of land on the waters of Bognard[?] Creek beginning at a White Oak corner to ESTER ODELL running thence with her line North fifty East one hundred poles to a spanish Oak on MARTHA DENTONS line then with her line North twenty west ten poles to a black Oak North thirty West Ninety four poles to a White Oak North twelve West twenty four poles with THOMAS DENTONS line to a pine North fifty six and an half West eighty poles to a post oak.
then with conditional lines with JOHN HOOD south six West Ninety six poles to a stake south twenty six and an half East twenty eight poles to a black Oak then with HOOD old lines south thirty one West One hundred and an 1/2 poles to a black Walnut thence south 38 E. 99 3/4 poles to the beginning Having such form as represented By the above Platt. Surveyed 19th day of November 1825.
WM GREGORY)
Jonathan Wood
HIRAM ALLEN) C.C. surveyor of
Cocke County

190
JOSEPH HUFF 50 ACRES

State of Tennessee Cocke County
By Virtue of an Entry Made in the entry takers office for said county at Newport dated 15th day of March 1825 I have surveyed for JOSEPH HUFF fifty acres of land on the waters of Cosby Creek. Beginning at a beech Marked J. H. at the foot of a steep Nobb and near a branch running thence along said Nobb south eighty and an half East forty poles to a hickory East seven poles to a buckeye south twenty Nine and a half East fourteen poles to a birch South twenty two East twenty two poles to a stake south fifty poles to a large hickory thence North Eighty one and an half East sixty two poles to a black Oak on the side of a ridge North eighty and an half West one hundred twenty six poles to a black Oak thence W direct to the beginning Having such form as is represented by the above platt. Surveyed 16th day of May 1826.
JOHN LILLARD)   Jno.
Woon
JAMES LILLARD) C.C.   surveyor of
Cocke County

191
ABEL LAFTY 50 ACRES

State of Tennessee Cocke County
By Virtue of an entry Made in the entry takers office for the county aforesaid at Newport of No. 435 dated 12th day of January 1826 I have surveyed for ABLE LAFTY fifty acres of land on the waters of Slate Creek including WAMACE[WOMACE] improvements. Beginning at a chesnut Oak on a ridge running thence south twenty three and an half Deg. West eighty four poles to a hickory on the North side of a ridge south sixty six and an half East eighty poles to a hickory thence North twenty three and an half East one hundred poles to a white Oak hickory and locust thence North sixty six and an half West eighty poles to a stake thence South twenty three and a half West sixteen poles to the beginning. Having such form as represented by the above platt. Surveyed the 5th day of May 1826.
JAMES WISE)
      Jonathan Wood
THOS. SMITH) C.C.   surveyor of
Cocke County

HENRY GARRETT 50 ACRES

State of Tennessee Cocke County
By Virtue of an entry Made in the entry takers office for said County at Newport of No. 281 dated the 30" day of September 1824. I have surveyed for HENRY GARRETT fifty acres of land on the west side of Big Pigeon River adjoining the lands of PRETHY and JAMES HARRIS old claim. Beginning on a dogwood on PRETHYS line formerly HARRIS running thence with said PRITHYS line North forty two and an half West sixty four poles to a black Oak on the side of a ridge thence south forty seven and an half West eighty Nine and a half poles to a spanish Oak south forty two and an half East eighty Nine and an half poles to a stake Near a dogwood on PRITHYS line then with the same North forty two and an half West twenty five nad an half poles to the beginning. Having such form as is represented by the above platt. Surveyed 17th day of May 1826.
JESSE GENNINGS)
      Jonathan Wood
SCOLFD MATTOX) C.C.   surveyor of
Cocke County

192
ABLE LAFTY 50 ACRES

State of Tennessee Cocke County
By Virtue of an entry Made in the entry takers office at Newport of No. 312 dated the 10th day of January 1825 I have surveyed for ABEL LAFTY fifty acres of land on the waters of Slate Creek including improvements where POGE LAFTY [or FOGE] formerly lived Beginning at a white Oak Marked with three marks running thence North thirty three East one hundred and ten poles to a stake on or near LAFTYS line then with or near with the same North eighty seven West one hundred and five poles to a locust then with conditional lines with THOMAS SMITH south two West forty one poles to a large hickory thence south twenty two West sixty two poles to a branch the same course continued in all eighty poles to a White Oak on a ridge thence W direct line to the beginning. Having such form as is represented by the above platt. Surveyed 5th day of May 1826.
THOMAS WISE)
Jonathan Wood
THOMAS SMITH) C.C. surveyor of
Cocke County

JOHN KELBEY 25 ACRES

State of Tennessee Cocke County
By Virtue of an entry Made in the entry takers office at Newport of No. 396 dated the 3rd day of January 1826. I have surveyed for JOHN KELBY twenty five acres of land on the waters of Slate Creek. Beginning at a hickory on a ridge running thence south forty four deg. East eighteen poles to a stake on ABEL LAFTYS line then with his lines South two deg. West eleven poles to a hickory black Oak and ash south twenty two deg. West sixty two poles to a small beech on the bank of a branch Near a steep Nobb then along said Nobb North, eighty one and an half deg. West fifty poles to a large black gum thence North eight and an half deg. East forty eight poles to a stake near three hickories thence a direct line to the beginning including the place known by the HARMON clearing and having such form as is represented By the above platt. surveyed the 5th day of May 1826.
ABEL LAFTY)
Jonathan Wood
JAS.[JOS.] WISE) C.C. surveyor of
Cocke County

193
THOMAS D. ADNEY 50 ACRES

State of Tennessee Cocke County
By Virtue of an entry Made in the Entry takers office for said county at Newport of No. 194 dated 5th day of July 1824 I have surveyed for THOMAS D. ADNEY fifty acres of land on the head waters of Indian Creek including his improvement Beginning at a locust Near a spruce pine on the East side of a branch running thence south thirty three degrees East crossing a road leading from Newport of Severeville[sic] at thirty poles in all One hundred poles to a locust on the side of a ridge thence North fifty seven East eighty poles to a stake thence thirty three West one hundred poles crossing said road to two black Oaks thence south fifty seven West eighty poles to the beginning.
Having such form as is represented by the above Platt. Surveyed 19th of October 1825
WM PRUETT)
Jonathan Wood
SAM P. PRUETT)
surveyor of Cocke County

194

JOSEPH WINTERS 50 ACRES

State of Tennessee Cocke County
By Virtue of an Entry Made in the entry takers office for said county at Newport dated the 3rd day of March 1825. I have surveyed for JOSEPH WINTERS fifty acres of land on the waters of long creek. Beginning at a chestnut corner and end of the fifth line of the tract of land whereon the said WINTERS now lives running thence south sixty four deg. and thirty minutes East eighty poles to a stake between two dogwoods two sourwoods and a white Oak all Marked Mouth and eyes thence south twenty four degrees and thirty minutes West one hundred poles to a stake in WOSLAN[???] old field thence North sixty four degrees and thirty minutes West eighty poles to a stake on the said WINTERS line in the edge of sinkhole then with his line North twenty four degrees and thirty five minutes East one hundred poles to the beginning. Having such form as is represented By the above Platt Surveyed 1st day of June 1826.

PETER OTTINGER)
Jonathan Wood
ANDREW WINTERS) C.C. surveyor of
Cocke County

JOSEPH WINTERS 50 ACRES

State of Tennessee Cocke County
By Virtue of an entry Made in the entry takers office for said county at Newport office dated 18th day of February of No. 478 - 1826 I have surveyed for JOSEPH WINTERS fifty acres of land on the waters of long Creek. Beginning at a white Oak on the first line of the tract ofland on which said WINTERS now lives on the North side of said tract running then with the lines thereof south sixty five West eighty poles to a post Oak south forty five West seventy seven poles to a black Oak South sixty nine West fifty nine poles to a black Oak corner to COOPER thence North thirty West forty two poles to a large black Oak on a ridge thence with or nearly with HUGH STUART [?] line North sixty East two hundred and thirteen poles to a sassafrass then sout thirty East thirty four poles to the beginning. Having such form as is represented by the above Platt. Surveyed the thirith day of May 1826

*ADEN WINTERS)
Jonathan Wood
PETER WINTERS)
surveyor of Cocke County

*Could be Oden or Arden Winters.

195

ABRAHAM McKAY 20 ACRES

State of Tennessee Cocke County
By Virtue of an entry Made in the Entry takers office of said county at Newport of No. [blank] dated the [blank] of 1826 for ABRAHAM McKAY twenty acres 3 rods and 9 poles of land it being all the vacant land that could be had for interfering lines said land situate on the North side of French broad river Beginning at a large poplar near the corner of a tract of land formerly owned by A McKAY SENR running thence with the line of a tract of land whereon GERIMIAH McKAY now lives North eighty one East twenty poles to a White Oak corner to WYLY WINFREE then with his line south twelve East twenty one poles to a gum West seventy eight poles to a White Oak on said McKAYS line then with the same North thirty two East seventy Nine poles to the beginning. Having such form as is represented by the above platt. Surveyed the 29th day of March 1826.

JEREMIAH McKAY)
Jonathan Wood
JAMES GRANT) C.C. surveyor of
Cocke County

JOHN WOOD 62 ACRES

State of Tennessee Cocke County
By Virtue of an Entry Made in the entry takers office for the aforesaid county at Newport of No. 468 dated the 9th day of February 1826 I have surveyed for JOHN WOOD sixty two acres of land on the dividing ridge on the waters of Clay Creek and Slate Creek Beginning at a hickory on said ridge running thence with conditional lines with MAT GEORGE south seventy six and an half West seventy one poles to a hickory on a ridge North four East forty six poles to two hickorys and an ash North eighty three West twenty six poles to a small black Oak North Eighteen East sixty six poles to two hickorys thence East (these the entry acres for the waters of Slate Creek) down to THOMAS SMITHS line which it cannot reach only in part one hundred and fourteen poles to a stake on the side of a steep Nobb then across high Nobb a direct line to the beginning. Having such form as is represented by the above platt. Surveyed 28th day of March 1826
WM McKAY   )
Jonathan Wood
MORTAIN GEORGE) C.C. surveyor of
Cocke County

METHODIST EPISCOPAL CHURCH 4 ACRES

State of Tennessee Cocke County
Pursuant to the Law in such case Made and provided I have surveyed Four acres of land on the waters of Clay Creek for the use of the METHODIST EPISCOPAL CHURCH Beginning at a large White Oak on the East side of the narrow road near THOMAS CHRISTIANS line running thence North eight East twenty seven poles to a small post Oak and sourwood North eighty Two West twenty three and three fourths poles to a White Oak and sourwood bushes south eight West seven poles to a small black Oak near said CHRISTIANS' line thence a direct line to the beginning. Having such form as is represented by the above platt. Surveyed the 28th day of March 1826.
M WM McKAY   )
Jonathan Wood
*MARTIAN GEORGE) C.C. surveyor of
Cocke County

*Or Mortain George.

197
JAMES POTTER 25 ACRES

State of Tennessee Cocke County
By Virtue of an entry Made in the Entry takers office for said county at Newport of 441 dated the 12th day of January 1826. I have surveyed for JAMES POTTER Twenty five acres of land on the waters of Clear Creek. Beginning at a large black Oak corner to JOHN HENDERSON on side of POTTERS line of a tract of land on which he now lives running thence with HENDERSONS line North One hundred and twenty two poles to a stake ten poles from OTTINGERS line thence West fifty six poles to a stake on NEAS[??] line then with his lines south ten poles to three black Oaks East twenty two poles to a hickory South thirty seven poles to a chestnut Grub south forty West twenty eight poles to a stake thence south sixty and an half East thirty four poles to a stake near a white Oak Marked Mouth and eyes south five East forty poles to a small hickory on POTTERS line then with his line North eighty three East seventeen and three fourths poles to the beginning. Having such form as is represented by the above platt. Surveyed the 29th of May 1826.
BENTLEY POTTER)
Jonathan Wood
*SAML[?] POTTER) C.C. surveyor of
Cocke County

*Actually looks like Some Potter.

JESSE SMITH 25 ACRES

State of Tennessee Cocke County
By Virtue of an entry Made in the Entry takers office forsaid county at Newport of No. [blank] dated [blank] day of 1826 I have surveyed for JESSE SMITH twenty five acres of land on the waters of McCowan[?] Creek. Beginning at a stake in a ridge on said SMITH line between a marked black oak and dogwood and sarvis running thence west Eleven poles to a stake on JESSES line then with ditto south Nineteen and an half West forty poles to a large __men[?] black Oak then south seventy and an half East eighty four poles to a stake in the head of a steep hollow North Nineteen and an half East fifty Nine poles to a stake on said SMITHS line near a sugartree then with his line west seventy four poles to a stake North Eleven poles to the beginning. Havinf such form as is represented by the above Platt. Surveyed the 2nd day of May 1826
THOMAS DRISKILL)
Jonathan Wood
ISAAC SMITH) C.C. surveyor of
Cocke County

SUSANAH LOKE 30 ACRES [or LAKE]

State of Tennessee Cocke County
By Virtue of an entry Made in the entry takers office at Newport of No. 317 dated 18th day of January 1825 I have surveyed for SUSANAH LOKE [or LAKE] thirty acres of land situated in the county aforesaid on the waters of Clear Creek adjoining the lands of ADAM NULL and others Beginning at a stake in the Middle of a branch near said NULES smith shop running thence with his line North 19 and an half East crossing the public road one hundred and twelve poles to a black Oak corner to said LOKES [LAKES] twenty acre tract then with the same South Seventy East thirty five poles to a stake four poles from a marked post Oak thence south ten West seventy five poles to a stake on the line HEIRS OF JOSEPH WILLIAMS DEC. then with the same south seventy eight West fifty two poles to a stake south thirty West Nineteen poles to the beginning. Having such form as is represented by the above Platt. Surveyed 30th day of May 1826.
JNO. JONES) Jonathan
Wood
CHRISTLY BLAZER[?]) C.C. surveyor of Cocke County

199
WILLIAM T. ELLIS 55 ACRES

State of Tennessee Cocke County
By Virtue of an entry Made in the entry takers office at Newport of No. 443 for one hundred acres dated the 30th day of January 1825. I have surveyed for WM T. ELLIS fifty five acres of land it Being all the vacant land that could be had for interfering lines on the waters of McCedun[?] Creek. Beginning at a stake on ROBERT McNOCKIM line running thence with the same North eighty seven East sixty poles to an elm and dogwood south eight poles to a poplar corner to DANEL OTTINGER then with his lines the same course seventy three and half poles to a black walnut on a ridge SAWRUAS[??] OTTINGERS corner then west supposed to be with OTTINGERS line Ninety six poles to a black Oak dogwood then with WINTERS line North twenty six west eighty three poles to a hickory & chestnut McCRACKINS and WINTERS corner, then with McCRACKINS line a direct course to the beginning. Having such form as is represented by the above platt. Surveyed the 29th day of May 1826.
ADAM COOK) Jno.
Wood
SAM[SOM] POTTER)
surveyor of Cocke County

200

JAMES HOLLAND 50 ACRES

State of Tennessee Cocke County
By Virtue of an entry made in the entry takers office for said county at Newport of No. 449, dated the 27th day of February 1826. I have surveyed for JAMES HOLLAND fifty acres of land on the south side of French Broad river Beginning at a stake at the foot of a Mountain on or Near the HOLLAND line and near a beech tree running thence with said Mountain seventy seven poles to a large chestnut on the spur of a ridge thence North eighteen East One hundred and two poles to a pine North seventy two west seventy five poles to a White Oak on or Near said HOLLAND line then with the same a direct line to the beginning. Surveyed the twenty second day of April 1826.

NATHAN MANOR) Jno. Wood
PERRY HOLLAND) C.C. surveyor of Cocke County

WM HARPER 20 ACRES

State of Tennessee Cocke County
By Virtue of an entry made in the entry takers office for said county at Newport of No. 206 dated 6th day of July 1824. I have surveyed for WM HARPER 20 acres of land on the waters of Cosbys Creek Beginning at a chestnut on the bank of said creek running thence south forty five West thirteen poles to a spruce pine at the foot of a mountain then with said Mountain south twenty one East one hundred and seventy poles to a Maple and a sourwood thence south forty five East fifty three poles to a spruce pine on the bank of said creek thence down the same North forty two West seventy eight poles to the beginning including the place whereon STEPHEN PRICEY now lives Having such form as is represented by the above platt. Surveyed the Twenty seventh day of June 1826.

JOHN GREEN) Jonathan Wood
HOHN PHILLIPS) C.C. surveyor of Cocke County

201

ABRAHAM LILLARD 40 ACRES

State of Tennessee Cocke County
By Virtue of an entry Made in the entry takers office for said county at Newport of No. 268, the 23rd of August 1824 I have surveyed for ABRAHAM LILLARD forty acres of land on Chavers Creek Beginning at a black Oak corner to WILLIAM GILES on the North bank of said creek running thence with his lines south five west Ninety eight poles to a poplar corner to JOEL DENNIS thence with his line North eighty five West sixty six poles to two dogwoods thence North five East Ninety eight poles to a gum Near a Mineral spring thence a direct line to the beginning, including the improvement that SAM CAMPBELL latly sold to EDOM HARRISON Having such form as is represented by the above Platt. Surveyed the 28th day of June 1826.

JOHN WEAVER) Jno. Wood
A. LILLARD) C.C. surveyor of Cocke County

202
JAMES JENNINGS 200 ACRES

State of Tennessee Cocke County
By Virtue of an entry made in the entry takers office for said county at Newport of No. 322 dated the 24th day of February 1825. I have surveyed for JAMES JENNINGS two hundred acres of land on the north side of French broad river part of which is covered with water of said river. Beginning at a stake near a white Oak sycamore at the Mouth of a branch on the north bank[?] of said river running thence down the said river North forty one and an half West forty two poles to a stake North fifty West eighteen poles North twenty four West twenty poles North forty West thirty four to a hickory bush at the Mouth of the long hollow then along the side of said hollow North thirteen West six poles to a stake supposed to be on the FORBION line then with the same North twenty seven East one hundred and twelve poles to a stake then along a rocky ridge North fifty five East forty poles to a stake to ELIZABETH CORUTHERS line Near a chestnut North ten West seventy two poles to a stake Near four postoaks North eighty East one hundred and thirty six poles to a stake on HEADRICKS line then with the same North twenty five West twenty eight poles to two hickorys West eighteen poles to WYMFREYS corner the same course continued two hundred and thirty five poles to a black Oak corner to said WYNFREYES on his fifteen acre tract then with the same seventeen East twenty six poles to a hickory then with the line of WYNFREYS new survey, south Ninety four poles to a hickory his corner the same course continued one hundred and two poles further to a stake on the bank of the river then a ditto south eighty one East forty five poles to a stake at the lower side of the long hollow then across the river south two West Ninety poles to a stake on the bank of an Island then up the bank of said Island south seventeen East Ninety two poles to a stake on the south bank of said river then a direct line North forty East Ninety poles to the beginning. Having such form as is represented by the above Platt. Surveyed the 3rd day of July 1825
WYLY WINFRE)
Jonathan Wood
JOHN HAYS) C.C. surveyor of
Cocke County

203
JOEL DAVIS 75 ACRES

State of Tennessee Cocke County
By Virtue of an entry Made in the entry takers office for said county at Newport of No. 126 dated the twenty Nineth day of June 1824 I have surveyed for JOEL DAVIS OR HIS HEIRS seventy five acres of land including the improvement Whereon his widow now lives Beginning at a White Oak on the line of JAMES DAVIS runing thence West twenty one poles to a black Oak south forty five West seventy poles to a stake in the Margin of the road leading from Newport to ESQ. TALLEYS Mill Near a white Oak on JOHN SMITH line then with his line south twelve East eighty four poles to two dogwood and a beech then North seventy eight East one hundred and twenty five poles crossing the aforesaid road to a hickory Ironwood and sarvis bushes North fifty eight poles to a white Oak on the line of JAMES DAVIS then with the same North fifty four West eighty five poles to the beginning. Having such form as is represented by the above platt. Surveyed the 9th day of August 1826
THOMAS BRIZENDINE) Jonathan
Wood
WM FOX) C.C. surveyor of Cocke County

REUBEN BLACK 15 ACRES

State of Tennessee Cocke County
By Virtue of an entry Made in the entry takers office for said county at Newport of No. 148 dated the 3rd day of July 1824 I have surveyed for REUBEN BLACK fifteen acres of land on the right fork of by creek [sic]. Beginning at a farnbean[hornbeam?] on the south side of said creek corner to the place whereon the said BLACK now lives runing thence south forty four and an half West fifty one poles to a stake then North forty four and an half West forty four poles to a chestnut at the foot of a Mountain thence along the same crossing said creek North seven East fifty Nine poles to an Ironwood East ten poles with his line to a hickory south eighteen poles to a stake on the bank of the creek south forty one East crossing the creek thirty one poles to the beginning, including his improvement. Having such form as is represented By the above Platt. Surveyed the 25th day of April 1826.
GEORGE BROOKS)   Jno. Wood
ELIJAH FREEMAN) C.C.   surveyor of Cocke County

ROYAL STOKELY 50 ACRES

State of Tennessee Cocke County
By Virtue of an entry made in the entry takers office for said county at Newport of No. XX Dated [blank] day [blank] 1826 I have surveyed for ROYAL STOKELY fifty acres of land on left hand fork of*by Creek. Beginning at a beech Near RUSSELL JONES corner thence North forty Nine West one hundred poles to a beech on the bank of June ball[hall] Creek Near the Mouth of the dry fork of big Creek on or Near said STOKELYS line thence North forty one East eighty poles to a black Oak and white Oak on the side of a ridge then south forty Nine East thirty two poles to a dogwood at the foot of a rocky ledge then with said river North eighty eight and an half forty poles to a white Oak south forty one East forty poles to a poplar at the foot of a Mountain then with said Mountain south seventy West fifty poles to a stake then a direct line to the beginning. Having such form as is represented by the above Platt. Surveyed the 24th day of April 1826.
REUBEN JUSTUS)   Jonn Wood
JOHN ELLISON) C.C.   surveyor of Cocke County

ELIJAH FREEMON 12 ACRES

State of Tennessee Cocke County
By Virtue of an entry Made in the entry takers office for said county at Newport of No. 234 dated the 14th day of July 1824. I have surveyed for ELIJAH FREEMON twelve acres of land on Big Creek beginning at a spruce pine on the bank of said creek Near WM BROOKS line running down said Creek with a Mountain as a boundry East thirty eight poles to a large white Oak and south fifty eight East twenty Nine to a spruce pine south forty five and an half West sixteen poles to a chestnut south sixty West forty seven poles to a stake thence a direct line to the beginning including the place where on said FREEMON now lives. Having such form as is represented by the above platt. N. B. the entry on which this survey is founded calls for JESSE FREEMONS lines which it down not or cannot touch in any place. Surveyed the 25th day of April 1826.
SAM YATES   )   Jonn Wood
GEORGE BROOKS) C.C.   surveyor of Cocke County

JOHN WOOD 50 ACRES

State of Tennessee Cocke County
By Virtue of an entry Made in the entry takers office for said county at Newport of No. [blank] dated day of [blank] 1826. I have surveyed for JOHN WOOD fifty acres of land on the waters of Clay Creek beginning at a White Oak corner to said WOOD ten acre tract then runing with the same East fifty poles to a stake North twenty four and three fourths poles to a stake on the line of his fifty acre tract then with the same East forty six poles to a gum North twenty and nine tenths poles to a stake corner to said WOOD new survey of fifty acres then with the same East fifty seven poles to a stake then with vacant land south eighty seven poles to a stake North eighty two West twelve poles to a sourwood and a post Oak corner to four acres of land owned by the METHODIST EPISCOPAL CHURCH the same course withtheir line fifty two poles further to a stake on DAVID WOOD line then with the same North thirty three West seven poles to a stake West fifty eight poles to a stake corner to DAVID WOOD Place on which he now lives then with the same North forty seven West thirty seven poles to the beginning. Having such form as is represented by the above platt. Surveyed the 27th day of March 1826.

WM RAY) Jno. Wood
RICHARD MANNING) C.C. surveyor of Cocke County

PHILLIP SWANSON 50 ACRES

State of Tennessee Cocke County
By Virtue of an entry made in the entry takers office for said county at Newport of No. 452 dated the 24th day of January 1826. I have surveyed for PHILLIP SWANSON fifty acres of land on a branch that leads or runs through the Dutch Bottoms Near FRANCIS J. CARTERS. Beginning at a stake Near Marked chestnut on Bliermound[?] E. SMITHS West line of a five hundred acre tract runing thence with steep Nobbs south forty five west thirty eight poles to a dogwood beech and fifteen poles to a poplar and beech south fifty six West crossing the road that leads from Newport of Clarks ford at thirty eight poles in all forty two poles to a stake at the foot of steep hill in the edge of a branch then with said Nobbs and branch North seventy three and an half west fifty four poles to a beech North twenty West forty two poles to a white Oal on the side of a hill then North fifty three East one hundred and thirty two poles to a stake on A. E. SMITHS line then with the same south ten East twenty poles to the beginning. Having such form as is represented by the above platt. Surveyed the 21st day of Mch 1827

ABRAHAM BROWN) Jonathan Wood
BERRY BIAZ[BIOZ]) C.C. surveyor of Cocke County

WM VINANT 25 ACRES [Vincent]

State of Tennessee Cocke County
By Virtue of an entry made in the entry takers office for said county at Newport of No. 374 dated 2nd day of January 1826. I have surveyed for WM VINANT twenty five acres of land. Beginning is said county on the East side of Pigeon River adjoining his own land Beginning at a hickory on a dry branch on his own line running thence up said branch south fifty seven and an half degrees East. sixty four poles to a bush at the foot of a rocky ridge then south thirty two and an half deg. West fifty five poles to a double chestnut on the brink of a small hill thence North fifty seven and an half West Ninety poles to a stake on said VINCENT line of his fifty acre tract then with the same a direct line to the beginning. Having such form

As is represented by the above Platt. Surveyed 22nd day of March 1827
W. VINCENT)
Jonathan Wood
JNO. VINCENT) C.C. surveyor of
Cocke County

209
SCIMEON CHANDLER 25 ACRES

State of Tennessee Cocke County
By Virtue of an entry made in the entry takers office of said county at Newport of No. 152 dated 3rd day of July 1824. I have surveyed for SCIMEON CHANDLER twenty five acres of land on the waters of Chavues[?] Creek. Beginning at a red Oak on his line runing thence south eighty six deg. West sixty poles to a small White Oak thence North four deg. West fifty two poles to a chestnut and poplar thence south four East fifty two poles to a stake thence south eighty six West seventeen poles to the beginning including the place whereon PRISSEY TURNER now lives Having such form as is represented by the above platt. Surveyed 28th day of June 1826.
ABRAHAM LILLARD)
Jonathan Wood
PRESLEY TURNER) C.C. surveyor of
Cocke County

JOHN RUNNER 150 ACRES

Stateof Tennessee Cocke County
By Virtue of an entry Made in the entry takers office for said County at Newport of No. 488 dated the 25th of February 1826. I have surveyed for JOHN RUNNER one hundred and fifty acres of land on Meadow Creek. Beginning at two chestnut Oaks the beginning corner of JOHN WILEYS old survey running thence with RUNNERS line East forty four poles to a stake on the line between Cocke and Green Countys then with said line south forty five and an half deg. East two hundred and thirty poles to a stake then across the spurs of a Mountain south forty four and an half West one hundred and eight poles to a stake North forty five and an half West one hundred and seventy seven poles to a chestnut hickory and chestnut Oak thence North one hundred and four poles to a chestnut Oak JOHN WILEYS corner North forty three and an half East thirty one poles to a locust North six West twenty nine and three fourths poles to a stake North sixty eight west three and one fourth poles to the beginning Boundary represented by the above diagram.
MARTIN WILEY)
Jonathan Wood
JEREMIAH HENSLEY) C.C. surveyor of
Cocke County

210
WM GRANT 500 ACRES

State of Tennessee Cocke County
By Virtue of an entry Made in the entry takers office at Newport of No. 436 dated the 10th of January 1826. I have surveyed for WILLIAM GRANT five hundred acres of land in said county. On the waters of Meadow Creek. Beginning at a dogwood on GEORGE NEAS line and on the line of a fifty acre tract entered in the entry takers office for COCKE runing thence West with NEAS line two poles to three chestnuts near McMURTREYS line then with or nearly GRANTS line south one hundred and sixty poles to a stake in the fiels West One hundred and seventy one poles to a stake near a chestnut Oak and White Oak and blackgum, on the side of a rocky ridge then along the same south fifty six West one hundred and sixty four poles to a black gum south fifteen

East two hundred and eighty five poles to a stake North sixty eight East one hundred and Ninety poles to a stake North fifteen West one hundred and twenty five poles to two gums and a dogwood North thirty two East one hundred and seventy poles to a chestnut then with conditional line with JOHN WILEYS North Nineteen West twenty three poles to a poplar North sixty one East forty four poles to a stake near a black Oak North thirty west forty one poles to a stake East thirty six poles to a sourwood North one hundred and seven poles to a stake West sixty three poles to the beginning. Having such form as is represented by the above Platt. Including the place whereon WILLIAM HANCOCKE now lives. Surveyed the 19th day of February 1827.
JAMES GRANT)
Jonathan Wood
JOHN NELTY) C.C. SURVEYOR OF
Cocke County

211
EORGE NEAS 150 ACRES

State of Tennessee Cocke County
By Virtue of an entry Made in the entry takers office for said county at Newport No. 117. dated the 26th day of June 1824. I have surveyed for GEORGE NEAS One hundred and fifty acres of land on the waters of Clear Creek. Beginning at a black Oak stump corner to said NEAS runing thence with his lines south twenty five west forty seven poles to two spanish Oaks south thirty one East thirty six poles to SHORTS corner the same course with SHORTS line in all one hundred and thirty one poles to a large white Oak then with vacant land west one hundred poles to a stake near a chestnut on COOPERS line then with the same North fifty three and an half poles to a stake south sixty seven and an half thirty six poles to a chestnut corner to the HEIRS OF JAMES WILLIAMS DEC. then with their lines North sixteen East one hundred and eighty poles to a hickory North eighty seven West one hundred and twenty poles to a stake North eighteen East Ninety six poles to a stake on a conditional line with BLAZER then with the same North three East fifty poles to a stake on said NEAS line then with the same a direct line to the beginning. Having such form as is represented by the above Platt. surveyed the 23rd day of December 1824.[sic]
DAN BLAZER)
Jonathan Wood
SAM NEAS) C.C.
surveyor of Cocke County

212
JOHN HEADRICK 100 ACRES

State of Tennessee Cocke County
By Virtue of an entry Made in the entry takers office for said county at Newport of No. 385. I have surveyed for JOHN HEADRICK one hundred acres of land in said county on the North side of French ______ river. Beginning at a stake the south East corner of a tract of land owned by said HEADRICK runing thence with his own line North twenty four deg. West fourteen poles to a stake HUFFMAN corner with his line North thirty five and an half East seventy eight poles to a black Oak his corner the same course with vacant land in all one hundred and six poles to a black Oak south fifty four and an half East one hundred and one poles to a white Oak south eleven and an half East sixty five poles crossing the spur of a ridge to a chestnut south thirty five and an half West eighty six poles to a chestnut thence a direct line to the beginning, having such form as is repre-

sented by the above Platt. surveyed the 18th day of April 1827.
JOHN BLANCHARD)
Jonathan Wood
WM FAUBION) C.C. surveyor of
Cocke County

213
JACOB PARROTT 35 ACRES

State of Tennessee Cocke County
By Virtue of an entry Made in the entry takers office for said county at Newport No. 473 dated 14th day of February 1826 I have surveyed for JACOB PARROTT thirty five acres of land on the North side of Clear Creek Beginning at a black gum on the North side of the lick branch it being the Northward corner of an 80 acre tract conveyed to GEORGE PARROTT by JOHN PARROTT SR. running thence North fifty deg. East one hundred and ten poles to a black Oak on the side of a ridge south fifty three East fourteen poles to an ash at the foot of a hill then along ditto south twenty six East sixty eight poles to two hickorys and a black Oak on a ridge thence with a conditional line with T. FOWLERS south sixty four West sixty six poles to a poplar in a hollow said to be on said PARROTTS line then with ditto North thirty two poles to a stake West sixty eight to the beginning Having such form as is represented by the above Platt surveyed the 19th day of May 1827.
GEORGE PARROTT) Jonathan
Wood
SPENCER LAWS[LOWS]) C.C. surveyor of Cocke County

WM FAUBION 50 ACRES

State of Tennessee Cocke County
By Virtue of an entry Made in the entry takers office for said county at Newport of No. 535 dated the 22nd day of May 1826. I have surveyed for WM FAUBION fifty acres of land on the North side of French broad river Beginning at a black Oak and runing thence North fifteen degrees West eighty Nine and an half poles to a stake near a marked post Oak and white Oak North seventy five East eighty Nine and an half poles to a white Oak south fifteen East eighty nine and an half poles to a black Oak thence south seventy five West eighty Nine and an half poles to the place of beginning, including a small spring represented by the above Platt. surveyed the 19th day of April 1827.
S. FAUBION)
Jno. Wood
C. SPENCER) C.C.
surveyor of Cocke County

ISAAC B. ALWARY [ALWAY] 4 ACRES

State of Tennessee Cocke County
By Virtue of an entry made in the entry takers office for said county at Newport of No. 243 dated 28th day of July 1824. I have surveyed for ISAAC ALWAY on the south side of Nolachucky River Beginning on a hickory on a clift or rocks running cornerways old line North thirteen West thirty eight to a stake North fifty East thirteen poles to a stake North twenty eight East thirty six poles to the bank of Nolychuckey river thence up the Meanders ditto and south a clift or rock to the beginning. Having such form as is represented by the above platt. Surveyed the seven day of August 1826.
WILLIAM HOLMER) Jno.
Wood
THOMAS DEAN) C.C. surveyor of
Cocke County

215
WM PARROTT 50 ACRES

State of Tennessee Cocke County
By Virtue of an entry made in the entry takers office at Newport of No. 214 dated the 7th day of July 1824. I have surveyed for WM PARROTT fifty acres of land in said county on west side of the Grassy fork of big Creek. Beginning at a large poplar on the west bank of said creek the corner of an improvement made by JAMES GINNINGS[?] lines south seventy eight and an half deg. East fifty six poles to a white Oak North fifty three East twenty three poles to a white walnut south eighty two and an half East fifty five poles to a white Oak North seventy nine poles to a black gum, poplar and white Oak in the head of a hollow West one hundred and twenty six poles and an half to a double chestnut then a direct line to the beginning. Having such form as is represented by the above platt. Surveyed the twenty six day of April 1826.
OSBON BALL)
Jno. Wood
ROYAL BALL) C.C.
surveyor of Cocke County

WM GARRETT 50 ACRES

State of Tennessee Cocke County
By Virtue of an entry made in the entry takers office for said county at Newport of No. 215 dated the 7th day of July 1824 I have surveyed for WM GARRETT fifty acres of land on Ravens Branch Being at a stake seventy poles below OATONS Camp and spring runing thence North seventy six East one hundred poles to a black on a ridge south fourteen East eighty poles to a pine on the bank of precipis then along ditto south seventy six west sixty poles to a spanish Oak North sixty West Ninety four poles to a stake then a direct line to the beginning. Having such form as is represented by the above Platt. Surveyed the 26th of April 1826.
OSBORN BALL) Jno.
Wood
ROYAL BALL) C.C. surveyor of
Cocke County

216
WM GARRETT 100 ACRES

State of Tennessee Cocke County
By Virtue of an entry Made in the entry takers office for said county at Newport of No. 212 dated the 7th day of July 1825. I have surveyed for WM GARRETT one hundred acres of land in said county on the two forks of Ravens Branch Beginning 40 poles below the Junction thereof Near two white Oaks on the Bank of said branch running North twenty five poles to a hickory at of [sic] Ravens Mountain along the same North seventy East one hundred and eighteen poles to a poplar south sixteen East ninety six poles to a stake at the foot of chestnut Mountain then with ditto south forty eight West one hundred and fifteen poles to a stake North forty two West seventy poles to a stake then North seventy poles to the beginning. Having such form as is represented by the above Platt. Surveyed the 26th of April 1826.
OSBORN BALL) Jno.
Wood
ROYAL BALL) C.C. surveyor of
Cocke County

217

JAMES ERWINE 70 ACRES

State of Tennessee Cocke County
By Virtue of an entry Made in the entry takers office for said county at Newport of No. [blank] dated 3rd day of November 1825. I have surveyed for JAMES ERVINE seventy acres of land in said county on the waters of long Creek. Beginning at a stake the second corner of a tract of land entered in the name of JOSEPH BLACK runing thence along the Mountain south fifty three West one hundred and eighty one poles to a stake North thirty West one hundred and Ninety one poles to a stake on the line of the land on which WM FAUBION now lives then with ditto East one hundred and six poles to a stake near a spanish Oak and dogwood on the line of said ERVINE seventy acre tract then with ditto south forty six and one fourth poles to a small hickory East one hundred and thirty three poles to a black Oak on the line of JOSEPH BLACKS then with ditto south seven poles to the beginning. Having such form as is represented by the above Platt. Surveyed the 16th day of May 1827.
WM ANDERSON)
Jonathan Wood
JNO. EBBS) C.C. surveyor of
Cocke County

ABRAHAM LILLARD 50 ACRES

State of Tennessee Cocke County
By Virtue of an entry Made in the entry takers office for said county at Newport of No. 269 dated the 23rd day of August 1824. I have surveyed for ABRAHAM LILLARD fifty acres of land between Cosbys Creek and Big Pigeon river Beginning at a hickory his Ground running thence North sixteen deg. East eighty seven poles to a double black Oak south seventy four East sixty six poles to a black Oak, south sixteen west one hundred and forty four poles to a hickory on McMAHANS line thence with ditto south seventy west thirteen and an half poles to a dogwood said LILLARDS corner then with his line a direct course to the beginning. Having such form as is represented by the above Plat. Surveyed the 2nd day of July 1827.
JAMES GARRETT) Jno.
Wood
A. MILTON) C.C. surveyor of
Cocke County

218

HOLLOWAY GILES 50 ACRES

State of Tennessee Cocke County
By Virtue of an entry Made in the entry takers office for said county of No. 427 dated the 10th day of January 1826 I have surveyed for HOLLOWAY GILES fifty acres of land on the Green brior fork of Cosbys Creek Beginning at a beech on the bank of said creek on or near his line runing with the same
south fifteen East Ninety four poles to a stake East twenty seven to a locust thence south twenty four poles to a sourwood West twenty six poles to two hickorys then along a Mountain North two west one hundred and ninety five poles to a large poplar then North seventy East seventy seven poles to the beginning Having such form as is represented by the above Platt. Surveyed the 4th day of July 1827.
WM VALENTINE) Jno.
Wood
WM COWAN[?]) C.C. surveyor of
Cocke County

JAMES BAXTER 37 ACRES

State of Tennessee Cocke County
By Virtue of an entry Made in the entry takers office for said county of No. 376 dated 2nd day of January 1826. I have surveyed for JAMES BAXTER Thirty seven acres of land on the left hand bank of Cosbys Creek Beginning at a Maple corner to said BAXTER runing thence across said Creek south seventy five East thirty four poles to a beech then along a Mountain south Eleven West fifty eight poles to a spruce pine near the falls of Creek, then south eighty west one hundred and Eleven poles to a stake then a direct line to the beginning Having such form as is represented by the above Platt. Surveyed 3rd day of July 1827.
J. GREEN   )   Jno. Wood
JESSEE GILES) C.C.   surveyor of Cocke County

219
WM GREEN 25 ACRES

State of Tennessee Cocke County
By Virtue of an entry Made in the entry takers office for said county of No. 403 dated 5th day of January 1826. I have surveyed for WM GREEN twenty five acres of land on the Middle fork of ground Hog Creek. Beginning at a poplar the bank of said creek running thence south seventy Eight West twenty two poles to a spruce pine North sixty nine West twenty six poles to a spruce pine at the foot of a hill south eighty one West twenty four poles to a beech and sourwood south fifteen East twenty five poles to a stake south five East seventy one to a bunch of Laral[?] on the bank of a branch corner to PHILIP JENKINS then with his line North twelve East six poles to a small spruce pine North seventeen west six poles to the beginning. Having such form as is represented by the above platt. Surveyed the 3rd of July 1827.
ROBERT McGAHA)
Jonathan Wood
JOSEPH PHILLIPS) C.C.   surveyor of Cocke County

220
JAMES TURNER 40 ACRES

State of Tennessee Cocke County
By Virtue of an entry Made in the entry takers office for said county at Newport of No. 432 dated the 15th day of January 1826 for seventy five acres of land I have surveyed for JAMES TURNER forty acres of land Bounded as follows Viz Beginning at a stake by a dogwood MARY TURNERS corner on the waters of Nelly Creek running thence with her line east one hundred poles to a hickory on a ridge then with conditional line with JOHN TURNERS south forty three poles to a spanish Oak south fifteen East twenty nine poles to a spanish oak south forty five east eleven poles to a white oak on said JOHN TURNERS line then with the same south eighty east one hundred and twenty three poles to a white oak ISAAC GILES line then with the same south with said TURNERS land a direct line to the beginning. Having such form as is represented by the above platt. Surveyed the 25th day of July 1827.
ABRAHAM FOX   )
Jonathan Wood
JAMES WAYMIRER) C.C.   surveyor of Cocke County

JAMES MILLER 50 ACRES

State of Tennessee Cocke County
By virtue of an entry made in the Entry takers office for said county of No 336 dated the 23rd day of April 1825. I have surveyed for JAMES MILLER fifty acres of land on the waters of Neelys Creek - Beginning at a locust on a ridge running thence along to the south twenty west thirty poles to a white oak south fifty three west one hundred poles to a spanish oak on a ridge north thirty seven west sixty three and one fourth poles to an ash - North fifty three East one hundred and thirty six and one and half poles with a conditional line to a stake in a field then a direct line to the beginning. Having such form as is represented by the above platt. Surveyed the 20th of July 1827.
Thos. Buttree)
Jonathan Wood
Jefferson Dwidht) C.C. Surveyor of
Cocke County

221
JERMIAH HILL 200 ACRES

State of Tennessee COCKE county
By virtue of an entry made in the entry takers office for said county at Newport of No 411 dated 7th day of January 1826. I have surveyed for JERMIAH HILL two hundred acres of land on the South side on Noly Chucky river beginning at a hickory on the bank of said river running thence West five poles to a rock in the river thence up the river North forty west fifty two poles North thirty five west forty two poles North twenty five west sixty four poles North ten East eighty poles to a lynn on the north of the cool branch then with a conditional line with JAMES SOLOMAN south sixty five East one hundred and twenty poles to a beech in a hallow below BROGGS sugar camp thence South twenty east two hundred poles to two small hickory bushes thence with the line of the land on which JEFFERSON DAUGHTY now lives west to the beginning. Having such form as is represented by the above plott. Surveyed the seventeenth day of July 1827.
WM. MCCONNELL) JON WOOD
JEFFERSON DAUGHTY) C.C. Surveyor of Cocke County

222
HARRISON REESE 50 ACRES

State of Tennessee Cocke County
By virtue of an entry made in the entry takers office for said county of No 446 dated the 16th day of January 1826. I have surveyed for HARRISON REESE fifty acres of land on the south side of Noly Chucky on the waters of Neelys creek. Beginning at a stake on the north corner of a tract of land on which said Reese having lived running thence the same East one hundred and twenty three poles to a stake then south forty six poles to a stake then along a steep prescifis south sixty five west forty three poles to a white oak, south thirty six west twenty poles to a hickory at Harrisons corner then with his line north twenty two west one hundred seventy nine poles to a stake near a hickory south sixty three to a stake on JOHN MARTINS line then with the same east ninty nine poles to a stake south two poles to the beginning. Having such form as is represented by the above platt. Surveyed the 25th day of July 1827.
John Martin) Jon
Wood

ABRAHAM FOX 25 ACRES

State of Tennessee Cocke County
By virtue of an entry made in the entry takers office for said county at Newport of No 497 dated the 28th day of February 1826. I have surveyed for ABRAHAM FOX twenty five acres of land on the waters of Neelys Creek. Beginning at a stake on HARRISONS REESUSE line near his corner on MARY TURNER line running thence with said REES line East thirty three poles to a stake on said MARY TURNER line then with the same north sixty four poles to the beginning.
Having such form as is represented by the above platt.
Surveyed 25th day of July 1827.

John Martin) Jno Wood
John Turner) C.C. Surveyor of Cocke County

223
HENRY CARMON 50 ACRES

State of Tennessee Cocke County
By virtue of an entry made in the entry takers office for said county at Newport of No 348 dated the 22nd day of November 1825. I have surveyed for HENRY CARMON FIFTY ACRES of land on the south side of French Broad river on the waters of Indian Creek beginning at a black ash on the line of GRAY GARRATT and SAM JENNINGS running thence with ditto south forty one and an half west one hundred poles to a black oak south forty eight and an half. East sixty poles to a stake corner to JONATHAN WOOD then with his line East forty poles to a stake north forty one and an half East sixty poles to a stake then direct line to the beginning.
Having such form as is represented by the above platt.
Surveyed the 7th day of July 1827.

GEORGE CAMERON) Jno Wood
BIRD FRANCIS) C.C. Surveyor of Cocke County

224
ISAAC JESTER 50 ACRES

State of Tennessee Cocke County
By virtue of an entry made in the entry takers office for the said county at Newport of No 398 dated 3rd day of January 1826. I have surveyed for ISAAC JESTER fifty acres of land on the waters of Neelys Creek. Beginning at a white oak at SHADRICK WILLIAMS corner to said Jesters line running thence with his line south eighty poles to a stake on JESSE SMITH line then with the said East one hundred poles to a mulberry on the side of a ridge north eighty poles to a stake near two white oaks on SHADRICK WILLIAMS line then with the same West one hundred poles to the beginning.
Having such form as is represented by the above platt.
Surveyed the 25th day of July 1827.

WM. B. TALLEY) Jno Wood
WM. WILLIAMS) C.C. Surveyor of Cocke County

225

HENRY CAMERON 46 ACRES

State of Tennessee Cocke County
By virtue of an entry takers office for said county at Newport of No 398 dated 3rd day of January 1826. I have surveyed for HENRY CAMERON forty six acres of land three rods and five punches of land on the waters of Indian Creek. Beginning at a black oak bush near GEORGE CAMERON corner in the margin of the road leading from Newport to Dandridge running thence with his line south eighty degrees west forty poles to a post oak South with DAVID LICHLITERS line four poles to a white oak south thirty seven west forty two poles to two post oaks thence with conditional line said to be made with JOHN HANCHERS south fifteen East seventy three poles south South forty seven East twenty four poles to two spanish oaks South seventy seven East thirty five poles to a black oak to Hancer corner south sixty five East seventeen to LEVI LINER corner to THOMAS MARTINS line North twenty five and one half west one hundred and six poles to a white oak North sixty four and half East fifty eight poles crossing the above road to a black oak and white oak on GEORGE CAMERONS line then with the same a direct line to the beginning. Having such form as is represented by the above platt.
Surveyed the &th[sic] day of July 1827
N. B. The entry on which this survey is found was for fifty acres and was bounded so now then hence the above numbers could be had. J.W.

Jno Wood

Surveyor of Cocke County

JAMES SCRUGGS 150 ACRES

State of Tennessee Cocke County
By virtue of an entry made in the entry takers office for said county at Newport of No 500 dated the 28th day of February 1826. I have surveyed for JAMES SCRUGGS one hundred and fifty acres of land on the south side of Nolly Chucky river beginning at a sourwood and a white oak corner to a tract of land formerly owned by JONATHAN ERVINS running up the river south eighty eight poles to an ironwood, hickory and black oak south twenty five poles to two white oaks on AARONS line then with his line west two poles to three white oaks south seventy and a half west one hundred and seventy poles to a hickory his corner the same course in all two hundred and forty eight to a beech bank Blar Creek near the junction of two branches then down the creek north thirty west seventy four poles to ISSAC ALWAYS line North twelve East sixty five poles to a dogwood the lower corner to said Scruggs land which he purchased of JONATHAN ERVIN aforesaid then with his line to the beginning Having such form as is represented by the above platt.
Surveyed the 7th day of August 1826.
WM. GILLIHORN)
Jonathan Wood
JOHN EDINGTON) C.C. Surveyor of
Cocke County

226
RICHARD SCRUGGS 2 ACRES

State of Tennessee Cocke County
By virtue of an entry made in the entry takers office for the said county at Newport of No 557 dated the 10th day of August 1826. I have surveyed for RICHARD SCRUGGS two acres of land principal course with the waters of Noly Chucky river. Beginning at a bunch of Lynns on the south side of said river first below there the said Scruggs is about erecting SELU and grist mill and on as near the line of a tract that JONATHAN ERVINS formerly owned running up the bank of the said river and with said line south sixty eight east twenty two poles to an ironwood south fifty east forty four to two black oak and two ironwood thence north twenty two degrees east thirteen poles and three fourths to a stake in said river supposed to be said Scruggs and ESQ. HALES line then with ditto north sixty eight west twenty six poles to a rock in said river thence south twenty two west twelve and eighteenth poles to the beginning. Including the place whereon the above mentioned mill is about to be built which tract has such form as is represented by the above platt, Surveyed the 18th day of August 1826.

WM. GALLIHAM)
Jonathan Wood
JNO EDINGTON) C.C. Surveyor of
Cocke County

227
ABEL LOFTY 25 ACRES

State of Tennessee Cocke County
By virtue of an entry made in the entry takers office for said county at No 501 dated the 28th day of February 1826. I have surveyed for ABEL LOFTY twenty five acres of land on the waters of McComer Creek. Beginning at a white oak on a ridge below his sugar camp running thence south eighty east fifty six poles to a large white oak on Kellys line then ditto east crossing the public road at four poles in all ten poles to a white oak and dogwood south five east twenty two poles to a dogwood and an elm corner to said Loftys eight acres tract east twenty poles to a beech and white oak south then east fifty four poles to two dogwood and a black oak north eight west eighty eight poles to a stake then a direct line to the beginning.
Having such form as is represented by the above platt.
Surveyed the 4th day of May 1826.
THOS SMITH)
Jonathan Wood
JNO WORTH) C.C.
Surveyor of Cocke County

228
JOHN HOLLAND JR. 25 ACRES

State of Tennessee Cocke County
By virtue of an entry made in the entry takers office for said county at Newport of No 346 dated the 26th day of September 1825. I have surveyed for JOHN HOLLAND JR. twenty five acres of land on the north side of French Broad River on the north side of the Little Howell Creek. Beginning at a white oak on the east line of 11 acre tract of said Holland running thence with the same east twenty one poles to a stake north sixteen poles to the foot of the mountain then along the same four poles to a

TO A RED OAK with north five and one fourth west twenty one east to a stake on a conditional line then with the same four poles to a birch north fifty west twenty seven and a half poles to a stake north twenty two and a half east fourteen poles to a stake north seventy five east seven poles to a Encumber corner to NATHANILL BOYSTON then along a mountain south six poles crossing a creek to a walnut south seventy six east twenty two poles to a black oak north sixteen and an half east forty six poles to an ironwood north thirty east sixteen poles to a stake south eighty eight west twenty poles to a white oak south forty nine west to fifty poles to an elm south fourteen and an half west sixteen poles to a hickory south thirty eight west nine poles to a white oak bush twenty one west seventeen poles to a stake south twenty two west thirty poles to a black oak north to a stake south sixty eight west sixteen poles to three small chesnuts south five west fourteen poles to two chesnut oak south forty seven east twenty poles to the beginning. Having such form as is represented by the above platt.
Surveyed the 21st day of April 1826.

JAMES NIAKOLS) Jno
Wood
W.B. LOKE) C.C. Surveyor of
Cocke County

229
ROYAL STOCKLEY 100 ACRES

State of Tennessee Cocke County
By virtue of an entry made in the entry takers office for the said county at Newport of No 518 dated the 23rd day of March 1826. I have surveyed for Royal Stockley one hundred acres of land on Big Creek on the left hand fork thereof beginning at a spruce pine near ELLISONS corner on the west side of the creek running thence south fifty eight and an half east five poles to a stake on the lines of a thirteen acre tract then with ditto south forty five west eight poles to a buckeye south fifty seven east forty two poles to a stake south thirty seven east twelve poles to a beech south fifty seven east twelve poles to a stake eighty eight east four poles to a stake north twenty six poles to a stake in a field south to a stake in the head of a steep hollow north forty five west twenty poles to a buckeye corner to ELLISONS north sixteen west sixteen west to a bush north thirty five west forty five west forty two poles to a large oak north ninety eight poles to a cucumber sourwood and dogwood north nineteen east forty two poles to the beginning.
Represented by the above platt,
Surveyed the 10th of March 1826.

BEN DAVIS) Jno
Wood
JNO ELLISON) C.C. Surveyor of
Cocke County

230
THOMAS HOLLAND SR. 100 ACRES

State of Tennessee Cocke County
By virtue of an entry made in the entry takers office for said county of No 459 dated 2nd day of February 1826. I have surveyed for THOMAS HOLLAND SR. one hundred acres of land on the south side of the French Broad River beginning at a stake on James MCHOES line running thence with the mountain north sixty seven East twenty three poles to a sourwood south fifty four east ninty six poles to a stake near a black oak at the foot of a hill then along ditto north twenty two east twenty eight poles to a white oak north sixty two poles to a water oak south forty nine East twenty three poles to a hickory north fifty one East sixty eight poles to a spanish oak south eighty five poles to a stake north one hundred and thirty six poles to a chesnut north forty five west fourteen to a black oak south seventy seven west twelve poles to a beech south five west twelve poles to a black oak south eighty two west eighteen poles to a black oak south seven one west eighty poles to white oak north forty five west eighteen poles to a hickory south sixty nine west sixty two poles to four pines north forty five west thirty eight poles to a black oak north seventy eight west twenty eight poles to a pine north forty three west sixty six poles to a stake. Near said Hollands line then a direct line to the beginning.
Having such form as represented by the above platt.
Surveyed the fourth day of May 1827.

NATHAN SHORPTON) Jno Wood
NATHAN HOLLAND) C.C. Surveyor of Cocke County

231
BUCKNER WOMMACK 200 ACRES

State of Tennessee Cocke County
By virtue of an entry made in the entry takers office for said county at Newport of No 418 dated 9th day of January 1826. I have surveyed for BUCKNER WOMMACK two hundred acres of land on the waters of Clay Creek. Beginning on a white oak on a conditional line with PETER HUCKER RUNNING thence north seventy one poles west eighty poles to a stake four poles from a large marked white oak on FOWLERS line then with his line north two hundred and sixty two poles to a white oak dogwood and two hickorys east one hundred and seventy three poles to two black oaks then a direct line the beginning including the place on now which he now lives.
Having such form as is represented by the above platt.
Surveyed the 23rd day of August 1826.

Page Lofty) Jno Wood
James Hall) C.C. Surveyor of Cocke County

JOHN BLANCHARD 50 ACRES

State of Tennessee Cocke County
By virtue of an entry made in the entry takers office for said county at Newport of No 534 dated 22nd day of May 1826. I have surveyed for JOHN BLANCHARD fifty acres of land in said county on the North side of French Broad River including the place which he now lives. Beginning at popular stump and a white oak SAPIN HARBIN corner running thence north twenty west seventy four poles to a stake MRS. CARUTHERS line with the same south eighty west eighty six poles to her corner the same in all one hundred and one poles to a black oak on or near JAMES JENNING line at the foot of a hill south forty two west to a stake south twenty four and a half East one hundred and two poles to a stake on the foresaid HARBISON line then with ditto a direct line the beginning.
Having such form as represented by the above platt.
Surveyed the 19th of April 1827.
JOHN HEADRICK) Jno Wood
IASAAC NICHOLESON) C.C. Surveyor of Cocke County

232
JAMES CLARK 25 ACRES

State of Tennessee Cocke County
By virtue of an entry made in the entry takers office for said county at Newport No 485 dated the 28th day of February 1826. I have surveyed for JAMES CLARK twenty five acres of land in said county on the south side of French Broad River on the waters of the Irish Branch and on the waters of a branch the impplies in the aforesaid river just below GEORGE LAREW mill. Beginning at a dogwood in the head of a hollow near a burnt cabin known by the name of BRUMICK cabbin on the drondys ridge running thence south eleven and one half west eighty poles crossing a road leading from CLARKS mill to the DUTCH BOTTOMS to a black oak thence north seventy eight and an half west crossing said road fifty poles to a small black oak eleven and an half East eighty poles to a beech on the west side of a small branch thence a direct line to the beginning.
Having such form as is represented by the above platt.
Surveyed the second day of April 1827.
SHIPPY PRICKETT) JNO N WOOD
GEORGE CAMPBELL) C.C. Surveyor of Cocke County

233
JAMES CLARK 10 ACRES

State of Tennessee Cocke County
By virtue of an entry made in the entry takers office for said county at Newport of No 460 dated the 3rd day of February 1826. I have surveyed for JAMES CLARK ten acres of land situate lying and being in said county on the south side of French Broad River adjoining the land on which the said Clark now lives in the DUTCH BOTTOM. Beginning at two oaks a shugar tree and hickory corner to GEORGE LAREW near a branch on his old line running thence with the same north twenty two west fifty six and one half poles to a beech on the North side of a dry branch near Clarks old field thence sixty eight East twenty eight and an half to a hickory and black oak in the edge of a guly on the East side of a ridge south twenty two east fifty six and one fourth poles to Larews line of a ten acre tract then with the same to the beginning.

Having such form as is represented by the above platt.
Surveyed the 2nd day of April 1827.

Shipp Puckett) JNO N
WOOD
O. Campbell) C.C. Surveyor of
Cocke County

234
JAMES CLARK 100 ACRES

State of Tennessee Cocke County
By virtue of an entry made in the entry takers office for said county at Newport of No-- dated the - day of -- 1826. I have surveyed for JAMES CLARK JR. one hundred acres of land on the south side of French Broad River on the Irish Branch. Beginning at a black oak on a ride near the head of a hollow running thence forty seven and an half east one hundred and seventy nine poles to a white oak and a chestnut oak on the east side of a hill north forty two and an half poles to a beech of a steep hill thence north forty seven and an half west one hundred and seventy nine poles to a hickory and two beeches in a hollow south forty two and an half west eighty nine and an half poles to a chestnut oak and black oak south forty seven and an half East two poles to the beginning.
Having such form as is represented by the above platt.
Surveyed the 24th day of February 1826.

Robt. Rogers) JNO n
Wood
Shelton Clark) C.C. Surveyor of
Cocke County

235
HIRAM ALLEN 100 ACRES

State of Tennessee Cocke County
By virtue of an entry made in the entry takers office for said county at Newport of No 197 dated the 5th day of July 1824. I have surveyed for HIRAM ALLEN one hundred acres of land in said county on the waters of BOGUARD CREEK. Beginning at a stake near a white oak on JOHN LANES line running thence with the same north thirty six east twenty five poles to a white oak stump north fifty five west seventy six poles to a white oak north eighteen and an half poles to a stake north twenty west forty one and one fourth poles to a double black oak north sixty eight poles to a line east one hundred and sixty four poles to two black oaks on or as near THOS ALLEN line then with the same ditto south forty nine east four poles to a black oak south one hundred and sixty two and three fourths poles to a stake on NANCY HICKS line thence with her lines south west eighty west ninty one poles to a stake south thirty five west seventeen poles to a white oak then a direct line to the beginning.
Having such form as is represented by the above platt.
Surveyed the 4th day of January 1826.

Thos. Allen) JNO n
Wood
Wm. Henry) C.C. Surveyor of
Cocke County

WM TAYLOR 150 ACRES

State of Tennessee Cocke County
By virtue of an entry made in the entry takers office for said county at Newport of NO 107 dated the 3rd day of June 1824. I have surveyed for WM. TAYLOR one hundred and fifty acres of land on the south side of French Broad River. Beginning at a sugar tree on the bank of said river corner to said Taylor running thence with his line south sixty west twenty poles over a strip nobb to his corner west fifty three poles to a stake near a marker hickory south twenty four poles to a white oak corner to EDWARD FRANCIS then with his line south nine East one hundred and sixty poles to an ash near the sugar hollow branch then south ten poles to a stake north fifty six east three hundred and ten poles to a beech on the bank of said river corner to the lines of JAMES HENSLEY then down the meanders of said river to the beginning.
Having such form as is represented by the above platt.
Surveyed the sixteen day of January 1826.

James F. Mann) JON
Wood
Alfred Taylor) C.C. Surveyor of
Cocke County

236
ELIJAH WYLEY 100 ACRES

State of Tennessee Cocke County
By virtue of an entry made in the entry takers office for said county at Newport of NO 225 dated the 9th day of July 1824. I have surveyed for Elijah Wyley one hundred acres of land on the waters of French Broad river on the south side thereof. Beginning at stake near two pines it being a corner of the tract whereon he now lives running thence south fifty three west one hundred and eighty poles to a hickory on a ridge then with conditional line with Keeny south thirty seven East thirty two poles to a stake near an oak south sixty five east sixty two poles south seventeen poles to a black oak south seventeen and a half. East ninety poles to a Red oak bush then east one hundred poles to a stake then north forty poles to a stake on the lines of the tract which he now lives then with the same west eighty three poles to a black oak north one hundred and sixty six poles to a stake in a field north thirty east forty six poles to the beginning.
Having such form as is represented by the above platt.
Surveyed the 10th day of September 1826.

George Wyley) Jon
Wood
Mitchal Keeney) C.C. Surveyor of
Cocke County

237

ARTHUR DAVIS 150 ACRES

State of Tennessee Cocke County
By virtue of an entry made in the entry takers office for aforesaid county at Newport of NO 424 dated the 10th day of January 1826. I have surveyed for ARTHUR DAVIS one hundred and fifty acres of land on both sides of Slate Creek. Beginning at a beech on the lick branch running north sixteen west ninety one poles to a mulberry west eighty poles crossing the creek to a white oak and beech at the foot of a steep hill then along the same as a boundary south seventeen and an half east forty poles to a popular south seventy seven east twelve poles to a stake south forty three east twenty eight poles to a beech south forty four poles to a hickory south thirty west fourteen and three fourths poles to a hickory south sixty five west thirty eight poles to two dogwoods at the foot of a steep nobb south sixty eight east twenty eight poles to a black walnut south fifty five East three poles to a buckeye south forty six East fifty poles to a birch south seventy eight poles to two white oaks then with DRISKILLS line East eighty three poles to a stake north sixty four poles crossing the aforesaid creek to a popular on the bank thereof East thirty eight poles to a large corner to said Davis six acre tract then with ditto north thirty two poles to a stake west four poles to an ash then with his fifty acre tract north five west thirty four poles to a white oak then a direct line to the beginning.
Having such form as is represented by the above platt.
Surveyed 4th day of May 1826.

Wm. Davis) Jon
Wood
A. Driskell) C.C. Surveyor of
Cocke County

JOHN HOLLAND 100 ACRES

State of Tennessee Cocke County
By virtue of an entry made in the entry takers office for said county at Newport of NO 541 dated the 3rd day of January 1826. I have surveyed for John Holland Sen. one hundred acres of land on the south side of French Broad. Beginning at a stake near a marked chestnut on his line just below the rich hollow running across the spurr of mountain south fifty west eighty nine and an half poles to a line on the west side of a ridge thence south fifty East one hundred and seventy nine poles to a stake North forty East eighty nine and an half poles to three white oaks bushes on the top of the mountain. On said Hollands line then with the same north fifty Wesr one hundred and seventy nine poles to the beginning.
Having such form as is represented by the above platt.
Surveyed the 1st day of May 1827.

Berry Holland) Jon
Wood
Wm. Holland) C.C. Surveyor of
Cocke County

WILLIAM CHAPMAN 7 ACRES 22 POLES

State of Tennessee Cocke County
By virtue of an entry made in the entry takers office for said county

AT Newport of NO 207 dated the 26th day of August 1824. I have surveyed for WILLIAM CHAPMAN seven acres and twenty two poles of land on the waters of Sinking Cane Creek. Beginning at a stake near a black oak and on JOHN NEAS northward corner running thence with his line south eight poles to a stake corner to Brood Hucks and said Chapmans line north eighty six poles to a stake East with Neas line thirty eight poles to the beginning.
Having such form as is represented by the above platt.
Surveyed the 20th day of January 1825.
Luna Chapman) Jon WOOD
Willis Morgan) C.C. Surveyor of Cocke County

239
JOHN ELLISON SEN. 50 ACRES

State of Tennessee Cocke County
By virtue of an entry made in the entry takers office at Newport of NO 527. I have surveyed for John Ellison fifty acres of land on the waters of the left hand fork of Cosbys Creek. Beginning at a spruce pine corner to stake running thence north fifty poles west thirty poles to a maple north thirty three west sixteen poles to a white oak corner to Ellison on the north side of the creek on Nichols line then with ditto north forty nine west thirty one poles to a gum corner to ROYAL STOKLEY then with his line north eighty two and an half west crossing said creek twenty six poles to a stake south fifty one west thirty six poles to a sourwood south eleven and an half west thirty four poles to a stake on said Ellisons line then with the same north fifty six East Eleven poles to a white oak south thirty four East forty four poles to a sarvis East sixty three poles to a stake near a white oak on Stokleys line north twenty three poles to a double dogwood and sourwood then a direct line to the beginning.
Having such form as is represented by the above platt.
Surveyed the 10th day of March 1826.
B. Davis)
JON Wood
J Ellison) C.C.
Surveyor of Cocke County

240
Alexander Driskell 6 Acres

State of Tennessee Cocke County
By virtue of an entry made in the entry takers office for said county at Newport of NO 350 dated the 8th day of March 1826. I have surveyed for ALEXANDER DRISKILL six acres of land in said county on the waters of Clear Creek. Beginning at a hickory corner to Joseph O'Neil then with said Driskills line north Eighty eight sixty eight poles to a stake in a field north twenty five west thirty five poles to a stake on O'Neils line then with the same south fifty west ten poles to a white oak corner to O'neils north eighty eight west six poles to a gum then a direct line to the beginning.
Having such form as is represented by the above platt.
Surveyed 31st day of July 1826.
Thos. Driskill) Jon Wood
Edward Holt) C.C. Surveyor of Cocke County

ALEXANDER DRISKILL 16 ACRES

State of Tennessee Cocke County
By virtue of an entry made in the entry takers office for said county at Newport of NO 145 dated the 2nd day of July 1824. I have surveyed for Alexander Driskill sixteen acres of land on the waters of Clay Creek. Beginning at a white oak running thence with conditional lines with JOHN GILLETT south sixty two west seventeen two poles to a hickory and Jarvis on a ridge south thirteen East twenty seven poles to two dogwoods then with a conditional line with Even More south twenty seven East fifty poles to a stake north sixty poles to a beech at the foot of a hill on said Driskills line then with the same a direct line to the beginning.
Having such form as is represented by the above platt.
Surveyed the 31st day of July 1826.
A. Driskill) Jon Wood
Edward Holt) C.C. Surveyor of Cocke County

241
SUSANAH LOKE 70 A

State of Tennessee Cocke County
By virtue of an entry made in the entry takers office for said county at Newport of NO 321 dated the 17th day of February 1825. I have surveyed for SUSANAH LOKE seventy acres of land in said county on the waters of Cleasr[sic] Creek. Beginning at a post oak supposed to be the line of hers of JOSEPH WILLIAMS ded running with the same south eighty seven East ninety eight poles to a black oak corner to GEORGR NEAS then with his line north twenty east eighty six poles to a post oak north sixty three and three fourths deg. west ninety four poles to a stake on the line of said Susannah ten acre tract then with ditto south fifty eight poles to a stake west twenty nine poles to a hickory then a direct line to the beginning.
Having such form as is represented by the above platt.
Surveyed the 12th day of February 1827.
Jacob Loke)
Jon Wood
Joel Wren) C.C.
Surveyor of Cocke County

242
A LOFTY 8 A.

State of Tennessee Cocke County
By virtue of an entry made in the entry takers office for said county at Newport of No 287 dated the 16th day of October 1824. I have surveyed for Able Lofty eight acres of land on Slate Creek beginning at a stake in the middle of said creek on WM. KELLYS line at the foot of a steep hill then along ditto north fifty eight east twenty eight to a stake north nine poles to a double Ironwood north fifty five East eighteen poles to an ash north eighty three and an half East twenty poles to a maple south sixty East twenty poles to a buckeye on Loftys line with ditto north eight poles to a stake west seventy poles to a stake on Kellys line then with ditto a direct line to the beginning.
Having such form as is represented by the above platt.
Surveyed the 24th day of May 1826.
Thomas Smith) C.C. Jonathan Wood - Surveyor

BENG LOUIS 82 A.

State of Tennessee Cocke County
By virtue of an entry made in the entry takers office for said county at Newport of NO 320 dated the 29th day of January 1825. I have surveyed for BENJAMIN LEWIS eighty two acres of land on the waters of CLOVERS Creek. Beginning at a hickory on THOMAS ALLEN line a short distance above said Allens field running thence with his line south one hundred and four poles to a black oak west forty three poles to a stake south five to Lewis line then with ditto west one hundred and thirty poles to a white oak thence north thirty seven poles to two hickorys and a black oak on HART GRAM line then with ditto north seventy eight north west twenty two poles to a hickory his corner north one hundred and thirty six poles to a black oak near a fence north eighty two west six poles to a stake to the beginning corner of Hasty Noll new survey which he bought of JOHN HOOD then with vacant land a direct line to the beginning.
Having such form as is represented by the above platt.
Surveyed 27th day of March 1827.
Randal Lane) Jno.
Wood
Thos. Allen) C.C. Surveyor of
Cocke County

243
POLLY JUSTUS 100 ACRES

State of Tennessee Cocke County
By virtue of an entry made in the entry takers office for said county at Newport of No 450 dated the 23rd of Jan. 1826. I have surveyed for POLLY JUSTUS one hundred acres of land on the waters of Meadow Creek. Beginning at a stake on THOS. GRIGGS line running thence with his line north fifty three east one hundred and fifteen poles to a popular and white oak on the side of a small branch north seventy two East forty six poles to a red oak south eighty six and a half East eighty five poles to a black oak thence north seventy poles to a black oak west one hundred and twenty four poles to a stake on her line then with ditto south thirty five east four poles to a stake south fifty five west seventy nine and one fourth poles to a pine north thirty five west twenty six poles to a pine south seventy west fourteen poles to a black oak south seventy six poles to a stake then a direct line to the beginning.
Having such form as is represented by the above platt.
Surveyed the 21st June 1827.
David Ottinger) Jon
Wood
Adam Ottinger) C.C. Surveyor of
Cocke County

244
JOHN PUCKETT 50 ACRES

State of Tennessee Cocke County
By virtue of an entry made in the entry takers office for said county at Newport of NO 449 dated the 19th day of January 1826. I have surveyed for JOHN PUCKETT fifty acres of land on the waters of Keneys branch. Beginning at a popular the upper corner of JOSEPH FRANCIS FIFTY ACRE TRACT RUNNING THENCE WITH A STEEP NOBB AS A BOUNDRY SOUTH fifty five west twenty nine poles to a white oak south forty one and an half west seventy three poles crossing a creek several times to two

And redbud bush at the foot of a hill thence north forty eight and a half. West eighty one poles to a locust and dogwood in the head of a steep hollow north forty one and an half East one hundred and thirty seven poles to a stake on the line of said Francis land then with the same south thirty five East sixty five poles to the beginning.
Having such form as is represented by the above platt.
Surveyed the 15th day of February 1826.

Wm. Reves)
Jon Wood
Sam Reves) C.C.
Surveyor of Cocke County

ABRNER HARRISON 50 ACRES

State of Tennessee Cocke County
By virtue of an entry made in the entry takers office for said county at Newport of NO 471 dated 12th day of Feby. 1826. I have surveyed for ABRNER HARRISON fifty acres of land on the waters of NOLY CHUCKY River. Beginning at a stake on JAMES HARRISONS line near a bush marked mouth and eyes running thence north seventy four west four poles to a stake then with WILLIAM and NANCY DAVIS line north seventy four west seventy three poles to a white oak corner to JOEL DAVIS line then with their lines south fifty eight poles to a Ironwood hickory and sassafras bushes south seventy eight west twenty poles to a white oak then south sixteen west seventy poles crossing the public road to two dogwoods and two hickory bushes then south seventy four East seventy four poles to a stake then a direct line to the beginning. Having such form as is represented by the above platt.
Surveyed the 8th Aug. 1826.

Clem Brientine) Jon Wood
Thos. Brizentine) C.C. Surveyor of Cocke County

245
JOHN HOLLAND 50 ACRES

State of Tennessee Cocke County
By virtue of an entry made in the entry takers office for said county at Newport of NO 442 dated the 3rd day of June 1826. I have surveyed for John Holland fifty acres of land on the south side of French Broad river on both sides of Creek beginning at a buckeye corner to a two acre tract of Benj. Holland near the foot of the mountain running along ditto as a boundry south twenty two East one hundred and fifty poles to a spruce pine maple and hickory near James Rood north eighty seven and a half East forty six poles to a beech and white oak north eighty six east forty poles to a white oak north sixty east ninety six poles to an ash then across a hollow north forty eight west forty two poles to a stake on the side of a mountain then along ditto south sixty west one hundred and eighty seven poles to a hickory north twenty three and an half west one hundred and fifty one poles to a mountain birch then west seven and a half poles crossing Rock Creek to the beginning.
Having such form as is represented by the above platt.
Surveyed 1st day of May 1827.

Wm. HOLLAND) Jon
Wood
Benj. Holland) C.C. Surveyor of
Cocke County

EDWARD VANN 150 ACRES

State of Tennessee Cocke County
By virtue of an entry made in the entry takers office for said county at Newport of NO 442 dated the 12th day of January 1826. I have surveyed for EDWARD VANN one hundred and fifty acre of land on the waters of Sinking Creek. Beginning at a black gum on the said Vanns line near a white oak corner to his old tract whereon he now lives then running south 16 1/2 west one hundred and fourteen poles to a white oak thence south forty three and an half east one hundred and ninety four poles to a chestnut on the speer of a mountain then along the same south forty six and an half East twenty poles to a hickory in a branch north eighteen east seventeen poles to a sourwood north thirty seven and an half east one hundred and twenty poles to two chestnuts north forty three and a half west ane hundred poles to a dogwood on the line of the place whereon said Vann now lives then with his line thereof south seventy four west eighty poles to a black oak south thirty four poles to a popular south fifty west thirty four poles to a white oak north sixty west twelve and three fourths poles to a white oak north sixty west twelve and three fourths poles to a chestnut oak north twenty eight poles to a hickory north twenty five west forty seven poles to the beginning.
Having such form as is represented by the above platt.
Surveyed 1st day of May 1826.

James Strange) Jona
Wood
James M. Vann) C.C. Surveyor of
Cocke County

246
EDWARD SPENCER 60 ACRES

State of Tennessee Cocke County
By virtue of an entry made in the entry takers office for said office at Newport of NO 600 dated the 29th day of January 1827. I have surveyed for EDWARD SPENCER sixty acres of land on the waters of Long Creek. Beginning at a hickory and white oak PETTY MCPEKS corner then with her line south sixty west forty one poles to a black walnut corner to JOHN FAUBION then with his line south thirty four west one hundred and ninety poles to a leaning white oak - JONES ERVINS line east seventy seven poles to a stake on the side of a mountain then along ditto north fourteen east seventy eight poles to a hickory corner to said Spencer then with his line north twenty one east eighty poles to a white oak north three east thirty four poles to the beginning corner.
Having such form as is represented by the above platt.
Surveyed the 20th day of April 1827.

Wm. Faubion) Jon
Wood
Spencer Faubion) C.C. Surveyor of
Cocke County

247
James Ervin 70 ACRES

State of Tennessee Cocke County
By virtue of an entry made in the entry takers office for said county at Newport of NO 350 dated the 3rd day of Nov. 1825. I have surveyed for JAMES ERVIN sixty acres of land on the north side of French Broad River on the waters of Long Creek beginning at a stake corner to a tract of land formerly belonging to JESSIE MCPIKE running thence with his lines north sixty and an half west one hundred and forty nine poles crossing the road leading from Warm Springs by Hollands to Newport to a stake to Wm. Faubions oats patch below his blacksmith shop south twenty eight and an half west four poles and nine links to a stake on the line of the tract of land on which William Faubion now lives. Then with the same east eight poles to a stake in the south side of said road south seventy six and an poles to his corner the same course continued in all one hundred and twenty three poles to a small hickory east one hundred and twenty five poles to a chestnut oak on the side of a ridge then a direct line to the beginning.
Having such form as is represented by the above platt.
Surveyed the 16th day of May 1827.
Wm. Anderson)
Jonathan Wood
John Ebbs) C.C. Surveyor of
Cocke County

248
JACOB FAUBION 100 A.

State of Tennessee Cocke County
By virtue of an entry made in the entry takers office for said county at Newport of NO 612 dated the 17th day of March 1827. I have surveyed for JACOB FAUBION one hundred acres of land on the north side of FRENCH Broad River beginning at a stake on the western line of a tract on which Wm. Faubion now lives and running thence south seventy west one hundred and forty six poles to a stake on Wm. Faubion 140 acre tract then with ditto south seventy six poles to a chestnut east one hundred and eighty poles to two small black oaks. And a dogwood north fifty five poles to a stake in a field on the line of a tract on which said Wm. now lives then with the same west forty six poles to his corner north seventy six poles to the beginning.
Having such form as is represented by the above platt.
Surveyed the 19th day of ---- 1827.
Spencer Faubion)
Jonathan Wood
George Hunchison) C.C. Surveyor of
Cocke County

249
JOSEPH HUFF 5 A.

State of Tennessee Cocke County
By virtue of an entry made in the entry takers office for said county at Newport of NO 351 dated 28th day of November 1825. I have surveyed for Joseph Huff five acres of land on the south side of French Broad River below the Trembling Shoals Branch of the said river running south twenty degrees east two poles to a chestnut oak at the foot of a mountain then along ditto as a boundary south forty six west fifty two poles to an ash and rattlewood south seventy west thirty poles to a black gum north eighty two west twelve poles to a hickory north ten west five poles to a locust on the bank of a river then up the mountain - meandors of ditto to the beginning.

Having such form as is represented by the above platt.
Surveyed the 4th day of May 1827.

Alfred MCGee)
Washington Bridges) C.C. Surveyor of Cocke County Jona Wood

CLABOURN PUCKETT 50 ACRES

State of Tennessee Cocke County
By virtue of an entry made in the entry takers office for said county at Newport of NO 492 dated the 28th of February 1826. I have surveyed for CLABOURN PUCKETT fifty acres of land on the south side of French Broad river including the place whereon SAMUEL DRINKWATER formerly had a sugar camp not for above where WILLIAM WITT formerly lived. Beginning at a white oak at the foot of a hill near the south east corner of NATHANIEL Mitchels old tract running thence along said hill south forty three east seventy and an half poles to a beech south nineteen east twenty poles to a large sweet gum and popular east seventy two poles to an ash and beech at the point of a ridge near the junction of two dry branches thence north twenty west one hundred and forty poles to a stake south forty seven west ninty poles to the beginning.
Having such form as is represented by the above platt.
Surveyed the 18th day of September 1827.

Francis Puckett)
Jonathan Wood
Isham Puckett) C.C. Surveyor of
Cocke County

JOHN WATSON 75 ACRES

State of Tennessee Cocke County
By virtue of an entry made in the entry takers office for said county at Newport of the NO 526 dated the 13th day of April 1826. I have surveyed for Watson seventy five acres of land on the waters of Clay Creek Beginning at a white oak near the land of NATHANIEL CHRISTIAN running north seventy five east eighty eight and one half poles to a black gum near H. HARDINS field south eighty and east ninety five poles to a stake south ninety five poles to a stake west eighty poles to a stake supposed to be near NATHANIEL CHRISTIANS line north forty west eleven poles to a black oak at the foot of a ridge north seventy west eighteen poles to a stake north fifty six west thirty and a half poles to a chestnut oak on the top of a ridge north thirty six west thirty seven poles to the beginning.
Having such form as is represented by the above platt.
Surveyed the 23rd day of May 1827.

Beny Holland)
Jonathan Wood
Wm Holland) C.C. Surveyor of
Cocke County

252
JACOB FAUBION 50 ACRES

State of Tennessee Cocke County.
By virtue of an entry made in the entry takers office for said at Newport of NO 610 dated the 17th day of March 1827. I have surveyed for Jacob Faubion fifty acres of land on the north side of French Broad river adjoining the land on which said FAUBION now lives beginning at a black gum stump the beginning corner of said WM. Faubion tract aforesaid running thence with his line one pole and five tenths to a stake in the margin of the road leading from Newport of Hollands ferry then west crossing said road twice one hundred and eight poles to a chestnut north crossing said road twice one hundred and eight poles in all sixty two poles to a stake on McPikes old line then with the same south sixty two and an half east crossing the aforesaid road at one hundred and ten poles in all one hundred and eighty three poles to a black walnut then south with vacant land fifty five poles to a post oak on a ridge said to be on or near a thirty acre tract of JAMES ERVIN west twenty two poles to a chestnut south eighteen poles to two small white oak sassafras and two hickory bushes west thirty six and an half poles to a popular north fifteen poles to a stake on said Wm. Faubion line with ditto east eight poles to a corner north seventy five and an half poles to the beginning.
Represented by the above platt.
Surveyed the 17th day of April 1827.

John Holand)
Jonathan Wood
Spencer Faubion) C.C. Surveyor of
Cocke County

253
SAMUEL BIRD 75 ACRES

State of Tennessee Cocke County.
By virtue of an entry made in the entry takers office for said county at Newport of NO 362 dated 2nd January 1826. I have surveyed for SAMUEL BIRD seventy five acres of land on the waters of English creek south of French Broad river. Beginning on a hickory running thence south eighteen east sixteen poles to a spanish oak on WM. DENTONS line then with his line south sixty poles to a black jack among some lime stone rocks thence west thirty two poles to a white oak corner to THOMAS WILLIAMS then north forty five west one hundred poles to four sourwoods thence north one hundred and eighty six poles to a stake east forty two poles to a stake east forty two poles to a stake on LAXTON CASES line then with his line south forty poles east fifty five poles to the beginning.
Represented by the above platt.
Surveyed the 21st day of July 1826.

Tarleton Bryant)
Jonathan Wood
Wm. Sneed) C.C. Surveyor of
Cocke County

JOHN BLANCHARD 20 ACRES

State of Tennessee Cocke County.
By virtue of an entry made in the entry takers office of said county at Newport of NO 623 dated -- of April 1827. I have surveyed for JOHN BLANCHARD twenty acres of land on the north side of French Broad River.

Beginning at a spotted oak corner to William Faubion near JAMES JENNINGS line running thence with the old line of said Faubions mill place south thirty four and one fourth degrees east one hundred and two poles to a stake corner to William Forbes and HENDERSONS line then with the same north sixty and an half east thirty four poles to stake corner to said Blanchard fifty acre tract then with ditto thirty four and one fourth west one hundred and twelve poles to a stake on Jennings line two poles from a marked black oak then with Jennings line a direct line to the beginning.
Having such form as represented by the above platt.
Surveyed the 21st of April 1827

John Headrick) Jonathan Wood
George Hutchinson) C.C. Surveyor of Cocke County

254
THOMAS ALLEN 100 ACRES

State of Tennessee Cocke County.
By virtue of an entry made in the entry takers office at Newport of NO 377 dated the 2nd day of January 1827. I have surveyed for THOMAS ALLEN one hundred acres of land on the waters of Cosbys Creek. Beginning at a stake on JOHN LANES line running with a line said to be a conditional line between him and Louis south one hundred and forty four poles to a black oak then west twenty six poles to a hickory an as near NANCY HICKS line with ditto north sixteen and an half west five poles to a post oak corner to said Allens ols tract then with ditto north one hundred poles to three hickorys north sixty five west fifty two to two hickorys corner to his fifty one acre entry then with ditto sixty east thirty six poles to a stake in a sink hole south sixty west one hundred and twenty poles to a stake north thirty four west thirty three poles to a stake north fifty two east one hundred and fifty poles with HICKS line to a dogwood east sixty eight poles to a stake south one hundred and twenty poles to a stake east thirty one and an half poles to the beginning.
Having such form as is represented by the above platt.
Surveyed the 20th day of July 1826.

SAML HALE) Jonathan Wood
TIMOTHY HICKS) C.C. Surveyor of Cocke County

255
SAMUEL BROYLES 50 A.

State of Tennessee Cocke County.
By virtue of an entry made in the entry takers office for said county at Newport of NO 350 dated the 3rd day of December 1825. I have surveyed for SAMUEL BROYLES fifty acres of land on the south side of Cosbys Creek beginning on a hickory corner to said Broyles line north fifty six west forty six poles to a stake south sixty one west eighteen poles to a dogwood south thirty seven west sixty poles to a black oak south fifty three east one hundred and three poles to a stake on said mountain and then north thirty seven east eighty three poles to a stake then a direct line to the beginning.
Having such form as is represented by the above platt.
Surveyed the 25th day of September 1827.

James Garrett)
Jonathan Wood
Joel Dennis) C.C. Surveyor of
Cocke County

P. LOYD 2 A.

State of Tennessee Cocke County.
By virtue of an entry made in the entry takers office for said county at Newport of NO 560 dated the 21st day of August 1826. I have surveyed for PLEASANT LOYD two acres of land principaly coursed with the waters of the Big Pigeon River. Beginning at a beech on the bank of said river on the east side thereof running thence up the bank of said river south twenty four west twenty two poles to two beeches on the bank of said river thence north sixty six west fourteen and a half poles to a rock in the river then down ditto south twenty four east twenty two poles to a rock in said river thence south sixty six east fourteen poles and a half to the beginning.
Having such form as is represented by the above platt.
Surveyed the 23rd day of September 1827.

Benned Arnold)
Jonathan Wood
Henry Inman) C.C. Surveyor of
Cocke County.

256
JAMES SWAGERTY 150 A.

State of Tennessee Cocke County.
By virtue of an entry made in the entry takers office for said county at Newport dated 14th day of January 1826. I have surveyed for JAMES SWAGERTY one hundred and fifty acres of land on the waters Oven Creek beginning at a stake on a line of a ten acre tract of said Swagertys near a white oak corner to said tract running thence north thirty eight and an half west twenty five poles to two white oaks then with conditional Etherton north seventy one east twenty two poles to a white oak south eighty two and an east twenty one poles to a stake on Ethertons old line thence south fifty five east sixty poles to two white oaks and a hickory north seventy three east and hundred and fifteen poles to a white oak on Ethertons line thence with the same south seventy nine eighteen poles to a stake north eighty four west four poles to a white oak south fifty six poles to a white oak west fifty six poles to a stake south eighty one poles to a stake west one hundred and sixty six poles to a stake north ninety three poles to a stake east sixty seven poles to two white oaks corner to said ten acre tract then with the same east forty two poles to two black oaks north forty poles to the beginning.
Having such form as represented by the above platt.
Surveyed the 16th day March 1826.

A. Swagerty)
Jonathan Wood
S.H. Swagerty) C.C. Surveyor of
Cocke County

257
JOHN JESTER 50 A.

State of Tennessee Cocke County.
By virtue of an entry made in the entry takers office for said county at Newport of NO 542 dated the 8th day of June 1826. I have surveyed for JOHN JESTER fifty acres of land lying between Big Creek and French Broad river the place known as FRANCES GAP. Beginning at a black oak on ROYAL STOCKLEY line running thence north one hundred poles to a chestnut in a flat hollow west eighty poles to a black jack on the side of a high mountain south one hundred poles to a post oak grub on Royal Stockley line then with ditto a direct line to the beginning.
Having such form as is represented by the above platt.
Surveyed the 3rd day of June 1827.

Wm. Bundy)
Jonathan Wood
Martin Davis) C.C. Surveyor of
Cocke County

258
WILLIAM GIBSON 200 ACRES

State of Tennessee Cocke County.
By virtue of an entry made in the entry takers office at Newport of NO 377 I have surveyed for WILLIAM GIBSON two hundred acres of land on the waters of Sinking Creek and Indian Creeks. Beginning at a stake his corner running thence with his line south eight poles to a white oak thence west seventy two poles to a chestnut to GARRETTE line north thirty three west crossing the servis road at three poles in all 26 poles to a white north forty two poles to a stake on Ellis line then with ditto east twenty poles to a stake north one hundred and fifty five poles to a stake north sixty six poles to a stake east one hundred and twenty poles to a white oak south twenty two poles to a stake on Ellis line then with his line east two hundred and forty four poles to a stake then with said Gibsons line south fifty four west and hundred and ten poles to a stake his corner south seventy seven poles to the beginning.
Having such form as is represented by the above platt.
Surveyed the 8th day of May 1826.

J.A. Massey)
Jonathan Wood
Charles Gibson) C.C. Surveyor of
Cocke County

ISSA MASSEY 150 ACRES

State of Tennessee Cocke county.
By virtue of an entry made in the entry takers office of said county at Newport of NO 487 dated 27th day of February 1826. I have surveyor for ISSAC MASSEY one hundred and fifty acres of land on the waters of Indian Creek. Beginning at a stake on WILLIAM T. ELLIS line near a hickory marked mouth and eyes running thence west seventy seven poles to two white oaks and a dogwood on ALLEN SARRATS line then with the same twenty east sixty seven poles to a stake his corner same course in all one hundred and thirteen poles to a black oak on said Masseys line south thirty six east

A STAKE FIFTY THREE AND AN HALF EAST ONE HUNDRED AND FIVE POLES TO A stake then with GARRETS line north twenty three west one hundred and thirteen poles crossing the public road to a locust north seventy six poles to a chestnut on ELLIS line west with ditto fifty two poles to a stake his corner north, fifty six poles to the beginning.
Having such form as is represented by the above platt.
Surveyed the 8th day of May 1826.

Allen Surratt)
Jonathan Wood
Charley Gibson) C.C. Surveyor of
Cocke County

259
THOMAS PHELEN 25 ACRES

State of Tennessee Cocke County.
By virtue of an entry made in the entry takers office for the aforesaid county at Newport of No 581 dated the 30th day of September 1826. I have surveyed for THOMAS PHELEN twenty five acres of land on the waters of MCCOWANS creek. Beginning at a stake corner to said Phelen and ELIZA MURPHY and the south bank of said creek running thence with said Phelens line east crossing said creek twice sixty seven poles to a holly south seventeen west fourteen poles south sixty two east eighteen poles north seventy three east thirty fout poles south eighty five east seven poles to a walnut then across a high nobb south thirty eight poles to a stake thence north thirty four poles to the beginning.
Including his improvements represented by the above platt.
Surveyed the 5th day of Oct. 1827.

A.N. Ramsey)
Jonathan Wood
Ruben Copeland) C.C. Surveyor of
Cocke County

260
EDWARD SPENCER 60 A.

State of Tennessee Cocke County.
By virtue of an entry made in the entry takers office for said county at Newport of No 600 dated the 29th of January 1827. I have surveyed for E. SPENCER sixty acres of land on the waters of Long Creek. Beginning at a white oak Betty McFikes corner then with his line south sixty west forty one poles to a black walnut corner to JOHN FAUBION then with his line south thirty four west one hundred and ninety poles to a leaning white oak near James Eran lines east seventy seven poles to a stake on the mountain then along ditto north fourteen east seventy eight poles to a hickory corner to the said Spencer then with his line north twenty one east eighty poles to the beginning.

Wm. Faubion)
Jonathan Wood
Spencer Faubion) C.C. Surveyor of
Cocke County

261
WM. C. STORY 50 A.

State of Tennessee Cocke County.
By virtue of an entry made in the entry takers office for said county at Newport of No. 516 dated the 22nd day of March 1826. I have surveyed for W.C. Story fifty five acres of land on Brooks the waters of Aven Creek. Beginning at a stake on MOSES easterly line one pole and seven links S.W. from a large white oak and twenty links N.W. of a beech marked mouth and eyes running thence with said easterly line west forty two poles to a white oak sis corner the same course continued in all one hundred sixteen poles to a dead white oak in the edge of an old field thence south niney poles to an ash south forty seven west thirty poles to a white oak south forty teen east twenty eight poles to a stake eight poles from a sourwood marked as a corner at the foot of a steep hill then a direct line to the beginning. Including the place where MCMILLION corner formerly lived.
Having such form as is represented by the above platt.
Surveyed the 3rd day of October 1827.

ALFRED Minas)
Jonathan Wood
John Fery) C.C. Surveyor of
Cocke County

HENRY JONES 50 A.

State of Tennessee Cocke County.
By virtue of an entry made in the entry takers office for said county at Newport of NO. 326 dated the 2nd day of March 1825. I have surveyed for Henry Jones fifty acres of land on the waters of English Creek. Beginning at a black oak on his corner and Pates old corner running thence with Pates old lines south forty one east nine poles to a hickory south twenty five east twenty two poles to a pine south seven and one half west twenty two poles to a stake south eight eat one hundred and two poles to a post oak and pine sixty two poles to a black oak in a flat near an old field north thirty three poles to a stake near a white oak then north eleven west eighty four poles to a stake near a post oak Pates corner on the aforesaid Jones line with his line south seventy five west twenty eight poles to a black oak north thirty three poles to a pine west forty four poles to the beginning
Having such form as is represented by the above platt.
Surveyed the 26th of March 1827.

Thos. Smart)
Jonathan Wood
Beng Coleman) C.C. Surveyor of
Cocke County

262
THOMAS CHRISTIAN 100 ACRES

State of Tennessee Cocke County.
By virtue of an entry made in the entry takers office at Newport of No 481 dated the 22nd day of February 1826. I have for Thomas Christian one hundred acres of land on the waters of Clear Creek on the south side at a white oak Anthony Christians line south one hundred and forty five poles to an ash stump east fifty poles to a large sweet gum thence north eighty four east thirty nine poles to a stake sox poles from a marked beech north thirty poles to a white oak the same course in all one hundred and seventy poles to a stake

on said Thomas Christians line six poles from a marked sycamore then with his line south forty two west twenty poles to a dead tree, then a direct line to the beginning.
Having such form as is represented by the above platt.
Surveyed the 4th day of October 1827.

Anthony Christian) JONATHAN WOOD
Wm. Fowler) C.C. Surveyor of Cocke County

263
JOHN GILLETT 75 ACRES

State of Tennessee Cocke County.
By virtue of an entry made in the entry takers office of said county at Newport of No. 626 dated 3rd day of May 1827. I have surveyed for John Gillett seventy five acres of land on the Dry fork of Clay Creek. Beginning at a large poplar near HEDGE COCKE spring running thence south twenty west twenty poles to a stake on DRISKILLS line south thirty five sixteen poles to a white oak corner to WILLIAM BIBEE then with his line north eighty west sixty nine poles to a stake south ninety poles to a stake near a small hickory on Gillett line then with his lines west sixty four poles to two cherry north nine poles to a double peach tree at the foot of a hill then along said hill north sixty eight east sixty four poles to a post oak north fifty four west twenty nine poles to a beech north fifty nine east thirty one poles to a black oak at the foot of a high nobb north thirty four west one hundred and two poles to a stake thence north fifty five east seventy eight poles to a stake south thirty five east seventy poles to a stake east forty poles to a stake south forty east ninety five poles with a conditional line with Holt to a dogwood south twenty seventeen poles to a stake corner to Driskills land then with his lines north forty four west one hundred and thirteen poles to a stake south forty six west forty two poles to a stake then a direct line to the beginning.
Represented by the above platt.
Surveyed the 4th day of October 1827.

Anthony Christian) Jonathan Wood
Wm. Broyls) C.C. Surveyor of Cocke County

ALEXANDER DRISKELL 100 ACRES

State of Tennessee Cocke County.
By virtue of an entry made in the entry takers office for said county at Newport of No. 454 dated the 27 day of January 1826. I have surveyed for Alexander Driskill one hundred acres of land on the waters of Clear creek. Beginning at a hickory on Fowlers line then with the same north twenty six poles to a black oak then with conditional lines with DANIEL GARRETT north twenty acres west one hundred and ten poles to a stake south sixty then west one hundred and eighty poles to a stake south twenty seven east forty seven poles to a stake at the foot of a hill near a hickory then along said hill a direct line to the beginning.
Having such form as is represented by the above platt.

Surveyed the 31st day of July 1826.

Edward Holt) John
Wood
Jas Driskill) C.C. Surveyor of
Cocke County

264
JAMES SWAGERTY 136 ACRES

State of Tennessee Cocke County.
By virtue of an entry made in the entry takers office of said county at Newport of No. 73 dated the 24th day of May 1824. I have surveyed for James Swagerty one hundred and thirty six in said county on the waters of Clear Creek. Beginning at a stake corner to 19 acre tract on said Swagerty running thence with ditto north one half a degree west twenty five poles to a black oak on JOHN SWAGERTYS line then with the same north fifty seven west thirteen poles to a pine corner to FOWLERS then with his line south 89 west 39 poles to a spanish oak south fourteen east 36 1/2 poles to a post oak south one east 21 poles to a pine south 72 west 22 poles to a post oak south 4 1/2 west 12 poles to a black oak south twenty nine east thirty to a stake south seventy four west 95 poles to a stake south 37 east fourteen poles to a pine thence south 16 1/2 east 6 1/2 poles to a spanish oak on a ridge north 66 east 71 poles to a stake among some rocks on Faubions line thence with his lines south five east twenty two poles to a stake south 85 east 48 poles to a black oak south 21 east 60 poles to a stake near a black oak then with Grants line north 58 east 37 poles to a stake corner to said Swagerty 138 acre tract then with ditto north 29 west 93 poles to a pine on a ridge north twenty east one hundred and thirty two poles to a stake on the line of his 36 acre tract then with ditto west sixteen poles to a pine and a black oak south 34 poles to a stake west 39 poles to a stake near a black oak north 16 1/2 east 95 poles to a stake east 20 poles to the beginning.
Having such form as is represented by the above platt.
Surveyed the 15th day of March 1826.

Jacob Parrott)
Jonathan Wood
S.H. Swagerty) C.C. Surveyor of
Cocke County

BENGIMAN DAVIS 40 ACRES

State of Tennessee Cocke County.
By virtue of an entry made in the entry takers office for said county at Newport of No. 595 dated the 2nd day of January 1826. I have surveyed for BENGIMAN DAVIS 40 acres of land on Big Creek. Beginning at a white oak cor. to the lines of JOHN STOKELY running thence with the line of ROYAL STOKLEY east 16 poles to a hickory south 56 east 34 poles to a stake north 62 poles to a white oak on a ridge north 54 west 89 poles to two white oaks and a sour wood on said Davis line then with his line south 41 1/2 west 50 poles to a stake on the line of the heirs of JOHN STOKLEY then with their line south 48 1/2 east 83 poles to the beginning.
Having such form as is represented by the above platt.
Surveyed the 3rd of May 1827.

George Williams)
Jonathan Wood
Jessee Jester) C.C. Surveyor of
Cocke County

265
JOHN EISENHOUR 200 ACRES

State of Tennessee Cocke County.
By virtue of an entry made in the entry takers office for said county at Newport of No. 439 dated the 11th day of June 1826. I have surveyed for JOHN EISENHOUR two hundred acres of land on the waters of Clay Creek. Beginning at a post oak corner to a 50 acre tract of said Eisenhour and on a line of a tract of land whereon he now lives running thence with the line of said fifty acre tract north five and an half east one hundred and twenty six and an half East one hundred and twenty six and an half poles to a white oak and maple north eighty four and an half west fifty poles to a stake north five and an half west fifty poles to a stake north five and an half east eighty eight poles to a stake south eighty two poles to a stake south eighty two and an half east eighty eight poles to a pine and black oak the same course continued fifty six poles further to a pine north twenty east twenty three poles to a post oak north eighty two and an half east twenty eight poles to a chestnut oak east twenty five poles to a white oak on ADAM BLAZERS line then with ditto south two west two hundred poles to a pine Blazers corner south eighty east eighteen poles crossing the public road to a take south eighty two and an half west one hundred and fifty nine poles to the beginning.
Having such form as is represented by the above platt.
Surveyed the 22nd day of June 1827.

George Allen)
Jonathan Wood
George Eisenhour) C.C. Surveyor of
Cocke County

266
BENGAMIN DAUGHTY 100 ACRES

State of Tennessee Cocke County.
By virtue of an entry made in the entry takers of said county of NO. 553 dated the 10th day of July 1826. I have surveyed the BENGAMIN Daughty one hundred acres of land in the said county on NEELYS Creek. Beginning at a stake on the east side of Neelys Creek on or near said Daughterys line running thence south seventy four east one hundred and fifteen poles to three Elms then with a conditional line with JAMES DAUGHTY south twenty west one hundred and thirty four poles to a beech in the head of a hollow north sixty west fifty two poles to an elm on the bank of a branch then down the same south seventy three west eighty poles to a beech north sixty west seventy two poles to a stake then a direct line to the beginning.
Having such form as is represented by the above platt.
Surveyed the 20th July 1827.

James Daughty) Jonathan
Wood
Jefferson Daughty) C.C. Surveyor of Cocke County

EDWARD HOLT 50 ACRES

State of Tennessee Cocke County.
By virtue of an entry made in the entrys takers office for said county at Newport of No. 149 dated the 3rd day of July 1824. I have surveyed for Edward Holt fifty acres of land on the waters of Dry Fork of Clay Creek Beginning at a white oak running thence south forty nine east thirty five poles to two white oaks then with his old line east one hundred poles to a redbud and hickory bushes and Joahannh Driskells line then with his line north eighty poles to two white oaks and two dogwoods west eighty poles to a stake then a direct line to the beginning.
Represented by the above platt.
Surveyed 22nd day of June 1826.

Alex Driskell)
Jonathan Wood
Jas Driskill) C.C. Surveyor of
Cocke County

267
BENJAMIN HOLLAND 25 ACRES

State of Tennessee Cocke County.
By virtue of an entry made in the entry takers office of said county at Newport of No. 545 dated the 10th day of June 1826. I have surveyed for BENJAMIN HOLLAND twenty five acres of land on the south side of French Broad River including the popular flatts. Beginning at a stake near a black oak on the spurr of a mountain running thence south thirty six west ten poles to a black oak on the brink of a frecipice then along ditto south forty eight west forty two poles to a chestnut oak south twelve west twelve poles to three chestnut oaks south eighty one east seventy poles to two white pines near a branch that runs into Rock Creek north thirty two east forty poles to a chestnut and Laurel Branch north twenty two forty four poles to four chestnuts south eighty eight west thirty six poles to a hickory south nine west eight poles to the beginning.
Having such form as is represented by the above platt.
Surveyed the 1st day of May 1827.

James Holand)
Jonathan Wood
Hugh Holland) C.C. Surveyor of
Cocke County

SUSANNAH LOKE 20 ACRES & 90 poles.

State of Tennessee Cocke County.
By virtue of an entry made in the entry takers office for said county at Newport of No. 347 dated the 5th day of October 1825. I have surveyed for SUSANNAH LOKE twenty acres and ninety poles of land on the waters of Lond Creek. Beginning at a white oak ROLEYS JUSTICES corner on JOHN EBBES LINE running thence with POLLY JUSTICES north sixty east forty eight poles to a stake west eighty poles to a stake said to be on HUGH SHULTS line then with his line north fifty east fifty poles to a poplar south thirty seven east thirty six poles to a leaning chestnut on the top of a ridge on JOSEPH WINTERS line then with ditto south fifty three west thirty four poles to a hickory south forty nine west sixty two poles to a white oak north forty nine west eighteen poles to a white

OAK CORNER TO JOHN EBBS then with his line north thirty eight west twenty one poles to the beginning.
Having such form as is represented by the above platt.
Surveyed the 21st day of Jan. 1827.

Henry Pack)
Jonathan Wood
J. Loke) C.C.
Surveyor of Cocke County

268
JOHN FAUBION 200 A.

State of Tennessee Cocke County.
By virtue of an entry made in the entry takers office for said county at Newport of NO. 611 dated the 18th day of March 1827. I have surveyed for JOHN FAUBION two hundred acres of land on the waters of Sinking Cane Creek on the north side of French Broad River. Beginning at a post oak corner to JACOB FAUBION SR. being the south east corner of a two hundred acre tract of land on which said Faubion now lives thence with a line of his east five poles to a stake corner of John Faubions seventy acre tract then with ditto south twenty four east twenty eight poles to two black oaks and a birchwood on JESSEE MCPIKES line then with the same forty eight poles to a poplar the same course continued in all crossing the warm springs road one hundred and eighty six poles to a stake near a marked pine south ninety eight poles to a post oak west one hundred poles to a stake on WM. FAUBIONS line then with his lines north thirteen west fifty six poles to four post oaks west eighty poles to a stake south forty seven poles to a stake north one hundred poles to a stake east ninety poles to a white oak north sixty five east seventy six poles to a stake near a white oak north twenty four poles to a hickory on JACOB FAUBIONS line then with ditto east one hundred and seventy five poles crossing the aforesaid road to the beginning.
Having such form as is represented by the above platt.
Surveyed the 9th day of April 1827.

John Headrick)
Jonathan Wood
Robert Graham) C.C. Surveyor of Cocke County

ROYAL BALL 46 A.

State of Tennessee Cocke County.
By virtue of an entry made in the entry takers office for said county at Newport of No. 510 dated the 11th day of March 1827. I have surveyed for ROYAL BALL forty six acres of land on Big Creek at the place the upper came. Beginning at a spruce pine running along a mountain south eight west forty one poles to a chestnut south twenty six west sixteen poles to a white oak south sixty five west crossing the creek eighteen poles to a white oak south twenty eight west sixteen poles to a haze bush south twenty four east fifty six poles to a stake south forty four east fourteen poles to a spruce pine south sixty two east

THIRTY FIVE poles to a stake north thirty seven east seventeen poles to a stake north thirty seven and a half west thirty poles to a white oak and pine on the brink of a presissice south sixty seven and a half west forty nine poles to a sourwood north ten east twenty poles to a stake north forty two east eighteen poles to a hornbean north seven west fifty four poles to a spruce pine then north eighty six west eighteen poles crossing the creek to the beginning including his improvements having such form as is represented by the above platt.
Surveyed 27th day of April 1826.

Martin Davis)
Jonathan Wood
Morymon Ball) C.C. Surveyor of
Cocke County

270
JAMES SWAGERTY 20 A.

State of Tennessee Cocke County
By virtue of an entry made in the entry takers office for said county at Newport of No. - dated - day of - 182-. I have surveyed for JAMES SWAGERTY twenty acres of land on the waters of Clear Creek. Beginning at a stake between three black oaks marked mouth and eyes said Swagerty corner running thence with his old line south sixty two and one half west one hundred and forty poles to a stake near two hickorys corner to LONA CHAPMAN then with his line north seventy five and an half east one hundred and eighty poles to a stake on ROBERT SMITHS line then a direct to the beginning.
Having such form as is represented by the above platt.
Surveyed the 14th day of March 1826.

Abraham Swagerty)
Jonathan Wood
Harry Swagerty) C.C. Surveyor of
Cocke County

271
JOHN EBBS 80 A.

State of Tennessee Cocke County.
By virtue of an entry made in the entry takers office for said county at Newport of No. 608 dated the 7th day of March 1826. I have surveyed for JOHN EBBS eighty acres of land on the waters of Long Creek. Beginning at a white oak near three springs on or near JOHN SHOLDS and Faubions line running thence along a rocky ridge south twenty nine est thirty five poles to two hornbeans south fifty eight east one hundred and forty poles to a stake thence across a mountain south seventy five east one hundred and ten poles to a stake in the edge of an old field Faubions line north crossing the Bull Spring Branch twenty eight poles to a small walnut north sixty east thirty eight poles to a chestnut and white oak on Faubions lines south four poles to a hickory east forty six poles to a stake then a direct line to the beginning.
Having such form as is represented by the above platt.
Surveyed the 15th day of May 1827.

Wm. Ebbs)
Jonathan Wood
George Ebbs) C.C. Surveyor of
Cocke County

REUBEN JUSTICE 50 A.

State of Tennessee Cocke County.
By virtue of an entry made in the entry takers office for said county at Newport of NO. 611 dated the 1st day of Feby 1827. I have surveyed for REUBEN JUSTICE fifty acres of land on the right hand fork of Big Creek on the north side then Beginning at a beech tree corner to DAVIS and ROYAL STOKLEY old tract now said Jessie running thence with MINSY DAVIS LINES north seventeen west seventeen poles to a black oak west twenty three poles to a black oak south sixty six west fifty poles to a beech thence north sixty three and one fourth poles to a black oak on a ridge north thirty three east nine poles to a chestnut north fifty five east one hundred and nine poles to a stake south fifty east fifty eight poles to a stake on said Justices line then with ditto south twenty west two poles to sugar tree south sixty three west thirty two poles to a hickory south eleven west sixteen to an ironwood south fifty three west twenty four poles to a dogwood south thirty four west sixteen poles to the place of beginning.
Having such form as is represented by the above platt.

Martin Davis)
Jonathan Wood
Jas Stokley) C.C. Surveyor of
Cocke County

272
SHELTON CLARK 200 ACRES

State of Tennessee Cocke County.
By virtue of an entry made in the entry takers office of said county at Newport of No. - dated the 2nd day of January 1826. I have surveyed for SHELTON CLARK two hundred acres of land on the south side of French Broad River on Irish Branch. Beginning at a black oak running thence north sixty eight west thirty four poles to a beech near the Irish Branch north eighty poles to black oak east eighteen poles to a spanish oak corner to ISAAC ROGERS the same and continued with his line forty poles further to a large poplar north sixty poles to a chestnut east twenty poles to a chestnut north twenty poles to a white oak of CALFEES line then with ditto south sixty one east one hundred and thirty poles to a red oak on a ridge east fifty and a half poles to a mulberry corner to CLARK then with his line south seventy poles to a beech corner to ROBERT ROGERS then with his line south fifty west one hundred thirty eight poles to a stake on JAMES CLARKS line near to two marked black oaks then with his line sorth forty seven and an half west ninety six poles to two beeches and a hickory his corner thence south fifty six west forty poles to the beginning.
Represented by the above platt.
Surveyed the 29th day of September 1827.

White Moore)
Jonathan Wood
Seth Rogers) C.C. Surveyor of
Cocke County

273
ROBERT ROGERS 40 A.

State of Tennessee Cocke County.
By virtue of an entry made in the entry takers office for said county at Newport of No. 393 dated the 3rd day of January 1826 for one hundred acres of land I have surveyed for ROBERT ROGERS forty four acres of land on the south side of the French Broad River bounded as follows Beginning on a stake near a birch corner to SHELTON CLARK thence with his south one hundred and twenty poles to an elm on the side of a steep hill west thirty poles to a chestnut oak south four poles to a sourwood west twenty nine poles to a black oak on JAS CLARK entry then with his new line north forty seven and an half west fifty five poles to a stake near two black oak corner to SHELTON CLARKS then with his line north fifty east one hundred and thirty eight poles to the beginning.
Having such form as is represented by the above platt.
Surveyed 30th day of September 1827.

White Moore)
Jonathan Wood
Seth Rogers) C.C. Surveyor of
Cocke County

274
LUNA CHAPMAN 75 A.

State of Tennessee Cocke County.
By virtue of an entry made in the entry takers office for said county at Newport of No. 602 dated the 2nd day of Feby 1827. I have surveyed for LUNA CHAPMAN seventy five acres of land on the south side of French Broad River on the waters of Long Creek. Beginning at a stake near a white oak on ABRAHAM FAUBION line of a tract of land willed by him FRUTHIAS will deod running thence south seventy five east sixty five poles to a dogwood near a ledge of lime stone rock then along ditto south fifty east nineteen poles along ditto south fifty east nineteen poles to a black oak south twenty eight east forty six poles to a large poplar and walnut near the Bull Spring the same course continued in all fifty five poles further to a stake west one hundred and twenty poles to a stake north thirty five west seventy poles crossing the bull spring branch to a mulberry at the foot of a hill north fifty five east forty five poles to a chestnut and white oak suposes to be on ABRAHAM FAUBIONS line with ditto east forty six poles to a stake on an old field then a direct line to the beginning.
Having such form as is represented by the above platt.
Surveyed the 14th day of May 1827.

Reece Busbbee)
Jonathan Wood
Thos. Kilgore) C.C. Surveyor of
Cocke County

275
WM. ELLIS 50 A.

State of Tennessee Cocke County.
By virtue of an entry made in the entry takers office for said county at Newport of No. 409 dated the 7th day of January 1826. I have surveyed for WM. ELLIS fifty acres of land on the waters of Sinking Creek

Beginning at a three white oaks south east corner of a tract of eighty six acres belonging to said Ellis running thence south fourty four east twenty four poles to two black oaks near JOHN BRYNS line south forty six east sixty nine poles and an half to three white oaks thence south forty four west one hundred and fifteen poles to a white oak in a hollow not far from Jones Field then north forty six west sixty nine and a half poles to a stake on the south of a ridge on said Ellis line then with ditto north forty six east ninety one poles to the beginning.
Having such form as is represented by the above platt.
Surveyed the 5th day of April 1826.

Nathaniel Potter)
Jonathan Wood
Moses Lane) C.C. Surveyor of
Cocke County

WM. GARRETT 50 ACRES

State of Tennessee Cocke County.
By virtue of an entry made in the entry takers office for said county at Newport of No. 213 dated the 7th day of July 1824. I have surveyed for WM. GARROTT fifty acres of land lying and being in said county on Big Creek at the north mouth of Raven Branch beginning at a spruce pine at the mouth of Raven Branch beginning running thence south sixty five east crossing said branch sixty poles to a beech on the bank of said branch then up ditto north eighty six east thirty four poles to a beech south fifty one east crossing the branch twenty eight poles to a large chestnut south seventy east nine poles to a spruce pine then north then west twenty nine poles to a spruce pine north twenty eight seventy west eighty one poles to a stake then a direct line to the beginning including the place whereon OSBURN BALL now lives.
Represented by the above platt.
Surveyed the 25th day of April 1826.

Osburn Ball) Jon.
Wood
Royal Ball) C.C. Surveyor of
Cocke County

276
ISSAC ALLEN 50 ACRES

State of Tennessee Cocke County.
By virtue of an entry made in the entry takers office for said county at Newport of No. 448 dated the 3rd day of August 1824. I have surveyed for Issac Allen fifty acres of land on the waters of the west side of Pigeon River. Beginning at an ash stump in the margin of the public road leading from Newport to Dandridge corner to ISSAC NEFF and JOHN ROGERS and Neens thence with Rogers line north forty eight and an half east fifty six poles to two post oaks north seven east one hundred and two poles to a white oak corner to ANDERSONS old survey the same corner continued twenty poles further to two hickorys and a dogwood on the

POint of a ridge south fifty six poles to a large white oak and black gum on ISSAC NEFFS line then with his line east ninety poles to a white oak his corner south fifteen west seventy eight poles to the beginning.
Having such from as is represented by the above platt.
Surveyed the 11th day of November 1825.

Jas. Allen)
J. Wood
Robin Hood) C.C. P.S.
of C.C.

277
TARELTON BRYANT 175 Acres

State of Tennessee Cocke County.
By virtue of an entry made in the entry takers for said county at Newport of No. 574 dated the 11th day of September 1826. I have surveyed for TARLETON BRYANT one hundred and seventy five acres of land on the waters of English Creek. Beginning at a gum hickory and chestnut. Running north twenty poles to a stake south seventy five poles to a stake south seventy five poles near a black oak LAXTON CASES corner then with his line east eighty nine poles to a stake on norths line north one hundred and ten poles to a hickory on said BRYANTS line of a 150 acre tract then with ditto south eighty two west one hundred poles to a white oak, hickory and double dogwood north eight west one hundred and thirty poles to a stake south sixty six west one hundred and thirty six poles to a stake thence south forty three east one hundred and sixty four poles to the beginning.
Having such form as is represented by the above platt.
Surveyed 29th day of March 1827.

Laxton Case) J.
Wood
James Click) C.C. Principal
surveyor of Cocke county

ISSAC ALLEN 100 ACRES

State of Tennessee Cocke County.
By virtue of an entry made in the entry takers office for said county at Newport of NO. 422 dated the 7th day of January 1826. I have surveyed for ISSAC ALLEN one hundred acres of land situated lying on the waters Sinking Creek corner to said Allens fifty acre tract running thence with same north forty five poles to a gum then west two hundred and two poles to three white oaks south eighty five poles to a large chestnut at the foot of a hill near a small branch then with SMITHS line north eighty two east one hundred and fifty poles to a white oak north twenty four east twenty four poles to a beech south forty seven east seventy six poles to a stake north nine west thirty poles to a stake north nine west thirty six poles to a post oak on a line of said Allens 50 acre tract then with the same west twenty four poles to the beginning.
Having such form as is represented by the above platt.
Surveyed the 1st day of February 1826.

Jas. D. Allen
Jonathan Wood

Surveyor of Cocke County

278
MURDOCK MCSWEENE 30 ACRES

State of Tennessee Cocke County.
By virtue of an entry made in the entry takers office for said county at Newport of No. 146 dated the 2nd day of July 1824. I have surveyed for MURDOCK MCSWEEN thirty acres of land on the west side of Big Pigeon River on the waters of the said river. Beginning at a black oak corner to said McSween near or on ESQ. FINES line running thence through a field with said McSween line north fifty one poles to a black oak north fifty six east eighty two poles to a pine stump corner to ROBERT HENRY then with his line south fifty eight west thirty poles to a stake south ninety poles to a stake on Fines lines then with the same to the beginning.
Having such form as is represented by the above platt.
Surveyed the 10th day of June 1825.

A. Fine)
Jonathen Wood
Wm. McSweene) C.C. Surveyor of
Cocke County

279
SCOFLE MATTOX 160 ACRES

State of Tennessee Cocke County.
By virtue of an entry made in the entry takers office for said county at Newport of No. 131 dated the 3rd day of June 1824. I have surveyed for SCHOFLE MATTOX one hundred and sixty acres of land in said county on the west side of Big Pigeon River. Beginning at a locust stump near JOHN RAINS corner on the bank of said river near the mouth of a gut running down the meanders of said river on the east side of an island north sixteen west twenty one poles to a stake north seven and one half west fifty poles north forty four and an half west thirty six poles to a stake at the mouth of a sluice then up ditto south seventy one and an half poles to a sycamore thence north eighty two and an half west crossing said small sluice twenty poles to a chestnut stump on the side of a hill then north thirty and an half forty poles to a dogwood on Harris line thence with ditto south thirty two deg. and twenty two minutes west sixty eight poles to a white oak south four west forty four and an half poles to a leaning white oak south seventy seven and an half west thirty poles to a white oak south forty four and an half west fifty four poles to a stake south one hundred and fourteen poles to a stake thence a direct line to the beginning including an island and improvements on which SCOLFLE MATTOX now lives.
Having such form as is represented by the above platt.
Surveyed the 10th day of September 1824.

Jessee Jennings)
Jonathan Wood
Shepherd Deaves) C.C. Surveyor of
Cocke County

280

JAMES DAUGHTY 50 ACRES

State of Tennessee Cocke County.
By virtue of an entry made in the entry takers office for said county at Newport of No. 450 dated the 1st day of February 1826. I have surveyed for JAMES DAUGHTY JR. fifty acres of land on the waters of Neelys Creek. Beginning at a white oak near BENGIMON DAUGHTY spring running thence north thirty one east one hundred and two poles to a stake south fifteen east eighty seven and an half poles to a white oak at the foot of a hill opposite the mouth of a branch then south sixty west one hundred and seventy six poles with a conditional line to a stake near a bush on the side of a hill north thirteen east sixty three poles and one fourth to a white oak north seventy seven east sixty poles to the beginning.
Having such form as is represented by the above platt.
Surveyed the 20th day of July 1827.

Benj. Daughty)
Jonathan Wood
James Miller) C.C. Surveyor of
Cocke County

JOHN WELTHY 50 ACRES

State of Tennessee Cocke County.
By virtue of an entry made in the entry takers office for said county at Newport of No. 319 dated the 24th day of January 1824. I have surveyed for JOHN WELTHY fifty acres of land on the waters of Meadow Creek beginning at a stake on WILLIAM GRANTS line and on the line between the said county and Green county running thence with Grants line south twenty two poles to a sourwood west thirty six poles west thirty six to a stake south sixty one west forty four poles to a poplar south nineteen east twenty three poles to a chestnut south forty east forty three poles to a small saafrass on RENNERS line then with the same north forty seven east sixty seven poles to a gum south forty and an half east thirty five poles to a gum south thirty four east twenty poles to a white oak south sixty three west eight and an half poles to a gum south fourteen east forty poles to a chestnut oak then with RENNERS lines north forty three and an half east thirty one poles to a locust north six west twenty nine and three fourths poles to a stake north sixty eight west twenty three and an fourth poles to a chestnut oak corner to G. WELTY SR. then with his line north eighteen and an half west sixty nine poles to a white oak on the county line then with the same north forty six west sixty two poles to the beginning.
Having such form as is represented by the above platt.
Surveyed the 20th day of February 1827.

Martin Welty)
Jonathan Wood
Jermiah Hensley) C.C. Surveyor of
Cocke County

281
<u>FRANCIS J. CARTER 75 ACRES</u>

State of Tennessee Cocke County.
By virtue of an entry made in the entry takers office for said county at Newport of No. 477. I have surveyed for FRANCIS J. CARTER seventy five acres of land on the south side of French Broad river. Beginning at a white oak corner to MARTAIN PHILLIPS running thence with the vacant land south sixty and an half west eighty poles to a chestnut oak and sourwood on ABRAHAM BOOKERS line then with same ditto south eleven east twenty eight poles to a stake near a dogwood and black oak south seventy eight west eighty and poles to a box elder on or near CARTERS line south nine east ninety poles to a ash stump in a hollow corner to JAMES KELLEYS old tract and ABRAHAM MCCLANHANS now CARTERS then with said MCCLANEHANS tract north forty five east one hundred and sixty poles to a white oak east eighty four poles to a white oak in the edge of an old field on WOODS line then with same ditto north thirteen and three fourths poles to a white oak north eighty east thirty six poles to a stake on the line of an eighty four acre tract of sd CARTERS then with same north sixty poles to a chestnut oak MARTAIN PHILLIPS corner then with his line west fifty eight poles to a black oak corner to sd PHILLIPS south thirty seven west sixty three and one fourth poles to a white oak the beginning corner.
Represented by the above platt.
Surveyed the 25th day of February 1826.

George Carter)
Jonathan Wood
Wm. Carter) C.C. Surveyor of
Cocke County

282
ROBERT MCGAHA 50 ACRES

State of Tennessee Cocke County.
By virtue of an entry made in the entry takers office for said county at Newport of NO. 309 dated the 2nd day of January 1826. I have surveyed for ROBERT MCGAHA fifty acres of land on the waters of Cosbys Creek and Ground Hog Creek. Beginning at a chestnut near a spring on the waters of Cosbys Creek running thence south seventy three east one hundred and thirty six and one half poles to a dogwood and an ironwood on the bank of Ground hog Creek north seventeen east sixty three and one fourth to a large bush near the road leading to MCMAHANS turnpike thence north seventy three west one hundred and twenty six and one half poles to a stake on the waters of Cosbys Creek then a direct line to the beginning.
Having such form as is represented by the above platt.
Surveyed the 3rd day of July 1827.

Francis Green)
Jonathan Wood
Wm. Green) C.C. Surveyor of
Cocke County

283

WILLIAM HARPER 12 1/2 ACRES

State of Tennessee Cocke County.
By virtue of an entry made in the entry takers office for said county at Newport of No. 262 dated the 18th day of August 1824. I have surveyed for WILLIAM HARPER twelve and one half acres of land including part of an island in Big Pigeon River beginning at a dogwood in said island on the west side thereof running thence south forty two east sixteen poles to a beech south thirty nine east twenty two poles to a sycamore south sixty eight east nine poles to a beech thence across said island north forty six east twenty six poles to the bank of a sluice same course crossing said sluice in all forty nine poles to an ash on the side of a mountain then along ditto north thirty four west thirty four poles to a stake south forty six west twenty two poles to a stake on the bank of a sluice then a direct line to the beginning.
Having such form as is represented by the above platt.
Surveyed the 25th day of September 1827.

Jas. Mattox)
Jonathan Wood
Jas. Denney) C.C. Surveyor of
Cocke County

JOHN ALLEN 180 ACRES

State of Tennessee Cocke County.
By virtue of an entry made in the entry takers office for said county at Newport of No. 188 dated 5th of July 1824. I have surveyed for John Allen one hundred and eighty acres of land on the waters of Cosbys Creek. Beginning at a black oak corner to said Allens and JOSEPH SHULTS running thence with HUFFS lines south forty six west eighty two poles to a stake north sixty two west fourteen poles to a stake corner to DENTON then with his line south three west one hundred and sixty to a stake south sixty one east forty four poles to a sourwood north forty three poles to a stake south forty seven east one hundred and sixty poles to a stake south sixty one east forty five to a sourwood north forty three east forty three poles to a stake south forty seven east one hundred and fifty five poles to a sourwood then with said Allens 110 acre tract south 21 deg. west one hundred and ninety poles to the beginning.
Having such form as is represented by the above platt.
Surveyed the 18th day of November 1824.

Abraham Denton)
Jonathan Wood
John Allen) C.C. Surveyor of
Cocke County

284
TARELETON BRYANT 150 ACRES

State of Tennessee Cocke County.
By virtue of an entry made in the entry takers office for said county at Newport of No. 401 dated 5th January 1826. I have surveyed for TARLETON BRYANT one hundred and fifty acres of land on the west side of Big Pigeon River on Englishes Creek. Beginning on two white oaks in a dog hollow above ELIAS SISKS field near said Sisks corner running thence south twenty seven east two poles to a white oak corner to said Sisks then with his line south eight east two hundred and two poles to three hickorys on north line then with his line south eighty two west one hundred and nineteen poles to a white oak hickory and double dogwood under the foot of English mountain then across the spur of ditto north eight west two hundred and four poles to a black walnut and red bud in the head of a steep hollow thence a direct line to the beginning.
Having such form as is represented by the above platt.
Surveyed the 21st day of July 1826.

Chrispopher Bird)
Jonathan Wood
Wm. Sneed) C.C. Surveyor of
Cocke County

285
WM. FAUBION SIXTY ACRES

State of Tennessee Cocke County.
By virtue of an entry made in the entry takers office for said county at Newport of No. 256 dated the 7th day of August 1824. I have surveyed for WM. FAUBION sixty acres of land in said county on the north side of French Broad river. Beginning at a stake corner to said Faubion on the north side of the road leading from Newport to the Warm springs near to where WM. HELTON formerly lived running thence with his old line west fifty seven and one half poles to a stake on MOSES FAUBION line then with the same north eighty six poles to a white oak north thirty five east fifty four poles to a stake near three black oaks and a hickory on said Faubions line then with the same a direct line to the beginning.
Having such form as is represented by the above platt.
Surveyed the 9th day of April 1827.

John Headrick)
Jonathan Wood
David Baley) C.C. Surveyor of
Cocke County

JOHN RUTHERFORD & E. CLEVENGER 12 ACRES

State of Tennessee Cocke County.
By virtue of an entry made in the entry takers office of said county at Newport of No. 345 dated the 20th September 1825. I have surveyed for JOHN RUTHERFORD & ELIAS CLEVENGER twelve acres of land including a small island and fish trap the bottom being principally covered with the waters of Big Pigeon River. Beginning at a spruce pine on the west bank of the said river below the ford nearly opposite where JOSEPH H. GREEN now lives running up the meanders of said river with Woods lines south fifty two east twenty seven poles to a willow south sixty five east thirteen and an half poles to a buckeye south eighty deg. east forty nine poles to a poplar then across ditto north eighteen east twenty five and one half to a stake on the east bank of said river awn ditto with a clift of rocks north eighty west forty nine poles to rock that projects some distance in the river below a fish trap then a direct line to the beginning.
Having such form as is represented by the above platt.
Surveyed the 24th day of July 1826.

Asa Wood)
Jonathan Wood
Abraham Wood) C.C.
Surveyor Of Cocke County

286
SUSANNAH LOKE 43 ACRES

By virtue of an entry made in the entry takers office of said county at Newport of No. 548 dated the 19th day of June 1826. I have surveyed for SUSANNAH locke forty three acres of land on the waters of Meadow Creek Beginning at a stake near at a stake near a white oak on OTTINGERS line running thence with ditto north fifty east sixteen poles to a hickory and sourwood on DAVID OTTINGERS line then with ditto north fifty six poles to a pine north thirty five west twenty poles to a post oak north three west forty two poles to a gum corner to DAVID OTTINGERS new survey then with ditto west sixty seven poles to a stake on PATTIES line south thirty east forty four poles to a post oak south thirty nine east seventy poles to a gum south one west thirty two poles to a white oak PATTIES corner west twenty six poles to a white oak corner to POTTER OTTINGERS then with the line of his new survey south fifty six poles to a black oak on old OTTINGER line then with the same a direct line to the beginning.
Having such form as is represented by the above platt.
Surveyed the 15th day of February 1827.
This survey was for 100 acres but could not be had for old lines.

John Elderman)
Jonathan Wood
J. Loke) C.C. Surveyor of
Cocke County

287
<u>JOHN PUCKETT 50 ACRES</u>

State of Tennessee Cocke County.
By virtue of an entry made in the entry takers office of said county at Newport of No. 457 dated the 1st day of February 1826. I have surveyed for JOHN PUCKETT fifty acres of land on the south side of the French Broad Keeneys Branch. Beginning at a lynn at the foot of a staap nobb near the mouth of the middle branch on JOSEPH FRANCES corner running thence with his line north thirty four and an half poles to a stake near a beech on the line of the HEIRS of JAMES KEENEY deed. then with their line north fifty five and an half east one hundred and twenty eight poles to a dead sugar tree near MCGILLS old still house corner to BENGIMON DAUGHTY then with his line north seventy seven east twenty six poles to an ash on the side of the Bear Branch then up ditto south one hundred and thirty five to a stake a direct line south thirty six west two hundred and twenty five poles to the beginning.
Having such form as is represented by the above platt.
Surveyed the 13th of February 1826.

WM. REANS)
Jonathan Wood
Sam Reans) C.C.
Surveyor of Cocke County

288
<u>JOHN ALLEN 200 ACRES</u>

State of Tennessee Cocke County.
By virtue of an entry made in the entry takers office for said county at Newport of No. 389 dated the 2nd day of January 1826. I have surveyed for JOHN ALLEN two hundred acres of land on the waters of Big Pigeon River. Beginning at a stake near a poplar on the bank of said river running thence up ditto south fifteen east twenty poles to a poplar south forty four east fifteen poles to a mulberry in an island corner to PRETTYS then with his lines south seventy eight and three fourths west seventy five poles to a white oak south thirteen west ninety four poles to a walnut south one hundred and sixty poles to a stake west one hundred and five poles to a stake then with HUFFS line north eight and an half west one hundred and fifty poles to two black oaks south eighty west seventy poles to a beech north twenty two poles to a beech in the edge of a branch above the WIDOW WOLF lives on said Allens line then with his own line to the river north forty three east fifty poles to a pine north five west two poles to a pine south eighty five east sixty poles to a stake north twenty four poles to a white oak north seventy nine east thirty two poles to a sourwood south fifty eight east forty four poles to a white oak north fifteen east thirty eight poles to a polar north sixty eight and an half east one hundred and twenty two poles to the beginning.
Represented by the above platt.
Surveyed 18th June 1827.

A.M. Wiliamson)
Jonathan Wood
Wade Houston) C.C.
Surveyor of Cocke County

289
JAMES SWAGERTY 114 ACRES

State of Tennessee Cocke County.
By virtue of an entry made in the entry takers office for said county at Newport of No. 34 dated 6th day of April 1824. I have surveyed for JAMES SWAGERTY SENR. one hundred and fourteen acres of land on the waters of Clear Creek. Beginning at a black oak on the line of a tract of land originally granted to FREDRICK SWAGERTY running thence with the same south three and an half west one hundred and seventy eight poles to a stake near two black oaks and a hickory on Grants line then with ditto south fifty west eighty poles to a stake near Faubions lie then with the same north twenty nine west ninety three poles to a pine on a ridge then north twenty east one hundred and thirty two poles to a stake on the line of a nineteen acre tract of Sr Swagertys then with the same east thirty one poles to a stake north thirty nine poles to a stake near a Grubb then with John Swagertys line a direct line to the beginning.
Having such form as is represented by the above platt.
Surveyed the 14th day of March A.D. 1826.

Abraham Swagerty*)
Jonathan Wood S
Harvey Swagerty) C.c.

CHRISTIAN RENNER 150 ACRES

State of Tennessee Cocke County.
By virtue of an entry made in the entry takers office for said county at Newport of No. 563 dated 28th of August 1826. I have surveyed for CHRISTIAN RENNER SEN. one hundred and fifty acres of land on the waters of Meadow Creek, Beginning at an elm his lower corner and corner to JOHN WILTY running thence with Wiltys line south forty one east thirty five poles to a gum and hickory east thirty nine poles to a chestnut oak Renners corner thence with his line south eighty five poles to a white oak in a hollow west sixty poles to a pine north eighty five west one hundred and twenty five poles to a stake on Grants line then with his line north fifty west thirty five poles to two gums and a dogwood north thirty two east one hundred and seventeen poles to a chestnut then with JOHN WILTYS line south forty two east forty three poles to a sassafras north seven east sixty seven poles to the beginning including the home and improvements where said

Renner formerly lived.
Represented by the above platt.
Surveyed the 2nd day of April 1828.

Samul Blazer)
Jonathan Wood
John Wilty) C.C. Surveyor of
Cocke County

290
JOSEPH NEAS 50 ACRES

State of Tennessee Cocke County.
By virtue of an entry made in the entry takers office of said county at Newport of No. 490 dated the 28th day of February 1826. I have surveyed for JOSEPH NEAS fifty acres of land on Oven Creek. Beginning at a horn bean on said Neas line in the edge of a small branch running thence with line north forty two east one hundred and twenty six and an half to a hickory north forty eight west sixty three and one fourth poles to a stake south forty two west one hundred and twenty six and an half poles to a stake south forty eight east sixty three and one fourth poles to the beginning.
Having such form as is represented by the above platt.
Surveyed 19 March 1828.

Jacob Easterly)
Jonathan Wood
Conrod Easterly) C.C. Surveyor of
Cocke County

291
WM. JONES 74 A. 2 R. 20 L

State of Tennessee Cocke County
By virtue of an entry made in the entry takers office for said county at Newport of No. 490 dated the 8th day of Feb. 1826. I have surveyed for JOSEPH NEAS THIS HAS BEEN COPIED SAME AS THE ABOVE INCLUDING CHAIN CARRIERS (A.M.)

JANDINE WILLIAMS 50 A

State of Tennessee Cocke County.
By virtue of an entry made in the entry takers office for said county at Newport of No. 589 dated the 27th day of Oct. 1826. I survey Jawdine Williams fifty acres of land on the west side of Big Pigeon River on Ground hog Creek. Beginning at a leaning poplar corner to GEORGE MATTOX old survey running thence south twenty poles to two beeches at the foot of a hill south sixty eight west thirty six poles to a large poplar north twenty eight west forty five poles to a leaning chestnut north thirty three east sixty six poles to a stake then along a mountain north seventy three east one hundred poles to a stake south forty five east sixty eight poles to a large white oak and poplar on the bank of Groundhog Creek then up ditto south eighty west one hundred and twenty poles where GEORGE MATTOX lives to a stake in a field his corner then with his line south twelve east thirty five poles to the beginning.
Having such form as is represented by the above platt. Surveyed the 3rd day of July 1827.

Wm. Green)
Jonathan Wood
Calvin Williams) C.C. Surveyor of
Cocke County

292
WM. C. STORY 100 ACRES

State of Tennessee Cocke County.
By virtue of an entry made in the entry takers office for said county at Newport of NO. 558 dated the 17th day of August 1826. I have surveyed for WM. C. STORY one hundred acres of land on the north side of ELAM KINDRICK dry land place running with his line north eight poles to a white oak then with his line north eight poles to a white oak then with his line north eight poles to a white oak then with said Storys line west one hundred poles to a white oak on FINES line then with his line south thirty nine poles to a stake east fifty poles to a hickory and a dogwood south fifty two poles to a post oak on the brink of a clift of rock then along ditto up the river north seventy one east forty two poles south sixty six east twenty four poles to a white oak east eleven poles to a white oak and cedar on the bank of the French Broad river then up the meanders north eighty two east eight poles to a Ironwood east sixteen poles to a --- north fifty five east eight poles to a line waterbirch then up a steep clift north thirty four poles to a pine north eighty east twenty poles to a white oak north fifty five east eighteen poles to a pine north forty nine east thirty three poles to a stake on the KENDRICKS line then west with the same to the beginning.
Having such form as is represented by the above platt.
Surveyed the 2nd day of Oct. 1827.

G. HOOKS)
Jonathan Wood
L.D. Potter) C.C. Surveyor of
Cocke County

293

TIPTON O. WOOD 100 A.

State of Tennessee Cocke County.
Pursuant to an entry made in the entry takers office for said county at Newport of No. 402 dated the 5th day of January 1826. I have surveyed for TIPTON O. WOOD one hundred acres of land on the waters of Sinking Creek. Beginning at a large poplar corner to JAMES STRANGE running thence south twelve east seventy four poles to a locust east sixteen poles to a green south ten west along a mountain thirty three poles to a black gum thence south forty one west twenty four poles to a chestnut oak south forty eight poles to two chestnuts north seventy west forty poles to a chestnut oak north twenty west eighty poles to a white oak north thirty poles to a pine north ten west twenty four poles to a gum corner to MILLER then with his line north five and one fourth east one hundred poles to a poplar his corner north twenty five west fifty poles to a chestnut oak on a ridge north eighty poles to a chestnut near NEWCOMBS old cabbin thence east fifty poles to a stake south one hundred and twenty five to two sourwood corner to JAMES STRANGE then with his line south one fourth to a degree east eighty nine poles to the beginning. Including the house and improvements where ANTHY PATE now lives. Having such form as is represented by me.
Surveyed the 10 April 1828.

A. Lane)
Jonathan Wood
T. Wood) C.C.
Surveyor of Cocke County

294

JAMES SOLOMAN 100 ACRES

State of Tennessee Cocke County.
Pursuant to an entry made in the entry takers office for said county at Newport of No. 404 dated the 5th day of February 1826. I have surveyed for JAMES SOLMON one hundred acres of land on the waters of Neely Creek and Noly Chucky river beginning at a stake corner to WILLIAM BUGG running thence with same south thirty east one hundred and twenty six poles to a dogwood Hills corner then with his line south sixty five west one hundred and twenty poles to a lynn at the mouth of the Cool Branch on the bank of Chucky thence up the measnsers[sic] therof north twenty eight- forty four poles to a hickory on Hales old line north thirty three west forty poles to a pawpaw north forty eight east twenty poles to a stake on the side of a hill then with Harles line of his new survey north one west one hundred and thirty seen poles to a stake on WILLIAM SOLOMONS line then with the same to a stake his and Jas Ragans corner then with Jarnagans (believe this is Jarnagan not Jas Ragan) line south sixty five east ten poles to a stake south twenty east twenty five poles to a beech south fifty eight east fifteen poles to a Elm same course in all forty six poles to a hickory. South five west twenty eight poles to a sugar tree on or near WM. BRIGGS line then with the same south thirty five west seventy three poles to the beginning.
Having such form as is represented by the above platt.
Surveyed the 17th of July 1827.

James Miller)
Jonathan Wood
And. Nelson) C.C. Surveyor of
Cocke County

295
CHRISTOPHER BENNER JR. 50 ACRES

State of Tennessee Cocke County.
By virtue of an entry made in the entry takers office for said county at Newport of No. 690 dated the 4th day of April 1828. I have surveyed for CHRISTIAN BENNER JR. fifty acres of land situate on the waters of Meadow Creek. Beginning at a pine corner to CHRISTIAN BENNER SEN running thence south eighty poles to a chestnut west eighty poles to a walnut north fifty six west fifty five poles to a chestnut oak. On the spur of a mountain north eighty poles to a stake on GRANTS line then with the same north fifteen west forty five poles to a stake corner to CHRISTIAN BENNERS SEN. then with his line a direct line to the beginning.
Having such form as is represented by the above platt.
Surveyed the - day of April 1828.

Samuel Beaner)
Jonathan Wood
Jas, Wilty) C.C. Surveyor of
Cocke County

296
WILLIAM MCCONNELL 400 ACRES

State of Tennessee Cocke County.
By virtue of an entry made in the entry takers office of said county at Newport of No. 550 dated the 10th day of July 1826. I have surveyed for WILLIAM MCCONNELL and RICE N. PUCKETT four hundred acres of land jointly on the waters of Neelys Creek, Lick Branch, and Nola Chucky River. Beginning at a beech near a JERAMIAH HILLS corner running thence with his line north twenty west two hundred and twenty poles to a beech on Braggs line then with ditto south sixty east thirty poles to three hickorys Braggs corner the same course continued and hundred and sixty poles to two spouis oaks on a ridge north fifty six east ninty two poles crossing Neelys Creek at the ford to a hornbean and two poplars south fifty one east nineteen poles to a ash at the foot of a hill south sixty one east eighty six poles to a stake on a ridge on or near JAMES DAUGHTYS line south two and twenty poles to a stake west two hundred and thirty poles to a stake north fifteen poles to a stake then with ELIJAH HILLS line north forty five eat fifty four poles to a stake north forty west eighty two poles to the beginning.
Having such form as is represented by the above platt.
Surveyed the 20th July 1827.

Abraham Hill)
Jonathan Wood
James Miller) C.C.
Cocke County

Surveyor of

297
GEORGE NELSON 20 ACRES

State of Tennessee Cocke County.
By virtue of an entry made in the entry takers office for said county at Newport of No. 167 dated the 3rd day of July 1824. I have surveyed for GEORGE NELSON twenty acres of land on the west side of Big Pigeon river on the waters of Sinking Creek Beginning at two white oaks running thence twenty wet nineteen poles to a hickory dogwood and spanish oak on JOHN BOYERS line then with his line north seventy two east fifty two poles to two black oaks south fourteen east fifty five poles to a black oak on said Boyers line crossing the public road north sixty six east twenty poles to a small hickory and limestone rock north thirty two poles to a pine north eighty poles to a fourteen poles to a dead pine and black ash north thirty two west fifty nine poles to a white oak and hickory pointers of NAVES line near his corner then with his line south sixty west forty six poles to a stake then a direct line to the beginning.
Having such form as is represented by the above platt.
N.B. The entry on which the survey is founded was for fifty acres but could not be had for interferring lines.
Surveyed the 12th day of November 1825.

no C.C. given
JONATHAN WOOD

Surveyor of Cocke County

JAMES HART 100 ACRES

State of Tennessee Cocke County.
By virtue of an entry made in the entry takers office of said county at Newport of No. - dated - day - of - 182-. I have surveyed for JAMES HART one hundred acres of land on the waters of Oven Creek. Beginning at a white oak about one hundred and fifty yards below the stone lick on a branch running thence south forty five degrees west one hundred and seventy nine poles to a stake on a ridge thence south forty five deg. east eighty nine and an half poles to a black gum and hickory near a dogwood near a dry branch thence north forty five deg. east one hundred and twenty nine poles to a stake thence north forty five west eighty nine and an half poles to the beginning. Including the place where the widow now lives.
Having such form as is represented by the above platt.
Surveyed the 18th day of March 1828.

Josiah Hart)
Jon. Wood
Spencer Lows) C.C.
Surveyor of Cocke County

298
JOSIAH HART & J.W. HART 200 ACRES

State of Tennessee Cocke County.
By virtue of an entry made in the entry takers office for said county at Newport of No. 631 dated the 28th day of May 1827. I have surveyed for JOSIAH HART AND JOHN W. HART 200 acres of land on the waters of Oven Creek. Beginning at a stake on the line of James Harts one hundred acre tract near a hickory and black gum on the side of his branch corner above the stone lick running thence east two hundred and forty poles to a stake then west one hundred and ten poles to a stake thence south ninety poles to a stake corner to said JAMES HART then with his line south forty five west one hundred and seventy nine poles to the beginning.
Having such form as is represented by the above platt.
Surveyed the 18th day of March 1828.

Jas. Hart)
Jon. Wood
Spencer Laws) C.C.
Surveyor of Cocke County

299
ISAAC ALWAY 16 ACRES

State of Tennessee Cocke County.
By virtue of an entry made in the entry takers office for said county at Newport of No. - dated - of - 182-. I have surveyed for ISAAC ALWAY sixteen acres of land on the south side of NOLA Chucky River. Beginning at an ash at a sink hole on the bank of said river in SCRUGGS cornfield running thence south forty three and an half east ninety poles to two hickorys and a white oak on the side of a steep hill south forty six and an half west seventy three poles to a stake near a lynn on the bank of a clear creek then north thirty two west sixty two poles to a stake three poles above a hickory and two marked dogwoods on the bank of the river then up the meanders thereof to the beginning.
Having such form as is represented by the above platt.
Surveyed the 17th day of August 1826.

Wm. Palmer)
Jonathan Wood
Thos. Dean) C.C.
Surveyor of Cocke County

ELI NEWLAND 50 ACRES

State of Tennessee Cocke County.
By virtue of an entry made in the entry takers office for said county at Newport of No. 143 dated the 1st day of August 1824. I have surveyed for ELI NEWLAND fifty acres of land on the waters of Sinking Creek including the house and improvements where on he now lives. Beginning at a stake in the middle of a spring branch running with north twenty eight east twelve poles to a stake near a white oak NELLY VEALS corner on JOHN ROGERS line then with ditto sixty three poles to a stake south eighty four poles to a stake on NEFFS line then with the same south eighty four east thirty five poles to Neffs corner same course continued in all fifty three poles to a black gum south four poles to a poplar in a sink hole south sixty east ten poles to a hickory north fifty five east sixty poles to a small white oak and two red buds saplings on a rocky ridge then a direct line to the beginning.
Having such form as is represented by the above platt.
Surveyed the 11th day of November 1825.

No c.c. given
J. Wood

Surveyor of Cocke County

300
SHADRICK SURGEON 50 A.

State of Tennessee Cocke County.
By virtue of an entry made in the entry takers office for said county at Newport of No. 678 dated the 14th day of Feby 1828. I have surveyed for SHADRICK SURGEON fifty acres of land on Toms Creek. Beginning at a poplar corner to SCOFLE MATTOX running thence above a mountain north eighty eight east sixty poles to a pine south eighty one east twenty two poles to a poplar south fifty five east twenty four poles to a cucumber south eighty three east eighty four poles to a chestnut same course continued thirty five poles further in all to a stake thence south twenty seven west thirty five poles to a stake north eighty west two hundred poles and five poles to a stake on MATTOXS line then with the same to the beginning.
Having such form as is represented by the above platt.
Surveyed the 6th day of May 1828.

Pettie Pretty)
Jonathan Wood
Jno Phillips) C.C.
Surveyor of Cocke County

301
JESSEE COLEMAN 100 A.

State of Tennessee Cocke County.
By virtue of an entry made in the entry takers office for said county at Newport of No. 520 dated the 7th of April 1826. I have surveyed for JESSEE COLEMAN one hundred acres of land on east side of Green Briar fork of Cosbys Creek. Beginning at a black oak near JAMES PHILLIPS line running with or nearly with his line north seventy one west one hundred poles to a sassafras north fifteen east twenty seven poles to a dead maple corner to J. RUNNIONS with his lines north sixty one west one hundred and ten poles to a poplar on the line of a lower tract then with ditto south sixty two west four poles to a spanish oak south fifty west forty poles to a beech then along a mountain south forty five east two hundred and seventy poles to a stake then a direct line to the beginning.
Having such form as is represented by the above platt.
Surveyed the 5th day of May 1828.

Nathaniel Mattox
Jonathan Wood
J. Phillips
Surveyor of Cocke County

NATHEN MATTOX 150 ACRES

State of Tennessee Cocke County.
By virtue of an entry made in the entry takers office at Newport of No. 365 dated the 2nd day of January 1826. I have surveyed for Nathe Mattox one hundred and fifty acres of land on Cosbys Creek beginning at a spruce pine on the bank of said creek running thence south sixty five west one hundred poles to a spruce pine on the west bank of Rock Creek south twenty five east one hundred and eighty eight poles to a dogwood north sixty five east one hundred and forty six poles to a large poplar on the bank of Cosbys Creek then a direct line to the beginning. Including his improvements.
Having such form as is represented by the above platt.
Surveyed the 7th day of May 1828.

James Garrett)
Jonathan Wood
Pettis Pretty) C.C.
Surveyor of Cocke County

302
NATHANIEL MATTOX 100 ACRES

State of Tennessee Cocke County.
By virtue of an entry made in the entry takers office of said county at Newport of No. 365 dated the 2nd day of January 1826. I have surveyed for NATHANIEL MATTOX one hundred acres of land on Cosbys creek. Beginning at a chestnut on the bank of said creek running thence south twenty poles east seventy four poles to a dogwood on the bank of a branch south seventy two eighteen poles to a chestnut north sixty three east one hundred and twenty four poles to a stake north twenty seven west nineteen poles to a -- then along a mountains south eighty four west one hundred and forty poles to a stake south forty five poles to a stake east ten poles to the beginning.
Having such form as is represented by the above platt.
Surveyed the 6th day of May 1828.

Nathaniel Mattox)
Jonathan Wood
Jas Phillips) C.C. Surveyor of
Cocke County

303
POLLY JUSTICE 25 ACRES

State of Tennessee Cocke County.
by virtue of an entry made in the entry takers office for said county at Newport of No. 632 dated the 23rd day of June 1827. I have surveyed for Polly Justice twenty five acres of land on the waters of Meadow Creek. Beginning at a leaning post oak corner to her fifty acre tract of which she now lives running thence with the same north fifty five east seventy nine poles and an half to a black jack north twenty five west forty four and an half poles to a stake in the margin of the road leading from Newport to Greenville to Newport south fifty five west eighty eight and a fourth poles to a pine and hickory south thirty five east forty four and an half poles to a stake north fifty five eleven poles to the beginning.
Having such form as is represented by the above platt.
Surveyed 23rd day of June 1827.

David Ottinger)
Jonathan Wood
Jno. Ebberty) C.C. Surveyor of
Cocke County

JOSEPH RUNION 25 ACRES

State of Tennessee Cocke County.
By virtue of an entry made in the entry takers office for said county of No. 654 dated the 26th of November 1827. I have surveyed for JOSEPH RUNION twenty five acres of land on the waters of Cosbys Creek. Beginning at a black oak on W. ADAMS old line running thence up a hollow conditional line with WILLIAM GILLILAND south seventy and one half East sixteen poles to a stake north eighty East eighteen poles to a sourwood south seventy three eleven poles north seventy one East nineteen poles to a chestnut south twenty eight and an half west one hundred and sixty poles over a mountain to a black oak and hickory on said W. ADAMS line then with the same north twenty west seventeen poles to a chestnut north twenty eight and one half west one hundred and sixty poles over a mountain to a black oak and hickory on said W. ADAMS line then with the same north twenty west seventeen poles to a chestnut north twenty east forty four poles to a black oak north ninety five poles to the beginning.
Having such form as is represented by the above platt.
Surveyed the 3rd day of June 1828.

William Gilliland)
Jonathan Wood
George Robinson) C.C. Surveyor of
Cocke County

304
JOHN LILLARD 125 ACRES

State of Tennessee Cocke County.
By virtue of an entry made in the entry takers office of said county at Newport of NO. 388 dated the 2nd day of January 1826. for one hundred and forty five acres. I have surveyed for JOHN LILLARD one hundred and twenty five acres it being bounded so no more could be had. Beginning at a sourwood on his own line running thence with the same north fifty six and one fourth west thirty eight poles to JOHN DENTONS corner south eighteen west twenty and one fourth poles to a white oak north seventy five and one fourth west two poles to a stake corner to Robert Gilliland then with his line sixty and one fourth poles to a gum south sixty and one fourth poles to a gum south eighty one west crossing the public road at twenty poles in all thirty poles to a small black oak south eighty six East forty two poles to a small black oak and maple on JOHN ALLENS line then with ditto north thirty seven and one half east sixty six poles to a white oak his corner south fifty two east eighty six poles to a black oak same course continued seventy four poles to a stake corner near HUFFS line north one hundred poles to a stake north twenty two west forty five poles to a sourwood corner to ABR DENTON then with his line to the beginning.

James Allen)
Jon. Wood
James Rose) C.C.
Surveyor of Cocke County

305, 306
FRANCES J. CARTER 436 ACRES

State of Tennessee Cocke County.
By virtue of an entry made in the entry takers office for said county at Newport of NO. 195 dated the 17" day of Aril 1828. I have surveyed for FRANCIS CARTER four hundred and thirty six acres of land on the south side of French Broad River. Beginning at a black oak dogwood and sourwood corner to MARTIN PHILLIPS one hundred acre tract running North thirteen poles to a white oak and chestnut oak East one hundred and thirty seven poles to a stake on JOHN WILCHS line then with his line south twenty east nine poles to a bush his corner of a 100 acre tract then with the same south one hundred and thirty poles to a dogwood in the head of a steep hollow east forty poles to a small white oak south one hundred and fifty five poles with vacant land to two small black oaks and a white oak on ALEXANDER E. SMITHS line with ditto south forty five and one half west one hundred poles to a sugar tree on the north side of branch south ten East ninty poles to a stake near a poplar corner to PHILLIP SWANSON then with his line south fifty three west one hundred and thirty two poles to a white oak south fifty three west one poles crossing the road leading from Newport to CLARKS ford to a beech on the bank of a branch then with ditto and steep nobbs north sixty five west Eleven poles two walnut south seventy five west fifty six poles to a beech on the side of a hill south thirty four poles to a beech west two hundred and ten poles to a small dogwood on BENJAMIN DAUGHTYS line then with his line north twenty five East seventy two poles to a white oak on a ridge north fifty west forty two poles to a sugar tree north eighty five west forty five poles to a stake near a markes beech on said Daughtys old line on the land on which he now lives then with same north seven and three quaters East six poles to a buckeye corner to said CARTERS MCCLANAHAN tract then with the same south eighty seven and an half East one hundred and forty poles to a beech by the side of the aforesaid road north thirty nine East twenty six poles to a black oak corner to a tract of land then with a line of NABBS north seventy eight East sixty poles to -- south seventy two East poles to a stake north seventy nine East sixteen poles north eighty two east thirty four poles to a beech north one hundred and seventeen and an half poles to a dogwood corner to said CARTERS new survey the same course continued with ditto one hundred and sixty poles further to a buckeye in a hollow West eighty two poles to a sweet gum and dogwood on PHILLIPS line then with ditto north forty eight and one fourth poles to the beginning.
Having such form as is represented by the above platt.
Surveyed the 20th day of April 1828.

JAMES WOOD) Jon
Wood
WILLIAM CARTER) C.C. Surveyor of
Cocke County

SAMUEL HANCE 25 Acres

State of Tennessee Cocke County.
By virtue of an entry made in the entry takers office for said county at Newport of NO 638 dated the 30th of July*1838. I have surveyed for SAMUEL HANCE twenty five acres of land on the head waters of a branch that runs through the long hollow which branch enters into the French Broad river. Beginning at a stake near a large black oak on the East side of a road leading from Clarks ford to Newport on SHEFFEY PUCKETTS line of a tract of land on which said HANCE now lives running thence north fifty two East thirty six poles to a white oak on CHUMES line north ten west fifty eight poles to a hickory then along precipice north twenty west thirty four poles to a stake on the side of a hill then south thirty eight west crossing the aforesaid road sixty two poles to a stake north eighty four East fifteen poles to a stake corner to said PUCKETT the same course continued with his line sixty three and one fourth poles further on crossing said road to a dead hickory south sixty East thirty four poles to the beginning.
Surveyed the 4th day of Sept. 1828 sure the above * was copied wrong.

THOS HEATON)
Jonathan Wood
WM HANCE) C.C.
Surveyor of Cocke County

308
WM GILLILAND 100 A.

State of Tennessee Cocke County.
By virtue of an entry made in the entry takers office for said county at Newport of NO 438 dated the 10th day of January 1828. I have surveyed for WM GILLILAND one hundred acres of land on the waters of Cosbys Creek beginning at a black oak on his own line running thence with his line north thirteen East four poles to a spanish oak North eleven west eighty poles to a birch north three and one half East twenty four poles north eighty west four poles to a white oak corner to McPIKES old tract thence with ditto south eighty five east forty five poles to a hickory north seventy East forty poles to a black oak & post oak then along DENNYS MOUNTAIN south fifty one East thirty seven south four poles to a poplar south twenty five East twenty poles to a stake south twelve west one hundred and fifty poles to a poplar corner to JNO RUNNIN then along with his lines south eighty one west sixteen poles to a chestnut south seventy one west nineteen poles north seventy three west Eleven poles to a sourwood south eighty west eighteen poles to a stake north seventy west sixteen poles to a black oak corner to said GILLILAND then with his own lines south thirteen East forty seven poles to the beginning.
Having such form as is represented by the above platt.
Surveyed the 4th June 1828.

JNO. RUNNIONS)
Jonathan Wood
ROBT. DENNIS) C.C.
Surveyor of Cocke County

309
WM. RAMSEY 75 Acres

State of Tennessee Cocke County
By virtue of an entry made in the entry takers office for said county at Newport of NO 622 dated the 28th of March 1827. I have surveyed for WILLIAM RAMSEY seventy five acres of land on the waters of NOBB CREEK beginning at a stake near a white oak on STARLING HUDSON line running north fifty five poles to an ash and dogwood East one hundred and eighty to a beech south thirty six-sixty poles to a stake eight poles from a marked chestnut oak north forty west fifty two poles to a dogwood DAVID SURHEYS line then with ditto north fifty five East six poles north sixty two East eight poles north thirty eight East eight poles north twenty two east twenty eight poles to a beech north forty three East eighteen poles to a walnut and mulby north eight poles to a beech and hickory north forty five west forty two poles to a white oak south seventy and a half west forty six poles to the beginning.
Surveyed the sixth day of October 1828.

HOWELL MORRIS) Jon. Wood
CHRISTIAN HUDSON) C.C. Surveyor of Cocke County

310
SIMON SMITH 50 A.

State of Tennessee Cocke County.
By virtue of an entry made in the entry takers office at Newport of NO 653 Dated November 26/1827. I have surveyed for SIMON SMITH fifty acres of land on the waters of Knob Creek & Slate Creek. Beginning at a white oak in a hollow running thence north sixty three & one half East one hundred & seventeen poles to a spanish oak on a ridge thence south seventy six and one half east sixty eight and an half poles to a black walnut on a ridge south sixty three and an half west one hundred & seventeen poles to a stake north twenty six and one half west sixty eight poles to the beginning.
Having such form as is represented by the above platt.
Surveyed the 9th day of October 1828.

Simon Smith) Jon. Wood
Wm. Colmon) C.C. Surveyor of Cocke County

311
ISAAC BURLSON 50 ACRES

State of Tennessee Cocke County.
By virtue of an entry made in the entry takers office for said county at Newport of NO 524 dated the 7th day of April 1826. I have surveyed for ISAAC BURLISON fifty acres of land on Cosbys Creek. Beginning at a white oak running thence south twenty east eight poles to a dogwood north seventy six and an half East forty poles south seventy eight poles to a beech north eighty five East fifty eight poles to a beech south forty two poles to a stake south eighty five west thirty poles to a gum on or near said Burlisons line north thirty five west one hundred poles to a beech on the bank of Cosbys Creek crossing Ditto north sixty three west sixteen poles to a stake then with his lines south fifty five west fifty six poles to a beech south twenty two poles to a white oak south fifty five west eight poles to a white oak north twenty six west twenty poles to a dogwood on the top of a ridge north forty five East eighteen poles

to a poplar north seven east forty three poles to a small spruce pine near the creek then north twenty west forty four poles to a beech corner to said Giles north eighty seven East crossing creek eighteen poles to the beginning. Having such form as is represented by the above platt.
Surveyed the 4th day of June 1828.

John Runnion)
Jonathan Wood
Jas Phillips) C.C. Surveyor of
Cocke County

DANIEL MOORE 10 Acres

State of Tennessee Cocke County.
By virtue of an entry made in the entry takers office for said county at Newport of NO 263 dated the 21st day of August 1824. I have surveyed for DANIEL MOORE ten acres of land on the south side of Noly Chucky river including the house and part of the improvement whereon he now lives. Beginning at a red oak on Conways line running thence with the lines of said Moores 11 tract west fifty nine poles to a stake East thirty poles to a stake on or near Conways line then a direct line to the beginning. with Conways line having such form as is represented by the above platt.
Surveyed the 10th day of October 1828.

GEORGE GREGORY)
Jonathan Wood
DAVID GREGORY) C.C. Surveyor of
Cocke County

GREENE S.W. ROSE 50 A.

State of Tennessee Cocke County.
By virtue of an entry made in the entry takers office for said county at Newport of NO 127 dated September the 30th 1828. I have surveyed for Greene S.W. Rose fifty acres of land on the south side of French Broad on the waters of By Creek. Beginning at white pine on the point of big ridge running thence north seventy five and an half East forty three poles to a stake thence to direct line to the beginning.
Having such form as is represented above. Surveyed the 18th day of November 1828.

HARRY YOUNG)
Jonathan Wood
ROBERT BLACK) C.C. Surveyor of
Cocke County

313
CAMPBELL SEALS 25 A.

State of Tennessee Cocke County.
By virtue of an entry made in the entry takers office for said county of NO 249 dated August 4th 1824. I have surveyed for CAMPBELL SEALS twenty five acres of land in said county on the waters of a creek commonly called Ground Hog. Beginning at a large poplar tree near said creek & running south fifty west forty two poles to a large chestnut on or near a line of a fifty acre tract entry of HENRY MILLERS on the spur of the SMOKY MOUNTAINS then across the spur of the same south eighty four East one hundred & twenty five poles to a stake thence a direct line to the beginning.
Having such form as is represented by the above platt.
Surveyed December 2nd day 1828.
JOHN SUTTON) Jonathan
Wood
AUGUSTINE JENKINS) C.C. Surveyor of Cocke County

NANCY HICKS 11 Acres

State of Tennessee Cocke County.
By virtue of entry made in the entry takers office for said county at Newport of NO 486 dated the 28th Feby 1826. I have surveyed for NANCY HICKS eleven acres of land in said county on the waters of Boguard creek Beginning at a stake on the line of a tract of land entered in the entry takers office for said county by HIRAM ALLEN and running with the same north eight East one hundred and thirty poles to a pine on or near THOMAS ALLENS line south eighty two east twenty poles to a hickory thence with Hicks line south thirteen poles west one hundred and thirty poles to a fence a direct line to the beginning.
Having such form as is represented by the above platt.
Surveyed the 10th day of September 1828.

THOMAS REYNOLDS)
Jonathan Wood
ABNER HICKS) C.C. Surveyor of
Cocke County
The above entry was founded on a certificate for 25 A. but the completement cannot be got for interferance of old lines. J.M.

EVEN FAGATT 100 A.

State of Tennessee Cocke County by virtue of an entry made in the entry takers office for said county at Newport of No 697 dated the 17th day of April 1828. I have surveyed for EVEN FAGATT. One hundred acres of land in said county fortly on the waters of by creek Beginning on a stake on a hill side in the dogwood flat running thence north fifty seven East fifty one poles to a white pine on a steep nobb south twenty two west thirty four poles to a stake and hickory on a ridge south seventy one and half west fifty five poles to a spanish oak on a precipice south thirty nine west one hundred and two poles to a dogwood in a hollow south twenty four east forty five poles to a birch at the foot of a steep nobb thence across the spur of the same east ninety six poles to a stake a direct line to the beginning.
Surveyed the 23rd day of January 1829.

JAS YOUNG)
Jonathan Wood
RICHARD NIGHT) C.C. Surveyor of
Cocke County

315
W. FIELDSS 25 A.

State of Tennessee Cock County.
By virtue of an entry made in the entry takers office for said county at Newport of NO 627. I have surveyed for WRAY FIELDS twenty five acres of land in county on the right fork of Big Creek. Beginning on a beech tree a corner to said W. FIELDS twenty four acre survey entered in the name of RUBEN JUSTICE running thence south fifty nine and a half west eighty poles to a sourwood sprout & bunch Ivy north thirty one & a half west fifty poles to a pine and black walnut north fifty nine & one half east eighty poles to a stake thence a direct line to the beginning.
Surveyed No. 17th 1828.

HARRY YOUNG) JOHN
MULLENDONE
MARTIN DAVIS) C.C. Dept
surveyor of Cocke county.

JOHN FUGATT 50 Acres

State of Tennessee Cocke County.
By virtue of an entry made in the entry takers office for said county at Newport of NO 401 dated the 3rd day of February 1826. I have surveyed for JOHN FUGATT fifty acres of land on the waters of BRUSH Creek. Beginning on a black oak on HENDERSONS line running north sixty three & one half East seventy one poles to a hickory on or near MOONEYHAMS line then with the same north forty west fifty five poles to a spanish oak on the side of a mountain north fifty two East thirty eight poles to a white oak near a branch south fifty eight and an half East sixty seven poles to a poplar & dogwood on a hill side south ninty four poles to a stake thence a direct line to the beginning.
Surveyed the 24th January 1827.

A. LOODEN(?)) John
Mullendone
T. BOYDSTON) C.C. Dept.
surveyor of Cocke County

DARIUS O NEIL 100 Acres

State of Tennessee Cocke County.
By virtue of an entry made in the entry takers office for Cocke county at Newport of NO 479 dated 2nd day of February 1826. I have surveyed for DARIUS O NEIL one hundred acres of land on the waters of Clay Creek. Beginning at a white oak marked with a cross near JOHN WOODS corner running thence south fifty five east seventy five poles to a hickory in a branch south eighty East one hundred and sixteen poles with a conditional line with WILLIAM GILLETT to a stake near a white oak and black oak said Gilletts corner then with his line East twenty two poles to a stake on THOMAS CHRISTIANS line then with the same south eight poles to a white oak south fifty nine west seventy nine poles to a white oak his corner near a branch then north six west two hundred and thirty four poles to a stake corner to JOHN WOOD then with his line north fifty two poles to the beginning.
Surveyed the 3rd day of January 1829.

WM TYRY)
Jonathan Wood
MARTIN GAUGE) C.C. Surveyor of
Cocke County

317
HENRY MILLER 50 Acres

State of Tennessee Cocke County.
By virtue of an entry made in the entry takers office for said county at Newport of NO 687 dated March the 26th day 1828. I have surveyed for HENRY MILLER fifty acres of land in said county on Ground Hog Creek Beginning on a large poplar near the creek running thence west sixty four poles to a poplar on JOHN JINKINS line south ninty seven poles to a beech on the spur of the Smoky Mountain then across the spur of the same East one hundred and six poles to a stake a direct line to the beginning.
Having such form as is represented by the above platt.
Surveyed December the 2nd day 1828.

JOHN SUTTON) John
Mullendene
AUGUSTINE JENKINS) C.C. Dept. Surveyor of Cocke County

318
WILLIAM GREEN 25 Acres

State of Tennessee Cocke County.
By virtue of an entry made in the entry takers office for said county of NO 549 dated June the 28th 1826. I have surveyed for WILLIAM GREEN twenty five acres of land on Ground Hog Creek running north thirty one East thirty four poles to a maple on the bank of said creek at the foot of the mountain south seventy six East one hundred and fifty poles to a stake south nineteen poles to a stake thence a direct line to the
Having such form as is represented by the above platt,
Surveyed the 2nd day of December 1828.

JOHN SUTTON) John
Mullendone
AUGUSTINE JENKINS) C.C. Dept. Surveyor of Cocke County

RUSSELL JONES 30 Acres

State of Tennessee Cocke County.
By virtue of an entry made in the entry takers office for said county at Newport of No 530 dated March the 2nd 1826. I have surveyed for RUSSELL JONES thirty acres of land in said county on the south side of french broad river on the dry fork of Big Creek. Beginning on a white oak on the north line of said Jones original tract running thence north fifty poles to a stake and chestnut East fifty two poles to a white oak south one hundred and thirty poles to a stake then a direct line to the beginning.
Surveyed the 13th of Nov. 1828.

JAMES SAWYERS) John
Mullendone
ERVIN FUGATE) C.C. Dept.
Surveyor of Cocke County.

319
ZACHARIAH KINNAMON 6 A.

State of Tennessee Cocke County.
By virtue of an entry made in the entry takers office at Newport of NO 630 dated the 8th day of May 1827. I have surveyed for ZACHARIAH KINNAMON six acres of land in said county adjoining the land of said KINNAMON bought of SAMUEL STUART. Beginning on a white oak on said Kinnamons line and running west twenty two poles to a stake north forty four poles to a post oak bush East twenty two poles to a black oak thence a direct line to the beginning. Having such form as is represented by the above platt.
Surveyed October the 15th 1828.

WASHINGTON KINNAMON) John
Mullendone
JOHN SMOTHERS) C.C. Dept. Surveyor of Cocke County

320
MICHEAL KEENEY 100 A.

State of Tennessee Cocke County.
By virtue of an entry made in the entry takers office at Newport of NO 577 dated the 26th day of September 1829. I have surveyed for MICHEAL

KEENEY one hundred acres of land between ELIJAH WHILEYS line & the beginning the big survey. Beginning on a hickory a corner to said Wyley Running then south forty six East one hundred poles to a stake and a black oak on said WHILEYS LAND (Maybe Thiley A.M.) south fourteen west eighty four poles to a dogwood and chestnut. On the line of the big survey then with the same west seventy one poles to a black oak on said line north thirty nine west one hundred and twenty six poles to a stake thence a direct line to the beginning.
Surveyed the 4th day of February 1829.

~~JOHN MILLER~~ (marked through) John Mullendone

Dept. Surveyor of Cocke County

CALEB WILHITE 100 Acres

State of Tennessee Cocke County.
By virtue of an entry made in the entry takers office for said county at Newport of NO 575 dated September 13th 1826. I have surveyed for CALEB WILHITE one hundred acres of land in said county on the waters of Big Pigeon River. Beginning at GEORGE McNABBS corner on a stake running thence with said McNabbs line North fifty five East one hundred and sixty poles to a stake and hickory at the foot of a mountain south thirty five East one hundred poles to a stake south fifty five west one hundred and sixty poles to a stake thence a direct line to the beginning.

John Mullendone

Dept. Surveyor of Cocke County

321
THOMAS DEAMES 100 A

State of Tennessee Cocke County.
By virtue of an entry made in the entry takers office of said county at Newport of NO 516 dated September 13th 1826. I have surveyed for THOMAS S. DEANES one hundred acres of land in said county on the waters of Middle fork of Cosby Creek. Beginning on a sourwood near the creek running thence North six deg. West eighty four poles to a white oak on or near MARY DEAMES line south eighty four west one hundred and eighty poles to a stake south six East eighty nine poles to a stake north eighty four East one hundred and eighty poles to a stake thence a direct course to the beginning.
Surveyed January the 9th 1829.

GEORGE MCNABB) C.C. John
Mullendone
J. DENNIS) Dep.
surveyor for Cocke County

322
THOMAS MOONEYHAM 30 A.

State of Tennessee Cocke County.
By virtue of an entry made in the entry takers office for said county at Newport of NO 383 dated 2nd day of January 1826. I have surveyed for THOS. MOONEYHAM thirty acres of land on rocks creek. Beginning at a white oak corner to WM. MOONEYHAMS running thence north ten west ninty six poles to a white oak near a branch south eighty west fifty poles to a sourwood near the creek above the mill south ten east ninty six poles to a stake then thence a direct line to the beginning.

Having such form as the above platt represents. Surveyed the 13 day of Nov. 1828.

WM. HOLLAND) C.C. John
Mullendone
WILLIAM MOONEYHAM) Dept.
surveyor of Cocke County

323
WM. HICKEY 50 A.

State of Tennessee Cocke County.
By virtue of an entry made in the entry takers office at Newport of NO 522 dated the 29th day of March 1826. I have surveyed for WM. HICKEY fifty acres of land in said county. Beginning on a black oak corner to NATHANIEL POTTS entry thence running East one hundred and ninty six poles to a black oak Potts corner south nineteen and one half west sixty poles to a black oak CAULTES line north seventy & one half west ninety seven poles to a black oak south 3 west forty eight poles to a stake in a road north eighty nine west fourteen poles to a stake on KENNAHANS line thence with the same north sixteen East fifty six poles to a stake on the same north one hundred and twenty six poles to a stake thence a direct line to the beginning. Having such form as is represented by the above platt. Surveyed the 15th of October 1828.

ZACHARIAH KINNAMER) JOHN
MULLENDONE
ISAAC HICKY) C.C. Dep.
surveyor of Cocke county
The location upon which this survey is founded was for one hundred acres but the completement cannot be got for the interfearance of older lines.
John Mullendone, Dep. Sur.

HENRY JONES 50 A.

State of Tennessee Cocke County.
By virtue of an entry made in the entry takers office for said county at Newport NO - dated 2nd day of January 1826. I have surveyed for HENRY JONES fifty acres of land on the waters of English Creek. Beginning at a stake on THOMAS STUART line running thence with the same west one hundred poles to a post oak on a ridge north eighty poles to a black oak saplin one hundred poles to a stake south eighty poles to the beginning. Represented by the above platt. Surveyed the 13th day of October 1828.

John Mullendone

Dep. surveyor for Cocke County

324
JOHN LOWELL 50 A.

State of Tennessee Cocke County.
By virtue of an entry made in the entry takers office for said county at Newport of No 433 dated January 10th 1826. I have surveyed for JOHN LOWELL fifty acres of land in said county on the waters of Clay Creek. Beginning at a stake on or near his own line running thence south twenty eight East seventy three poles to a stake & dogwood. Monnie pine north sixty three sixty eight poles to a stake on a line north eight East one hundred Eleven & one half poles to a stake thence a direct line to the beginning. Having such form as is represented by the above platt.

Surveyed the 10th day of October 1828.

JAMES CHRISTIAN) C.C. John
Mullendone
HIRAM CORNAWELL) Dep.
surveyor of Cocke County

JACOB SMITH 12 Acres

State of Tennessee Cocke County.
By virtue of an entry made in the entry takers office of said county at Newport of NO 466 dated the 8th day of February 1826. I have surveyed for JACOB SMITH twelve acres of land in said county on a branch of the waters of long creek joining the lands whereon said Smith now lives. Beginning at a white oak and running south forty west eighty eight poles to a post oak on the side of a mountain south fifty East twenty two poles to a stake and Elm on the bank of said branch at the foot of the mountain north forty East up said branch and foot of the mountain eighty eight poles to a stake thence a direct line to the beginning.
Having such form as in represented by the above platt.
Surveyed the 10th day of November 1828.

JOHN FRESHOUR) C.C. John
Mullendone
RICHARD HAKY) Dep.
surveyor for Cocke County

325
MOSSES HICKS 50 Acres

State of Tennessee Cocke County.
By virtue of an entry made in the entry takers office of said county at Newport of NO 339 dated the 2nd day of January 1826. I have surveyed for MOSES HICKS fifty acres of land in said county on the waters of English Creek. Beginning on a pine corner of SAMUEL LORGE and running north fifty three and an half deg. west one hundred and eighty poles to a stake north 36 1/2 East one hundred poles to a stake south thirty East thirty poles to a stake on or near MARTHENS old line thence a direct line to the beginning. Having such form as is represented by the above platt.
Surveyed the 5th day of January. A.D. 1829.

S. HICKS) C.C. john
Mullendone
N. HICKS)
Dep. Surveyor of Cocke County

326
JOHN RUNION & GEORGE RUNION 100 Acres

State of Tennessee Cocke County.
By virtue of an entry made in the entry takers office of said county at Newport of No 710 dated the 5th day of June 1828. I have surveyed for JOHN RUNION & GEORGE RINION one hundred acres of land in the said county on the waters of Cosbys Creek on the Green Grassy fork thereof. Beginning at a stake on or near the upper line of an entry made by ISAAC BURLISON for fifty acres on the north side of said creek and running north fifty five East one hundred and twenty seven poles to a chestnut oak on the top of a ridge south thirty five East one hundred and twenty six poles to two dogwood bushes on a hillside near a large chestnut South fifty five west one hundred and twenty seven poles to a stake thence a direct line to the beginning.
Having such form as is represented by the above platt.
Surveyed the 3rd December 1828.

JOSEPH PHILLIPS) John
Mulldendone
JOHN BANKS) C.C. Dep.
surveyor of Cocke County

327
THOMAS MOONEYHAM 30 Acres

State of Tennessee Cocke County.
By virtue of an entry made in the entry takers office for said county at Newport of NO 382 dated the 2nd day of January 1826. I have surveyed for THOMAS MOONEYHAM thirty acres of land on the north side of French broad River. Beginning at a white oak WM MOONEYHAM-on the bank of said river running thence south thirteen & a half west ninty eight poles to a black oak north seventy six and an half west forty nine poles to a hickory north thirteen and an half deg. East ninety eight poles to a stake thence a direct line to the beginning.
Surveyed the 15th day of November 1828.

WILLIAM MOONEYHAM) John
Mullendone
WILLIAM BLACK) C.C. Dep. surveyor of Cocke County

JAMES ALLEN 50 Acres

State of Tennessee Cocke County.
By virtue of an entry made in the entry takers office of said county at Newport of NO 378 dated 2nd January 1826. I have surveyed for JAMES ALLEN fifty acres of land in said county. Beginning on a stake on his own line running thence south eighteen East eighty poles to a stake and black oak south sixty five East twenty four poles to a stake and post oak on a ridge on LEAUES(?) line north one hundred poles to a stake thence a direct line to the beginning.
Surveyed January 6th 1829.

TIMOTHY HICKS) C.C. John
Mullendone
ABRAHAM ALLEN) Dep.
surveyor of Cocke County

328
ROBERT McGAHA 50 Acres

State of Tennessee Cocke County.
By virtue of an entry made in the entry takers office of said county at Newport of NO 734 dated the 18th October 1821. I have surveyed for ROBT. McGAHA fifty acres of land on the waters of Ground Hog Creek. Beginning at a white oak on his own line running thence south fifty six East fifty two poles to a pollar on the spur of the turkey hill then along Ditto thirty four poles to a beech south forty five East twenty two poles to a spruce pine south fifty nine East forty poles to a chestnut oak south twenty poles to a stake north eighty five west one hundred and twenty five poles to a stake north seventeen East seventy four poles to a horn bean his corner same course continued with his line forty three poles further to the beginning.
Having such form as is represented by the above platt.
Surveyed the 2nd of December A.D. 1828.

HENRY MILLER) Jon.
Wood
JOHN SUTTON) C.C. Surveyor of
Cocke County

329
ABRAHAM ALLEN 40 A.

State of Tennessee Cocke County.
By virtue of an entry made in the entry takers office for said county at Newport of NO -- dated ---- I have surveyed for ABRAHAM ALLEN forty acres of land on the waters of Cosby and English Creek. Beginning at a post oak THOMAS DENTON corner running thence with JONATHAN DENTON line North nine and a half poles to a black oak north seventy East twenty poles to a post oak on or near North line North thirty five West twelve poles to a stake near two black oaks supposed to be north corner thence north twenty four four west forty three poles to a black oak corner field south seventeen East fifty poles to a locust THOMAS DENTENS corner thence with his line south thirty seven East fifty four poles to a post oak East eighty one poles to the beginning.
Represented by the above platt. Surveyed the 6th day of January 1829.

A. ALLEN) C.C. Jon.
Wood
C. BIRD)
Surveyor of Cocke County

330
EVAN FUGIT 50 A.

State of Tennessee Cocke County.
By virtue of an entry made in the entry takers office for said county at Newport of NO 506 dated the 2nd day of March 1826. I have surveyed for EVAN FUGIT fifty acres of land on the waters of Big Creek. Beginning at a stake on or near on the stake of dry fork of said creek running thence west one hundred poles to a pine and hickory north eighty poles to a stake south eighty poles to a stake east one hundred poles to a stake south eighty poles to the beginning.
Represented by the above platt. Surveyed the 17th day of November 1828.

THOAMS YOUNG) C.C. John
Mullendone
NATHON SHARPTON) Dep.
surveyor of Cocke County

331
THOMAS & DANIEL WARDON 50 A.

State of Tennessee Cocke County.
By virtue of an entry made in the entry takers office for said county at Newport NO 436 dated the 12th day of January 1826. I have surveyed for DANIEL WARDON and THOMAS WARDON jointly fifty acres of land in said county on the waters of Meadow Creek. Beginning on a chestnut on Andrew near the LEGION FURNACE COOLING GROUND. Running south seventy six west one hundred and two poles to a white oak & hickory on a ridge near WINTERS line to a stake McCRACKINS line north seventy six East one hundred and two poles to a stake thence a direct line to the beginning.
Having such form as is represented by the above platt.
Surveyed the 28th November 1828.

RITTIS ISENHOUR) C.C. John
Mullendone
JOHN GREGG) Dep.
Surveyor for Cocke County

JOHN & THOMAS BRYANTS 100 A.

State of Tennessee Cocke County.
By virtue of an entry made in the entry takers office for said county at Newport of NO 826 dated January the 2nd 1826. I have surveyed for JOHN & THEMAS BRYANT one hundred acres of land in said county on the Middle fork of Cosbys Creek, adjoining their own land. Beginning on a white oak running thence south forty one west one hundred and forty poles to a stake and a black gum on said Bryants line of an entry of fifty acres south forty nine East one hundred and fifteen poles to a stake north forty one East one hundred and forty poles to a stake thence a direct line to the beginning.
Surveyed January 9th 1829.

R. DEAVOR) C.C. John Mullendone
R. GILLILAND)
Dep. surveyor of Cocke County

332
JAMES TAYLOR 50 A.

State of Tennessee Cocke County
By virtue of an entry made in the entry takers office for said county at Newport of NO - dated --- day ---. I have surveyed for JAMES TAYLOR fifty acres of land situate lying on the waters of Nobb creek. Beginning a stake on JOHN FRESHOURS line near said Taylors corner running thence with Freshour line south fifty west one hundred and five poles to an Elm corner to THOMAS DRISKELL then with his line East nine poles to an elm south fifty East forty poles to a stake north sixty five East one hundred poles to a stake south twenty eight East twenty two poles to a stake on said Talleys line then with his ditto south sixty five west ninety six poles to a stake Talleys corner north twenty eight west sixty five poles to the beginning.
Having such form as is represented by the above platt.
Surveyed the 8th October 1828.

LEVI SMITH) C.C. Jon. Wood
THOMAS SMITH)
Surveyor of Cocke County

333
A. FRY 16 Acres

State of Tennessee Cocke County.
By virtue of an entry made in the entry takers office for said county at Newport of NO - dated ----- I have surveyed for A. FRY sixteen acres of land East side of Big Pigeon River. Beginning at a stake near a maple post below a spring on the bank of said river running then East four poles to a dogwood at the foot of the mountain then along the same south twenty six west fifty poles to a beech west twenty poles to a chestnut oak then down the meanders of the river to the beginning. including the house and improvements where SHE now lives. Having such form as is represented by the above platt. Surveyed the 24th day of September 1827.

JAMES DUNNEY) C.C. Jon. Wood
GEORGE MATTOX)
Surveyor of Cocke County

DANIEL BLAZER 25 Acres

State of Tennessee Cocke County.
By virtue of an entry made in the entry takers office for said county at Newport of N) 599 dated the 26th January 1827. I have surveyed for DANIEL BLAZER twenty five acres of land on the waters of sinking creek. Beginning on a white walnut corner of JOHN BORDER and running north forty nine west forty five poles to a white oak and dogwood on a hillside south forty one eighty East forty five poles to a stake then a direct line to the beginning. Having such form as is represented by the above platt.
Surveyed the 27th November 1828.

JOHN OTTINGER)
John Mullendone
HENRY BLAZER) C.C. Dep.
surveyor of Cocke County

334
GEORGE McNABB 100 Acres

State of Tennessee Cocke County.
By virtue of an entry made in the entry takers office of said county of NO 678 dated the 25th of February 1828. I have surveyed for GEORGE McNABB one hundred acres of land in said county on the waters of Cosbys Creek Beginning at a chestnut near a branch and running south sixty eight west sixty two poles to a maple at the foot of a mountain south twenty two East thirty poles to a chestnut south eighty west one hundred and one poles to a large poplar south eighty two one hundred and sixty nine poles to a stake west sixty one pole to the beginning.
Having such form as is represented by the above platt.
Surveyed the 4th day of December 1828.

JAMES GARRETT) C.C. John
Mullendone
JOHN RUNNION)
Dep. surveyor of Cocke County

335
ABRAHAM ROLLING 75 Acres

State of Tennessee Cocke County.
By virtue of an entry made in the entry takers office for said county at Newport of NO 738 dated the 17th day 1828. I have surveyed for ABRAHAM ROLLINGS seventy five acres of land in said county on south side of French Broad river on the waters of Big Creek. Beginning on a white oak running thence north sixty East one hundred and thirty two poles to a stake thence a direct line to the beginning.
Surveyed the 23rd January 1829.

B. HOLLAND) C.C. John
Mullendone
J.R. DENNING)
Dep. surveyor of Cocke County

336
DEMPSEY MOORE 100 Acres

State of Tennessee Cocke County.
By virtue of an entry made in the entry takers office of said county at

Newport of No 373 dated the 5th September 1826. I have surveyed for DEMPSEY MOORE one hundred acres of land in the said county on the waters of Nobb Creek. Beginning on a stake near CONWAYS line running thence north forty west ninety six poles to a white oak north eight east twelve poles to a dogwood NELSONS line north forty one west twenty six poles to a stake north seventy four west forty three poles to a white oak on said Nelsons line south forty nine west seventy four poles to a stake thence a direct line to the beginning.
Having such form as is represented by the above platt.
Surveyed the 10th October 1828.

DAVID DRISKILL) C.C. John
Mullendone
MOSES DRISKILL)
Dep. surveyor of Cocke County

JOHN THOMPSON 100 Acres

State of Tennessee Cocke County.
By virtue of an entry made in the entry takers office for said county at Newport of NO 564 dated August 28th 1826. I have surveyed for JOHN THOMPSON one hundred acres of land in said county on the waters of Noly Chucky river. Beginning on the beginning corner of ABRAHAM ARONS tract of land joining RICHARD POTTERFIELDS land running thence -------------- no more given.......

337
JOB PARROTT 44.

State of Tennessee Cocke County.
By virtue of an entry made in the entry takers office for said county at Newport of NO 664 dated the twelth day of December 1827. I have surveyed for JOB PARROTT forty four acres of land in said county on the south side of Clear Creek. Beginning on a white oak supposed to be the second corner.
.............no more given...

338
WILLIAM REYNOLDS 75 A.

State of Tennessee Cocke County.
By virtue of an entry made in the entry takers office for said county at Newport of No 346 dated the 15th day of June 1826. I have surveyed for WM. REYNOLDS seventy five acres of land in said county on the north side of French Broad River. Beginning at some rocks the name of the chimney on the bank said river north seventy east thirty poles to an elm on the bank of the same north forty six and one half east fifty six poles to a spanish oak on the bank of said river north eighty nine East fifty poles to a rock in the river north forty five west one hundred poles to a rock on the side of the Paint Mountain then a direct line to the beginning. Having such form as is represented by the above platt.
Surveyed the 12th of Nov. 1828.

STEPHEN REYNOLDS) C.C. John
Mullendone
WM. P. HARREN)
Dep. surveyor of Cocke County

JOBE MURRELL 50 A.

State of Tennessee Cocke County.
By virtue of an entry made in the entry takers office for said county at Newport of NO - dated --- 1826. I have surveyed for JOB MURRELL fifty acres of land on the waters of Bogard Creek. Beginning at a white oak corner to JOHN SUTTERS near the Cave road running thence with his line north fifty nine east crossing said road one hundred and six poles to a black gum south seventy nine East twenty poles to a black oak south thirty one East sixty four poles to a white oak near the Shastas mountain then across the spur of ditto south fifty nine then a direct line to the beginning. Represented by the above platt surveyed the 5th day of January 1829.

Jon. Wood

Surveyor of Cocke County

339
JAMES WILLIAMS & LAXTON CASE 100 Acres

State of Tennessee Cocke County.
By virtue of an entry made in the Entry takers office of said county at Newport of NO 537 dated March 29th day 1826. I have surveyed for JAMES WILLIAMS & LAXTON CASE one hundred acres of land in said county on the waters of English Creek at a black walnut on said cases line & running north sixty one East thirty poles to a hickory in NAITHS line thence with the same south fifty four East seventy six poles to a stake on or near said line & HIRAM ALLENS line then with said Allens line then with said Allens line south seventy six & one half west sixty two poles to a hickory WILLIAM DENTONS line north seventy five west forty three poles to a stake on said line north thirty eight west sixteen poles to a poplar a corner of said line north thirty two west forty eight poles to a post oak corner of the said ---- south seventy one --- to a rock south fifty nine west forty poles to a stake on said WILLIAMS line north forty two & a half west thirty two poles to a black oak corner of said line south thirty five & one half west one --- to a spanish oak north forty west fifty two poles to a hickory & north twenty five East forty -- to a stake north eighty three East eighty eight poles to a stake south forty eight East nineteen poles to a stake LAXTON CASES corner then with his line East one hundred and twenty poles to two black oaks then ---- to the beginning ---- Having such form as represented by the above platt. ---

340
MOSES HICKS 16 Acres

State of Tennessee Cocke County.
By virtue of an entry made in the entry takers office for said county at Newport of NO -- dated January 2nd 1826. I have surveyed for MOSES HICKS sixteen acres of land in said county on the waters of Cosby Creek. Beginning on a black gum -- corner to the survey of SAMUEL MATHEWS dec.---south seven and one half east sixteen poles---white oak LARGIS old line and a branch ---with some south forty east twenty poles---south five west twenty two poles to ---line south thirty five and one half East---two dogwoods north forty nine East---white oak conditional line to Hicks--forty six poles to a stake and white oak--seventy five East eighty five poles Knobb on or near Thomas---thirty three west twenty one poles---fifty six acre entry of sd Hicks---north sixty four poles to a ---lines thence a direct line to the beginning. Having such form as is represented by the above platt.

Surveyed 3rd January 1829.

John Mullendone

Dep. surveyor of Cocke County

341
NATHANIEL BOYSTON 50 Acres

State of Tennessee Cocke County.
By virtue of an entry made in the entry takers office of said county at Newport of NO 452 dated February the 6th 1826. I have surveyed for NATHANIEL BOYSTON fifty acres of land in said county on the north side of French Borad River. Beginning at a white oak on or near a line of JOHN FUGATTS running thence north eighty East seventy four poles to a line---oak south thirty six & an half East---poles to a stake on FUGATTS line----eight & an half East thirty one----white oak on the side--north twenty west twelve poles---south eighty two---an half west---to a black oak THOMAS MOORES----thirty acres entry thence with----seventy one and an half---poles to a hickory north-----half East one hundred---poles to a stake thence---BEGINNING. Surveyed November -----.

JOHN FUGATTE) C.C. John
Mullendone
M. EASTERS) Dep.
Surveyor of Cocke County

342
RICHARD TURNER 100 Acres

State of Tennessee Cock County.
By virtue of an entry made in the entry takers office for said county at Newport of NO 405 dated the 6th of January 1826. I have surveyed for RICHARD TURNER one hundred acres of land in said county on both sides of the waters of Neeleys Creek on the south side of Noly Chucky. Beginning at a stake on BENGIMAN DAUGHTYS line thence south one hundred and sixty two and a half poles to a stake thence north one hundred and six poles to a beech on the side of a hill on or near BENJAMIN DAUGHTYS line north sixty seven East one hundred and thirty poles crossing Neelys Creek to the beginning. Having such form as is represented by the above platt.
Surveyed the 5th of October 1829.

WILLIAM BRAGG) C.C. Jonathan
Wood
JAMES DAUGHTY)
Principal surveyor of Cocke County

GEORGE HOLT 15 Acres

State of Tennessee Cocke County.
By virtue of an entry made in the entry takers office of said county at Newport of NO 614 dated March the 21st 1827. I have surveyed for GEORGE HOLT fifteen acres of land in said county on the north side of dry fork Beginning on a white oak EDWARD HOLTS west corner running thence south thirty eight poles to a stake & sweet gum East sixty three & one half poles to a black oak sprout & two dogwoods north thirty eight poles to a stake west three & one fourth poles to the beginning.
Surveyed the 7th day of November 1828.

ASA HOLT) John
Mullendone
J.W. BEELMON) C.C. Dep.
surveyor of Cocke County

343
JOEL DAVIS 30 Acres

State of Tennessee Cocke County.
By virtue of an entry made in the entry takers office for said county at Newport of NO 491 dated February the 27th 1827.
Beginning on a black oak near Suttons line thence with said line north eighty East ninety & an half poles to a black oak on a hill side north eighty two west fifty eight poles to a stake south eighty west ninety poles to a stake thence a direct line to the beginning.
Surveyed January 10th 1829.

J. DRISKELL) C.C. John
Mullendone
D. TURNER) Dep.
surveyor of Cocke County

344
EPPY LEA 60 Acres

State of Tennessee Cocke County.
By virtue of an entry made in the entry takers office for said county at Newport of NO 671. I have surveyed for EPPY LEA sixteen acres of land in said county in the forks of French Broad & Chucky adjoining his own land & an entry made by ELIJAH & JERMIAH HILL Beginning at a stake & beech on said Leas line near his corner running thence west forty poles to a stake south six west nine poles to a stake south seventy nine west sixty seven poles to a white oak north twenty seven poles to a stake on a hill line thence with the same north fifty five east two hundred and four poles to a stake thence a direct line to the beginning. Having such form as is represented by the above platt.
Surveyed October the 21st 1828.

JAMES CLARK) C.C. John
Mullendone
WM. McCONNELL) Dep.
surveyor for Cocke County

WILLIAM BRAGG 100 Acres

State of Tennessee Cocke County.
By virtue of an entry made in the entry takers office for said county at Newport of NO 705 dated May 28 1828. I have surveyed for WILLIAM BRAGG one hundred acres of land in said county on the waters of Neeleys creek adjoining his own lines and the lines of PRESTON JARNIGANS on the Bank of the creek on Jarnigans line & running with same north one and one half west ninety two poles to a sake north seventy and three fourths East forty poles to a beech north two East forty six poles to a stake on said Braggs line south sixty poles to a stake thence a direct line to the beginning.
Having such form as is represented by the above platt.

AMOS DAYLES) John
Mullendone
JAMES DAUGHTYS) C.C. Dep.
surveyor of Cocke County

345
JAMES GARRETT 25 Acres

State of Tennessee Cocke County.
By virtue of an entry made in the entry takers office for said county at Newport on NO - dated --. I have surveyed for JAMES GARRETT TWENTY five acres of land in said county on Cosby Creek. Beginning on a black oak & running south nineteen twenty one poles to a sweet gum on the said river bank north seventy three East seventeen poles to a gum bush on J. SUTTONS line thence with the same north twenty six & one half East thirty four poles to a stake on said line south eighty six & one half East forty poles to a black gum on the point of a ridge north fifty five East sixty five poles to a stake thence a direct line to the beginning. Having such form as is represented by the above platt.
Surveyed the 3rd December 1828.

JOHN RUNIONS) C.C. John
Mullendone
WM BRAYLESS) Dep.
surveyor of Cocke County

HENRY VALENTINE 50 Acres

State of Tennessee Cocke County.
By virtue of an entry made in the entry takers office for said county at Newport of NO 728 dated the 29th of September 1828. I have surveyed for HENRY VALENTINE fifty acres of land in said county fork of Cosbys creek. Beginning on a spruce pine & running thence south fifty six East one hundred four poles to a chestnut oak south thirty four East thirty poles to a spruce pine on the bank of said creek north forty four west sixty poles to a large poplar south seventeen West fifty poles to a large poplar south seventeen West fifty poles to a stake West one hundred and eighty poles to a stake thence a direct line to the beginning.
Having such form as is represented by the above platt.
Surveyed December 3rd 1828.

RUBEN McGAHA)
JOHN MULLENDONE
H. BALENTINE)
Dep. surveyor of Cocke County
(don't know if this is Valentine
or Balentine)

347
A. WOODY 100 Acres

State of Tennessee Cocke County.
By virtue of an entry made in the entry takers office for said county at Newport of NO 407 dated January the 6th 1826. I have surveyed for WOODY one hundred acres of land in said county on the waters of Bush Creek Beginning at a stake near the pine branch and near JOHN WOODYS line running thence north sixty five East one hundred and fifty poles to a stake & white oak on a hill side near GREEN COUNTY line south twenty five East one hundred and seven poles to a white oak near a branch south sixty five west one hundred and fifty poles to a stake thence a direct line to the beginning.
Surveyed January the 24th 1829.

T. MOONEYHAM)
John Mullendone
F. BOYSTON) C.C. Dept.
surveyor of Cocke County

DAVID WARDEN & THOS. WARDEN 100 Acres

State of Tennessee Cocke County.
By virtue of an entry made in the entry takers office of said county at Newport of NO 407 dated January the 6th 1826. I have surveyed for DAVID WARDEN & THEMAS WARDEN jointly one hundred acres of land in said county on the waters of long creek. Beginning on a black oak on a ridge on the south side of the creek running thence south forty five West one hundred and forty poles to a hickory in a hallow on the bank of a small branch south forty five East one hundred and forty poles to a stake thence a direct line to the beginning.
Surveyed November the 28th 1828.

PETER EISENHOUR)
John Mullendone
JOHN GREGG) C.C. Dep.
surveyor of Cocke County

JONATHAN FOX 50 Acres

State of Tennessee Cocke County.
By virtue of an entry made in the entry takers office for said county at Newport of NO 453 dated January 24th 1826. I have surveyed for JONATHAN FOX fifty acres of land is said county adjoining the land of the late WILLIAM FOX. Beginning on a hickory and Red oak on the side of a hill it being his own corner south sixty two poles to a stake on his line south eighty seven west thirteen poles to a stake on the same north thirty four west eighteen poles to a white oak corner to the same south sixty six west twenty three poles to a stake north eighty eight west seven poles to two post oaks among some rocks north twenty poles to a sourwood on or near the line of the big survey thence with the same north forty five East one hundred poles to a stake thence a direct line to the beginning.
Surveyed February 4th 1829.

WILLIAM MORRIS) C.C. John
Mullendone
E. FOX)
Dep. surveyor of Cocke County

349
HUGH D. HALE 100 Acres

State of Tennessee Cocke County.
By virtue of an entry made in the entry takers office for said county at Newport of No 596 dated January the 8th 1827. I have surveyed for HUGH D. HALE one hundred acres of land in said county on the south side of Nolee Chuckey river adjoining the land of JOHN THOMPSON & said HALE & RICHARD CURETON. Beginning at a stake on his corner running thence south forty two East one hundred and twenty four poles to a bush near a branch at the foot of a large knobb north sixty two East six poles to stake on said Hales line thence with the same south thirty four & one half East one hundred and nine poles to a stake on a conditional line between him and Cureton-North thirty one west one hundred & fifty six poles to a stake thence a direct line to the beginning.
Surveyed the 6th of November 1828.

J.A. THOMPSON)
John Mullendone
WM. THOMPSON) C.C. Dep.
surveyor of Cocke County

GEORGE NEAS 23 Acres

State of Tennessee Cocke County.
By virtue of an entry made in the entry takers office of said county at Newport of No 655 dated Nov. 27th day 1827. I have surveyed for GEORGE NEAS twenty three acres of land in said county on the waters of Clear Creek. Beginning on a large black oak a corner to PHILLIP NEAS land running thence with his line west forty six poles to a stake at OTTINGERS corner south eighty three poles to a stake and white oak on or near BLAZERS line East forty four poles to a stake on said GEORGE NEAS original line thence with the same a direct line to the beginning.
Nov. 28th 1828.

WILLIAM NEAS) C.C. John Mullendone
JOHN NEAS)
Dep. surveyor of Cocke County
N.B. The entry on which cirtificate is founded is for twenty five acres but complement cannot be got for the interference of old lines.

John Mullendone.

EASTER ODELL 25 Acres

State of Tennessee Cocke County.
By virtue of an entry made in the entry takers office of said county at Newport of No - dated -- 182- I have surveyed for Easter O Dell twenty five acres of land on the waters of Cosbys Creek. Beginning on LEWIS line running thence with the same south eighty four deg. west crossing a branch twenty four poles to a poplar south seventy five deg. west twenty poles to a bush thence south twenty three and an hal deg. west eighty poles to a spanish oak on a ridge thence south eighty deg. East forty six and one fourth poles to a stake near ROBERT LILLARDS line to the beginning.
Surveyed the 19th of December 1828.

COBB ODELL) C.C.
Jonathan Wood
JESSEE JENNINGS)
Surveyor of Cocke County

ASA HOLT 50 Acres

State of Tennessee Cocke County.
By virtue of an entry made in the entry takers office for said county at Newport of NO 621 dated April 6th 1827. I have surveyed for ASA HOLT fifty acres of land in said county on the waters of Bear Creek. Beginning on a white oak POTTERFIELDS line running thence north seventeen East eighty poles to a stake & black walnut on the point of a ridge north seventy three west one hundred poles to a stake and sugar tree near SCRUGGS line south seventeen west eighty poles to a stake thence a direct line to the beginning.
Surveyed Nov. 7th 1828.

BUSDLE HOLT) C.C. John Mullendone
JOHN D. BULMON)
Dep. surveyor of Cocke County

352
WM. L. MAYNOR 25 Acres

State of Tennessee Cocke County.
By virtue of an entry made in the entry takers office at Newport of No 597 dated the 8th day of January 1827. I have surveyed for WILLIAM LORD MAYNOR twenty five acres of land in said county on the waters of Big Creek. Beginning at a white oak on the old Ann mountain running thence south twenty five East eighty poles to a stake on the side of said mountain south sixty five west fifty poles to a stake north twenty five west eighty poles to a stake thence a direct line to the beginning.

B. HOLBORD) C.C.
John Mullendone
J. MAYNOR)
Dep. surveyor of Cocke County

RUFUS JAMES 100 Acres

State of Tennessee Cocke County.
By virtue of an entry made in the entry takers office of said county at Newport of No 598 dated the 20th day of October 1826. I have surveyed for RUFUS JAMES one hundred acres of land in said county on the waters of Big Creek. Beginning at a beech running north eighty poles to a black oak east thirty poles to a mulberry and beech at the foot of the Pine mountain south eighty six poles to a beech east twenty poles to a stake and two birches on a branch a conditional line between--& SHARPTON thence up the branch forty two and half East ninty eight poles to a beech south one hundred and forty five and an half poles to a stake thence north one hundred and eighty two poles to the beginning.

JAMES HOLLAND) C.C. John
Mullendone
NATHAN SHARPTON)
Dep. surveyor of Cocke County

353
EDWARD HOLT 50 A.

State of Tennessee Cocke County.
by virtue of an entry made in the entry takers office for said county at Newport of No dated----. I have surveyed for EDWARD HOLT fifty acres of land in said county of the waters of Clay Creek. Beginning on a white oak at the mouth of a hollow thence north forty west seventy five poles to a dogwood and a white oak in a howwlow south fifty west one hundred and seven poles to a dogwood and a large white oak south forty East seventy five poles to a stake a direct line to the beginning.
Surveyed the 9th of December 1828.

ASA HOLT) C.C. John
Mullendone
J.W. BULMON)
Dep. surveyor of Cocke County

354

JOHN JINKINS 50 A.

State of Tennessee Cocke County.
By virtue of an entry made in the entry takers office for said county at Newport of No 635 dated the 9th day of July 1827. I have surveyed for JOHN JINKINS fifty acres of land in said county on the waters of Ground hog creek. Beginning at a beech a corner to PHILLIP JINKINS and running thence with his line south thirteen west eighty four poles to maple at the foot of a mountain then with the same as a boundry south sixty four west thirty five poles to a poplar west eighty one poles to a poplar west eighty one poles to four chestnuts. North fifty five poles to a stake. Thence a direct line to the beginning.
Having such form as is represented by the above platt.
Surveyed the 2nd day of December 1828.

JOHN SUTTON) C.C. John
Mullondene
R. JINKINS)
Dep. surveyor of Cocke County.

GEORGE MILLER 300 A.

State of Tennessee Cocke County.
By virtue of an entry made in the entry takers office for said county at Newport of NO 646 dated the 22nd day of August 1827. I have surveyed for GEORGE MILLER three hundred acres of land on the head waters of Sinking Creek. Beginning at a stake near marked line running thence south forty nine west thirty four poles to a white oak one hundred and thirty poles to a stake south two hundred and twenty five poles to a stake south seventy four East two hundred poles to a black oak thence a direct line to the beginning.
Including what is usely called the Cold Spring home.
Having such form as is represented by the above platt.

GEORGE MILLER) C.C. JON.
Wood
JOHN GORMAN)
Surveyor of Cocke County

355

DAVID & THOMAS WARDEN 50 A.

State of Tennessee Cocke County.
By virtue of an entry made in the entry takers office of said county at Newport of No 437 dated January 12th 1826. I have surveyed for DAVID & THEMAS WARDEN jointly fifty acres of land in said county on the waters of long creek. Beginning on a black oak and running thence sixty eight west seventy three poles to a white oak and dogwood on a hill side south twenty two poles to a East hundred and twelve poles to a stake north sixty eight East twenty two poles to a stake then a direct line to the beginning.
Surveyed November the 28th 1828.

PETER ISENHOUR) C.C. John
Mullendone
JOHN GREGG)
Dep. surveyor of Cocke County

356

GEORGE FRESHOUR 100 A

State of Tennessee Cocke County.
By virtue of an entry made in the entry takers office for said county at Newport of NO 644 dated the 21st day of August 1827. I have surveyed for GEORGE FRESHOUR one hundred acres of land in said county on the waters of Clear Creek. Beginning at a black oak & locust near WILLIAM GORDENS line running thence north fifty seven east twenty two poles to a poplar south twenty eight east one hundred and seventy poles to a post oak on a ridge north twelve East one hundred and seventeen poles to a hickory on a ridge north twenty eight west one hundred and twenty nine poles to stake thence a direct line to the beginning.

SAMUEL HICKS)
John Mullendone
K. HARMON) C.C. Dep.
surveyor of Cocke County

JAMES ETHERTON 50 Acres

State of Tennessee Cocke County.
By virtue of an entry made in the entry takers office for said county at Newport of NO 652 dated November the 26th 1827. I have surveyed for JAMES ETHERTON fifty acres of land in said county near the waters of Oven Creek. Beginning at a stake joining Etherton line & the land of JAMES SWAGERTY running thence East sixty four poles to a stake on said Ethertons original line south one west four poles to a black oak said Ethertons corner east fifty five poles to two dogwoods north fifty and a half East thirty six poles to a white oak south four west twenty two poles to a stake on Swagertys line thence -------------no more given------------

357

JAMES DAUGHTRY 150 A.

State of Tennessee Cocke County.
By virtue of an entry made in the entry takers office of said county at Newport of NO 430 dated the 10th day of January 1826. I have surveyed for JAMES DAUGHTEY one hundred and fifty acres of land in the said county on the waters of Knobb Creek. Beginning at a stake at or near said Daughtrye corner to a tract of land on which he now lives south twenty west two hundred poles to a stake & two post oaks north seventy west eighty poles to a stake & dogwood sprout. North twenty East one hundred & ten poles to an ash bush north forty seven and one half west forty six poles to a chestnut oak north twenty East one hundred and sixty three poles to a stake south thirty one East one hundred and forty three poles to the beginning.
As is described the above platt.
Surveyed the 6th day of October 1828.

John Mullendone

Dep. surveyor of Cocke County

358

JAMES BAXTER 100 Acres

State of Tennessee Cocke County.
By virtue of an entry made in the entry takers office of said county at Newport of NO 489 dated 27th day of February 1826. I have surveyed for JAMES BAXTER one hundred acres of land on the waters of Cosby Creek. Beginning at a white oak on or near his old line running thence with the same East one hundred & sixty poles to a dogwood & white oak GILLES corner then with Gilles line seventy eight poles to a hickory on a ridge south twenty four East twenty poles to a stake south forty eight East thirty poles to a black oak on or near a ridge to North thirty East twenty six West thirty four poles to a stake North thirty six East twenty four poles to a black oak north fifty seven west along a mountain one hundred & six poles to a spanish oak south twenty poles to the beginning. Represented by the above platt.
Surveyed the 3rd day of July 1821.

JESSIE GILLIS) C.C.
Jonathan Wood
GUS GREEN)
Principal Surveyor for Cocke County

E. BREEDING 50 A.

State of Tennessee Cocke County.
By virtue of an entry made in the entry takers office for said county at Newport of No -- day --- I have surveyed for ELIJAG BREEDING fifty acres of land on the waters of English Creek. Beginning at a poplar his corner running thence with his line west forty eight poles to a post oak north forty five west sixteen poles to a black oak thence with MOSES HICKS line of the steep hollow tract south thirty five East thirty five poles to a stake south fifty two west thirty four poles to a dogwood corner to THOMAS ALLEN East seven poles to a stake south thirty and an half poles to a black oak corner to JOHN LANE then with his line north fifty two and an half East seventy one poles to a white oak north fifty seven poles to a hickory north forty six East seventeen poles to a black --Lanes corner near Breedings line then with the same west seventy three poles to a line south sixty four to a post oak and black oak thence a direct line to the beginning. Having such form as above represented. Surveyed the 5th day of January 1829.

JOHN LANT) C.C.
Jonathan Wood
E. BREEDING)
Surveyor of Cocke County

360

Beginning at a locust and a white oak running thence forty and an half deg. west one hundred and twenty poles to a stake & black gum in a hollow north forty and an half west sixty four poles to a stake and dogwood in a hollow north forty nine and an half East one hundred and twenty six poles to a stake then a direct line to the beginning.
Surveyed 13th day of November 1828.

WM. BLACK
John Mullendone
WM. BAYLSON
Dep. surveyor of Cocke County.

Wm. BIBEE 50 A.

State of Tennessee Cocke County Tennessee.
By virtue of an entry made in the entry takers office for said county at Newport of NO 625 dated the 22nd day of April 1827. I have surveyed WILLIAM BIBEE FIFTY ACRES of land in said county on the waters of dry fork of Clay Creek. Beginning on a hickory and small white oak a corner to said Bibee land running thence south fifty eight west eighty poles to a white oak north twenty two west one hundred poles to a post oak on a ridge north fifty eight East eighty poles to a stake then a direct line to the beginning.
Surveyed July 3rd 1828.

JOHN WOOD) C.C. John Mullendone
ANSBERRY PART)
Dep. surveyor of Cocke County.

361
JOSEPH YOUNG 50 A.

State of Tennessee Cocke County.
By virtue of an entry made in the entry takers office for said county at Newport of No 505 dated the 2nd day of March 1826. I have surveyed for JOSEPH YOUNG in said county on the south side of French Broad River on the waters of Big Creek beginning at this corner of RUSSEL JONES upper entry on fifty acres running thence south ninety poles south ninety poles to a white pine on a ridge East ninety poles to the beginning.
Surveyed November 15th 1828.

Nathan Thompson) C.C. John Mullendone
Evan Fugatt)
Dep. surveyor for Cocke County

362
JOHN FUGATT 25 A.

State of Tennessee Cocke County.
By virtue of an entry made in the entry takers office for said county at Newport of No 721 dated the 11th day of September 1828. I have surveyed for JOHN FUGATT twenty five acres of land on the rocky branch on the flat top mountain. Beginning at a stake running thence north thirty eight and an half East fifty six poles to a maple and pine north fifty one and one half west seventy two poles to a stake south thirty eight and an half west fifty six poles to a stake thence a direct line to the beginning.
Surveyed the 14th day of November 1828.

EVAN FUGATT) C.C. John Mullendone
-----------)
Dep. surveyor for Cocke County

-- West forty poles to stake north twenty three and an half west three poles to a stake and sourwood south seventy west ninety six poles to a stake thence a direct line to the beginning.
Having such form as is represented in the above platt.
Surveyed the 8th day of November 1827.

ADAM NEAS) C.C. John Mullendone
JOHN FANCHER)
Dep. surveyor of Cocke County.

C. STEPHEN 50 A.

State of Tennessee Cocke County.
By virtue of an entry made in the entry takers office for said county at Newport of No 675 dated the 26th day of January 1828. I have surveyed for CLEMENT STEPHENS fifty acres of land in said county on the waters of Wolf Creek. Beginning at a white oak on the south side rich hollow running thence south twenty six East one hundred and twenty poles to a stake north twenty six west one hundred and two poles to a stake thence a direct line to the beginning.
Surveyed the 19th day of July 1829.

B. HOLLAND) C.C.
John Mullendone
-- RUSSELL)
Dep. surveyor of Cocke County.

363
JOHN McNABB 150 A.

State of Tennessee Cocke County.
By virtue of an entry made in the entry takers office for said county at Newport of NO 576 dated September the 20th day of 1826. I have surveyed for JOHN McNABB one hundred and fifty acres of land in said county adjoining the land of said McNabb. Beginning on a pine on or near said McNabb line running thence south five west two hundred poles to a stake on the point of a ridge south eighty five East one hundred and twenty poles to a chestnut on the top of McNabbs mountain north five East two hundred poles to a stake thence a direct line to the beginning.

GEORGE McNABB) C.C. John Mullendone
JOHN McNABB)
Dep. surveyor of Cocke County

364
JAMES ETHERTON 100 A

State of Tennessee Cocke County.
By virtue of an entry made in the entry takers office for said county at Newport of No 414 dated the 14th day of February 1826. I have surveyed for JAMES ETHERTON one Hundred acres of land in said county on the waters of Oven Creek. Beginning on a stake on his own line running thence west one hundred and thirteen poles to a stake south ninety eight poles to a stake East one hundred and three poles to a stake on or near said Ethertons old line thence a direct line to the beginning.
Surveyed November 8th 1828.

ADAM NEAS) C.C. John Mullendone
JOHN FRANCHER)
Dep. surveyor of Cocke County

JOHN S. GARRETT 50 Acres

State of Tennessee Cocke County.
By virtue of an entry made in the entry takers office for said county at Newport of NO 506--. I have surveyed for JOHN S. GARRETT fifty acres of land in said county on the head waters of WOLF CREEK in WALNUT Gap between the Bluff and the Little rock mountain. Beginning on a chestnut on the state line running north sixteen west sixty seven poles to a large spanish oak. by a branch south seventy four west one hundred and twenty poles to a stake thence a direct line to the beginning. Having such form as is represented by the above platt. Surveyed January 20th A.D. 1825.

B. HOLLAND) C.C. John
Mullendone
C. STEPHENS)
Dep. surveyor of Cocke County.

365
JOSEPH BLACK 50 Acres

State of Tennessee Cocke County.
By virtue of an entry made in the entry takers office at Newport of No 684 dated the 3rd day of March 1828. I have surveyed for JOSEPH BLACK fifty acres of land in said county on the East side of French Broad River on the ridge known by the name of Widows ridge. Beginning on a black oak marked near DOCTOR FOWLERS black oak corner running thence south six west fifty eight poles to a stake on an old line to three black oaks marked WILLIAM FAUBIONS corner then with the same East one hundred and four poles to a stake on the same north one hundred three and one half poles to a stake on DALTON FOWLERS line joining WILLIAM FOWLERS line joining WILLIAM FAUBIONS dry land tract thence a direct line to the beginning.
Having such form as is represented by the above platt.
Surveyed the 16th of October 1830.

JOHN BLANCHARD)
John Mullendone
NOAH H. JOHN) C.C. Dep.
surveyor of Cocke County.

366
NATHAN SHARPTON 50 Acres

State of Tennessee Cocke County.
By virtue of an entry made in the entry takers office of said county at Newport of NO 687 dated Feb. 25, 1828. I have surveyed for NATHAN SHARPTON fifty acres of land in said county on the south side of French Broad river on the waters of Big Creek. Beginning at two beeches corner to RUSSELL JONES running thence south thirty two and one half East seventy poles to a black oak north fifty seven and one half East one hundred and fifteen poles to a stake north forty two to a stake south forty six and one half west one hundred and fifteen poles to the beginning.
Surveyed November the 15th 1828.

JOHN HOLLAND) C.C. John
Mullendone
JOSEPH YOUNG)
Dep. surveyor for Cocke County

367

JOS SUTTON 50 Acres

State of Tennessee Cocke County.
By virtue of an entry made in the entry takers office of said county at Newport of NO 726 dated the 26th day of September 1828. I have surveyed for JOSEPH SUTTON fifty acres of land in said county on Chavis Creek. Beginning at a hickory on the north side of the creek running south thirty seven and one half west one hundred and twenty six poles and a half to the side of a mountain south fifty two and one half east sixty three and one fourth poles to a stake north thirty seven and one half east one hundred and twenty six poles and a half to a stake thence a direct line to the beginning.
Having such --- as represented by the above platt.
Surveyed the 3rd day of December 1828.

ELIJAH NOLAND) C.C.
Jonathan Wood
JOSEPH SUTTON)
Principal surveyor of Cocke County

JOHN FOWLER 100 Acres

State of Tennessee Cocke County.
By virtue of an entry made in the entry takers office for said county at Newport of NO 464 dated the 6th day of February 1826. I have surveyed for JOHN F. FOWLER one hundred acres of land in said county on the waters of --- creek. Beginning at a black oak being the west corner of two hundred acre tract ------ by THOMAS FOWLER running thence East one hundred and forty poles to a pine corner to said Fowlers original tract south fifty five west fifty one poles to a hickory on a conditional between --- and THOMAS HODGES thence south two west thirty four poles to a stake south eighty three and one half west thirty four poles to a beech Bryants line south twenty five west one hundred and forty four poles to a stake near a stream. North thirty one west sixty eight poles to a stake crossing road thirty poles thence a direct line to the beginning.
Having such form as is represented by the above platt.
Surveyed 10th day of October 1828.

John Mullendone

Dep. surveyor of Cocke County

369

GEORGE METLER 50 Acres

State of Tennessee Cocke County
By virtue of an entry made in the entry takers office for said county at Newport of No 639 dated October 1827. I have surveyed for GEORGE METLER fifty acres of land on the south side of French Broad river on the bear branch. Beginning at a poplar near said branch running up ditto south thirty one west one hundred and six poles to a hickory north seventy two west seventy poles to a poplar in a hollow then down north ditto twenty two west nineteen poles to an ash north fifty five west thirteen poles to a dogwood fourteen East four poles to a Lynn near the mouth of a branch north thirty four west fifteen poles to a lynn corner to JOHN BENTRY seventy three East one hundred and four poles to a stake near a beech thence south twenty poles to the beginning.

Having such form as represented by the above platt.
Surveyed the 13th day of October 1828.

JOHN HEATON) C.C. John
Wood
DANIEL PRUETT)
Surveyor of Cocke County

GEORGE BUCKNER 55 A.

State of Tennessee Cocke County.
By virtue of an entry made in the entry takers office for said county at Newport of NO 378 dated the 3rd day of January 1825. I have surveyed for GEORGE BUCKNER fifty five acres of land in said county on the waters of Clay Creek on the north side of French Broad river. Beginning on a white oak on said Buckners line -------------

370
R BLACK 50 A

State of Tennessee Cocke County.
By virtue of an entry made in the entry takers office for said county at Newport of No 609 dated the 10th day of March 1827. I have surveyed for ROBERT BLACK fifty acres of land in said county on the west fork of by creek. Beginning on a white oak pine running thence north five east one hundred poles to a white pine on a hill side north eighty west eighty poles to a stake thence a direct line to the beginning.
Surveyed November 18th 1828.

REUBEN BLACK) C.C. John
Mullendone
GREEN L. B. ROSE)
Dep. surveyor of Cocke County

JAMES SAWYERS 150 A.

State of Tennessee Cocke County.
By virtue of an entry made in the entry takers office for said county at Newport of NO 498 dated the 27th day of February 1826. I have surveyed for JAMES SAWYERS one hundred and fifty acres of land in said county on the waters of Neelys Creek. Beginning at a stake on HARRISONS REEMES line running thence north seventy five East one hundred and seventy six poles to a hickory south fifteen East one hundred and twenty four poles to a dogwood bush black oak and black gum south seventy six poles to a stake thence a direct line to the beginning.
Having such form as represented by the above platt.
Surveyed 22nd October 1828.

WM. C. COLLINS) C.C. John
Mullendone
CLEM BRIGENDENE)
Dep. surveyor of Cocke County

371
WM FELKER 50 A.

State of Tennessee Cocke County.
By virtue of an entry made in the entry takers office for said county at Newport of NO -- dated January 2nd 1826. I have surveyed for WILLIAM FELKER fifty acres of land on the waters of English Creek. Beginning

ON A STAKE ON Thomas Poles line north eighty eight poles to a stake three poles from a marked post oak bush north fifty eight deg. west ninety four poles to a stake on JAMES CLICK line south forty one poles to a stake south six East seventy two poles to a stake East nineteen poles to a post oak south fifty poles to a black oak on BRYANTS line then with the same East forty poles to the beginning.
Having such form as is represented by the above platt.
Surveyed the 4th day October 1828.

JOHN CLEVENGER) C.C. John Mullendone
WM FELKER)
Dep surveyor of Cocke County

372
WM. GANCH 100 A.

State of Tennessee Cocke County.
By virtue of an entry made in the entry takers office for said county at Newport of No 470 dated Feb. 10th 1826. I have surveyed for WM. GANCH one hundred acres of land in said county on the waters of Clay Creek. Beginning on a black oak a corner of a tract of land on the said William Canches and running south seventy nine East seventy poles to a pine north fifty three ------ black oak conditional line between him and Potter field south one hundred and ninety poles to a chestnut oak in the head of a hollow at the foot of a large nobb north thirty East one hundred and eighteen poles to a stake thence a direct to the beginning.
Surveyed November 6th 1828.

WILLIAM THOMPSON) C.C. John Mullendone
JOHN HUGHS)
Dep. surveyor of Cocke County

373
JOHN LENOX 200 Acres

State of Tennessee Cocke County.
By virtue of an entry made in the entry takers office for said county at Newport of No 543 dated January the 7th 1826. I have surveyed for JOHN LENOX two hundred acres of land in said county south of French Broad river on the head of the hollow that leads down to LERNER? sugar camp Beginning on a white oak on the top of a ridge and near foth that leads from JOHN WOODS to the Dutch Bottoms and running south seventy five west one hundred and twenty six poles to a black oak near PUCKETTS line south fifteen East one hundred and forty six poles to a sourwood on the top of a ridge East two hundred poles to a stake north thirty East fifty fifty two poles to a stake thence a direct line to the beginning. Having such form as is represented by the above platt.
Surveyed the 21st day of November 1828.

WM? SLIDER) C.C.
John Mullendone
-- MILLER)
Dep. surveyor of Cocke County

JOHN OTTINGER 28 1/2 Acres

State of Tennessee Cocke County.
By virtue of an entry made in the entry takers office of said county at Newport of NO 694 dated the 8th day of April 1828. I have surveyed for JOHN OTTINGER twenty eight and a half acres of land on the waters of Clear Creek. Beginning at a stake on or near a corner to his own land and adjoining HENRY BUSTERS land running thence north forty poles to a stake on Busters line to a post oak bush corner thence with his line north sixty two west forty eight poles to a stake on said line near said BORDENS black oak corner south thirty four west ninety two poles to a stake and white oak bush on said Ottingers original line thence a direct line to the beginning. Having such form as is represented by the above platt.
Surveyed 27th day of Nov. 1828.

DANIEL BLAZER) C.C. John
Mullendone
HENRY BLAZER)
Dep. surveyor of Cocke County.

N.B. the entry on which this certificate is founded was for fifty acres but the completement could not be got for the interferearance of old lines.

John Mullendone

HENRY EASTER 100 Acres

State of Tennessee Cocke County.
By virtue of an entry made in the entry takers office for said county at Newport of NO 713 dated - day of -- 1827. I have surveyed for HENRY EASTER one hundred acres of land in said county on the waters of Knobb creek. Beginning on a hickory a corner to his forty acre tract running thence south five west eighty poles to a stake south thirty and a half East one hundred and fourteen poles to a stake at the foot of a large hill north fifty nine and a half East one hundred and thirty poles to a stake on the side of a mountain north forty nine and one half west one hundred and sixty poles to a stake near serseys platt thence a direct line to the beginning. Having such form as is represented by the platt.
Surveyed the 7th of October 1828.

JAMES DAUGHTY
John Mullendone
NATHIAS D. EASTON
Dep. surveyor for Cocke County

HENRY EASTON (given this way here but Easter above) died Friday on the 25th of July 1834. Attest. Wm. Dean, John F. Faubs

JAMES BAXTER 25 Acres

State of Tennessee Cocke County.
By virtue of an entry made in the entry takers office of said county at Newport of NO - dated day of -- 1828.
I have surveyed for JAMES BAXTER twenty five acres of land on the waters of Cosbys Creek. Beginning at --- JOHN BAXTERS and FRANCES GREEN --- thirty four west thirty poles -----

THOMAS JENKINS 25 Acres

State of Tennessee Cocke County. By virtue of an entry made in the entry takers office of said county at Newport of NO 637 dated July 20th --- I have surveyed for THOMAS JENKINS twenty five acres of land on the north side of Groundhog Creek. Beginning at a chestnut on the north side of one prong of said creek running thence across the same south sixty three East eighty nine poles to a white oak north twenty seven east 44 3/4 poles to a stake near a maple north 63 west 89 poles to a stake thence a direct line to the beginning. Having such form as is represented by the above platt.
Surveyed the 3rd day of December 1828.

NATHANIEL MARMON 25 Acres

State of Tennessee Cocke County.
By virtue of an entry made in the entry takers office for said county at Newport of NO 689 dated the 4th day of April 1828. I have surveyed for NATHANIEL MARANOM twenty five acres of land in the fork of Rock Branch on the flat top mountain. Beginning at a black oak running thence north eighty five west sixty poles to a stake south twenty four and a half east one hundred and twenty two p. along a mountain to a stake then --- a direct line to the beginning. Having such form as is represented by the above platt.
Surveyed the 4th day of November 1828.

John Mullendone

Dep. surveyor of Cocke County

JAMES GARRETT 75 Acres

State of Tennessee Cocke County.
By virtue of an entry made in the entry takes office for said county at Newport of No 506 dated Aug. the 11th 1826. I have surveyed for JAMES GARRETT seventy five acres of land on the waters of Cosbys Creek. Beginning on a spanish oak at or near JOHN SUTTONS line running south fifty nine East eighteen poles to a spruce pine on the bank of said branch south thirty eight to a spruce pine S. 30 W. 88 P. to a dogwood near PEARLYS line N. 46 E. 47 P. to a bunch of witch hazel on the bank of said creek thence with a conditional line between JOHN SUTTON S. 38 E. 13 P. to two chestnuts on the bank of the creek South twenty west 20 P. to a stake near the foot of round mountain West 120 P. to a stake thence a direct line to the beginning.
Having such form as is represented by the above platt.

JOHN RUNION) C.C. John
Mullendone
WM. BROYLS)
Dep. surveyor of Cocke County

WILLIAM YEAT 187 Acres

State of Tennessee Cocke County. By virtue of an entry made in the entry takers office of said county at Newport of NO 440 dated the 26th day of January 1826. I have surveyed for WILLIAM YEAT 187 acres of land in said county on the waters of Clear creek. Beginning at a post oak on JOHN JORDONS line running with said line west 69 P. to a post oak north thirty seven East seventy five poles to a --- East seventy five -- North 31 East 76 P to a post oak in a flat 66 1/2 E. 100 poles to a stake and ash on DANIEL BLAZERS line thence with same south -- twenty two poles to a post oak on the top of a ridge -- ninety two poles to a stake S 20 -- thence a direct line to the beginning. --------------

376
JOHN COOPER 25 Acres

State of Tennessee Cocke County.
By virtue of an entry made in the Entry takers office for said County at Newport of NO 594 dated December 13th day 1828. I have surveyed for JOHN COOPER twenty five acres of land on the waters of long creek in said county adjoining the lands of JOHN EBBS. Beginning at the beginning corner of said Ebbs entry and survey running thence south forty seven west one hundred and forty poles to a stake and white oak and black oak south sixty five East seven poles to a white oak north forty eight and one fourth poles to a stake on Robers line thence a direct line to the beginning. As described by the above platt.
Surveyed 14th of October 1828.

JAMES D. COOPER) C.C. John
Mullendone
WM. KELLEY)
Dep. surveyor of Cocke County.

FREDERICK SMELSER 100 A.

State of Tennessee Cocke County.
By virtue of an entry made in the entry takers office for said county at Newport of NO 647 dated -- I have surveyed for FREDERICK SMELSER 100 Acres of land in said county. Beginning on a corner of PHILLIP NEAS land running thence with his line fifty seven poles to a post oak said Snelsers original corner thence with his line north twenty five west two hundred and eighteen poles to a stake and black oak north sixty five East twenty six poles to a post oak East one hundred and forty eight poles to a stake south one hundred and forty eight poles to a stake south one hundred & forty six poles to the beginning. Having such form as is represented by the above platt.
Surveyed 27th November 1828.

DANIEL BLAZER) C.C. John
Mullendone
BENJAMIN BLAZER)
Dep. surveyor of Cocke County

------------------- a stake south seventy west ----- one hundred poles to a stake ---- south twenty East eighty eight poles to a stake on said BUCKNERS line then a direct line to the beginning.
Having such form as is represented by the above platt.
Surveyed October 7th 1828.

D. EATON) C.C.
John Mullendone
--- DEAN)
Dep. surveyor of Cocke County

379
THOMAS JENKINS 25 A.

State of Tennessee Cocke county.
By virtue of an entry made in the entry takers office for said county at Newport of NO 636 dated 20th day of July 1827. I have surveyed for THOMAS JENKINS twenty five acres of land on the north side of Ground Hog Creek. Beginning at a stake ---- running thence up the creek south sixteen west thirty --- to a Tis wood south thirteen East fourteen poles to a spruce pine south six west seventy --- to a stake near a black oak north sixteen East ninety poles to a stake south sixty seven East fifty six poles to the beginning.
Surveyed the 2nd day of Dec. ----

JOEL JENKINS) C.C. John Wood
WM. JENKINS)
Surveyor of Cocke County.

RUSSELL JONES and JOSEPH YOUNG 25 A.

State of Tennessee Cocke County.
By virtue of an entry made in the entry takers office for said county at Newport of NO 504 dated the 2nd day of March 1828. I have surveyed for RUSSELL JONES & JOSEPH YOUNG jointly twenty five acres of land in said county on the trail fork of big creek.
Beginning on a beech running thence south seventeen and one half East nineteen poles to a stake thence a direct line to the beginning.
Surveyed November 15th 1824.

N. SHARPTON) C.C. John Mullendone
F. FUGATE)
Dep. surveyor of Cocke County

380 381 382
State of Tennessee Cocke County. Personally appeared before me J.W. WILLAFORD chairman of county court of Cocke county. ALLEN G. BRYANT, Register of Cocke to who made oaths in Due form of law that he has Transcribed the Book or Books Delivered to him without any change or Devation to the Best of his knowledge. Sworn to and subscribed before me this Jan. 1st 1837.
J. W. H. WILLAFORD, chairman of ct.

ALLEN BRYANT
blank

blank

383
JACOB PACK 5000 A.

State of Tennessee Cocke County. Surveyors office.
By virtue of an entry made in the office of the entry takers for said county in the name of JACOB PECK oak land the seventh of June 1830 NO 823 I have this 4 day of May 1831 surveyed for JACOB PECK 5000 acres of land situate in the north East corner of Cocke County. Beginning on the pointed rock in the state line corner of Cocke & Green county then with the meanders of the mountain & state line the various courses thereof 1047 poles to the road which leads from Bumcombe C. by the Warm Springs to Knoxville in the year 1799 continuing with said mountain 292 poles to a gum in a gap of the same then west 800 poles horizontal

measure to a stake then north 1200 poles crossing French Broad river then north 45 east 400 poles to the county line and with the same to the beginning.
Surveyed 20th August 1831.

Joseph c. Green C.S.

By his Deputy J. Peck

ISHAM T. PECK 2000 A.

State of Tennessee Cocke County. Surveyors office.
By virtue of an entry made in the office of the Entry taker of Cocke County the 7th June 1830 NO 824 I have surveyed for IHAM T. PECK two thousand acres of land situated in the said county on the line of the state of Tennessee & North Carolina. Beginning at a gum tree in a gap of the Smokey mountain in the state line corner of JACOB PECK then with the state line and the top of said mountain the various windings seven hundred and seventy five poles to the top of a knob where the mountain turns East then West six hundred poles horizontal measure to a stake then north six hundred & thirty poles to the line of JACOB PECK and with the same East 555 poles to the beginning as by the above platt is represented.
Recorded 20th August 1831.

Joseph H. Green C.L.

By his deputy Jacob Peck.

384
ADAM C. PECK 2000 A.

State of Tennessee Cocke County. Surveyors office.
By virtue of an entry made in the office of Entry takers for said county in the name of ADAM C. PECK of Oakland the seventh of June 1830 NO 825 I have surveyed for ADAM C. PECK of Oakland 2000 acres of land. Beginning at the north East corner of ISHAM T. PECKS survey of 2000 acres on Smokey mountain on the top of a knob where the mountain East then with the top of the mountain and state line the various courses 904 poles at a point where the mountain has run south 44 poles then west 440 poles horizontal measure then north 400 poles to a stake then East 120 poles to a stake then north 220 poles to a stake the corner of ISHAM T. PECK then East with his line to the beginning.
Recorded August the 20th 1831.

Joseph H. Green C.S.

By Peck his deputy

ELIZA JANE, JULIT N. & MARTHA A.N. PECKS 5000 A.

State of Tennessee Cocke County. Surveyor office.
By virtue of an entry made in the entry takers office for said county in the name of ELIZA JANE, JULIET N. & MARTHA A.N. PECKS 5000 acres of land situated in the county of Cocke Beginning on the top of Smokey mountain in the line of the state of the corner of WILL & JOHN & L. PEKCS then with the windings of the mountain which when reduced to a straight line will be 1230 poles to the corner of FOREST & MORRISON then north 700 poles horizontal measure then East 800 poles then south 45 East 330 poles to the line of WILLIAM R. & JOHN H.L. PECK with the same south 45 west 210 poles to his corner then south 45 East 600 poles to the beginning.
Recorded 25 August 1831.

Joseph H. Green C.S.

By his Deputy Jacob Peck

385
<u>FROST & MASON 5000 A.</u>

Surveyors Office. State of Tennessee Cocke County.
By virtue of an entry made in the Entry takers office for said county in the name of <u>GARRSON FRAUST</u> and WILLIAM L. MASON the 7th June 1830 NO 827. I have this 4 day of May 1837 surveyed for said <u>GERRAD FROST</u> and WILIAM MASON 5000 acres of land in said county of Cocke on the line of the state. Beginning at the corner of the Miss Pecks 5000 acres survey on the top of the Smokey mountains and with the same a line of the state crossing the river Big Pigeon Denneys creek at the Distance of 800 poles when Reduced to a straight line from said beginning then with the river Pigeon 320 poles then north 45 West 320 poles then north 45 East to a point from which a line from the south west of the Miss Pecks will intersect the same run then with said line to the corner and then south to the beginning.

JOSEPH H. GREEN
Recorded 25 August 1831. COUNTY SURVEYOR by Jacob Peck Deputy

<u>WM. R. PECK 2000 A.</u>

State of Tennessee Cocke County. Surveyors office.
By virtue of an entry made in the entry takers office for said county. In the name of WILLIAM R. PECK the 7th day of June 1830 NO 828. I have this 4 day of May 1831 surveyed for William R. Peck 2000 acres of land situated in Cocke county. Beginning on the top of Smokey mountain at the corner of ADAM C. PECK of Oakland then with said mountain & state line 272 poles to the top of the big Bluff containing said line & mountain 310 poles to the low gap at the foot of the Big Bluff between Spring Creek and Wolf Creek head same line continued 234 poles being 106 poles beyond the top of a high Nobb between the waters of Spring, Wolf and Big Creek in all with the mountain 816 poles to Rock then west 390 poles horizontal then north 60 poles to a pine west of a Pecks corner then East passing said corner to the beginning.

J. H. Green C.S.

By his Dept. Jacob Peck

386
<u>MILES & JOHN HENRY L. PECK 4000 A.</u>

State of Tennessee Cocke County. Surveyors office.
By virtue of an entry made in the entry takers for said county in the name of MILES AND JOHN HENRY HENRY L. PECK 4000 acres of land situated in Cocke County. Beginning at the corner of WILLIAM R. PECK on the top of the Smokey Mountains at same rock then with said mountain and line of the state 142 poles beyond the low gap at the head of big creek which Distance of the line 640 poles on a straight line thence north 45 East 375 poles to a joint Due west of WILLIAM RAINS PECKS corner survey of 2000 acres then East passing said corner to the beginning.

Joseph H. Green C.S.

By his dep. Jacob Peck

387
<u>ISHAM TALBERT & ADAM CLAYTON PECK 5000 A.</u>

State of Tennessee Cocke County. Surveyors office.
By virtue of an entry made in the entry takers office for said county

in the name of ISHAM TALBERT & ADAM CLAYTON PECK of Oakland the seventh day of June 1830 NO 832. I have this 4 day May 1831 surveyed for said ISHAM & ADAM PECK five thousand acres of land in Cocke county. Beginning at the corner of N. S. PECK and brothers on the SMOKEY Mountain in the line of the state then with sd mountain as it winds 850 poles passing the fifth mine tree on said line then north 45 west horizontal meanderors four miles then south 45 west two miles north west of the corner of N.S. PECKS and brothers then south 45 East four miles passing their corner and with their line to the beginning.

Joseph H. Green C.S.

by his Dep. Jacob Peck

E. EMBREE 5000 A.

State of Tennessee Cocke County. Surveyors office.
By virtue of an entry made in the entry takers office for said county in the name of E. EMBREE the 30 day of June 1830 NO 838. I have this 4 day of May 1831 surveyed fro said ELIZA EMBREE 5000 Acres of land in said county. Beginning at the corner of WILLIAM R. and brothers on the Smokey mountain then with the windings of said mountain and line of the state 150 poles beyond some rocks supposes to be split with lighting the place that the surveyor Ended the running said line 1799 then North 45 west four miles and one half horizontal measure to a stake then south 45 west 640 poles to a line of the aforesaid PECKS then south 45 East with same line to the beginning.

Joseph H. Green C.S.

By his depty. Jacob Peck

388
THOMAS Y. REED 5000 A.

By virtue of an entry made in the entry takers office of said county number 1006 in the name of THOMAS Y. REED dated the 4th day of May 1831. I have surveyed for the said THOMAS YATEMON REED 5000 acres of land in said county adjoining the state line. Beginning on the top of Smokey Mountain in said line at the north East corner of E. EMBREE then with said mountain twelve hundred poles with the winder of said mountain to the river Big Pigeon corner to MANSON FROOST then down said river one mile then north 40 degrees west nine hundred and thirty poles to the line of E. EMBREE and with the same south 45 East to the beginning.

Joseph H. Green C.S.

By his dep. Jacob Peck

JOHN ALLEN five acres & fifty poles

State of Tennessee Cocke County. Surveyors office.
By virtue of an entry made in the entry takers office for said county in the name of JOHN ALLEN the 16 August 1830 I have surveyed for said JOHN ALLEN five acres and fifty poles of land in said county. Beginning on a stake on the south bank of Big Pigeon River on said Allens line thence with Madas line south twenty one East fifteen poles to a white oak Madas corner thence with said line north fifteen poles to a pine on the bank of the river then down the meanders of said river to the beginning.
Recorded the 8th Feb. 1832.

Joseph H. Green - County Surveyor

ADAM MADOX 50 A.

State of Tennessee Cocke County. Surveyors office.
By virtue of an entry made in the entry takers office for said county in the name of ADAM MADOX 27 day December 1828 NO 744 I have surveyed this 3 day February 1831 for said Madox fifty acres of land situated in said county on the south side of Big Pigeon river near Ground Hog creek Beginning on a poplar at the foot of the mountain then with said mountain and down said creek then north seventy two East two hundred poles to a stake on COLMON line forty poles to a stake then with the spur of the mountain south seventy two west two hundred poles to a stake then a direct line to the beginning.

RECORDED the 3rd Feb. 1832 Joseph H. Green

Surveyor for C.C.

JANE BUSH 25 A.

State of Tennessee Cocke County. Surveyors office.
By virtue of an entry made in the office of the entry takers for said county in the name of JANE BUSH the 15th day of December 1831. Surveyed for JANE BUSH twenty five acres of land situated on the south side of French Broad river. Beginning on a white oak at the mouth of the Pigeon Roost branch thence up the river East 124 P. to a stake corner at JOSEPH five acre entry thence with his line to the foot of the mountain south thirty three and one fourth poles thence with spurs of said mountain west 124 poles to a stake thence north thirty three and one fourth poles to the beginning.

Recorded this 20 January 1832

Joseph H. Green C. C.

By Dept. Thomas Gann

ANDREW HOOPER 25 A.

State of Tennessee Cocke County. Surveyors office.
By virtue of an entry made in the entry takers office for said county in the name of ANDREW HOOPER the 7th day of December 1829 of No 783 I have this 25 day of February 1830 surveyed for said ANDREW HOOPER twenty five acres of land in said county on the waters of Brush Creek. Beginning on his corner of old survey on a holly and chestnut stump at the mouth of the branch near the bank of French Broad thence running N 47 west 70 p. to white oak crossing said creek thence S 52 W 70 p. to a stake thence south 68 East 96 P. to the Buffalow hollow Rock on the river South E. 6 East 38 poles to the beginning.

Joseph Green C.C.

By his dep. Thomas Gann

391
JOHN EBBS 50 A.

State of Tennessee Cocke County. Surveyors office.
By virtue of an entry made in the office of the entry takers for said county in the name of JOHN EBBS this 29 day of April 1831 of NO 1005. I have surveyed this 18th day of November 1831 for JOHN EBBS fifty acres of land in said county on the waters of long creek. Beginning on a stake on JOHN COOPERS line near his corner which is a post oak thence N. 42 west 53 1/2 P. to a large chestnut Coopers corner thence with Coopers line S. 51 West 52 poles to a stake Coopers corner thence S. 6 E. 172 P to hickory and mulberry thence S. 88 E. 60 P. to stake corner of said Coopers old tract of land then N 40 west 113 P. to three sourwoods then N 50 E. 90 P. to stake then a direct line to the beginning.

Joseph H. Green C.S.

By his dep. Thomas Gann

392
JOHN HOLLEN 200 Acres

State of Tennessee Cocke County. Surveyors office.
By virtue of an entry made in the office of the Entry takers for the county in the name of JOHN HOLLEN the 15 May 1830 of NO 816. I have surveyed for JOHN HOLLEN two hundred acres of land in said county on French Broad river. Beginning on a stake on sd Hollands own line of old survey running thence with sd line N. 52 W. 118 P. to a chestnut thence with THOMAS HOLLENS line at the new Entry N. 74 W. 22 P. to a black walnut in a hollow thence with sd Hollan old tract S. 47 W. 22 P. to two chestnut oaks on the side of the mountain thence with said mountain S 10 W 160 P. to a pine thence with sd mountain thence with said mountain S. 43 W 60 P. to a chestnut oak thence 66 E. 140 P. to a stake on the side of said mountain thence a direct line to the beginning.
Recorded the 8th Feb. 1832.

Joseph H. Green C.C.

By his dep. Thomas Gann.

JERMIAH JENKINS 25 A.

State of Tennessee Cocke County. Surveyors office.
By virtue of an entry made in the office of Entry takers of said county in the name of JERMIAH HENKINS the 20 day of Sept. 1828 NO 725. I have surveyed for sd Jenkins twenty five acres of land in said county on the waters of Scorere Creek. Beginning on a buckeye on the bank of sd creek running south 6 E. 26 poles to white oak then south 64 E. 40 P. to chestnut thence N 61 E 40 P. to dogwood north 55 West 53 p. to a stake thence south sixt six west 64 poles to the beginning. of said survey. Recorded 4 Feb. 1832.

Joseph H. Green surveyor

By his Dept. Thomas Gann

393
GUY GAMMONS 30 A.

State of Tennessee Cocke County Cocke County Surveyors office.
By virtue of an entry made in the entry takers office in the name of --------------------- (cannot be read from copy). I have surveyed for

said Gammons thirty acres of land in said county lying on the north side of French broad river adjoining the lands of GEORGE OTTINGER and others. Beginning on a red oak and white oak running S. 41 W. 34 p. to a post oak on sd Ottingers line thence with said Ottingers line thence S. 66 1/2 East 150 poles to ANDREW SLIVERS line to a stake thence N 35 west with said line 108 poles to Gammons own corner of old survey thence Dew west 50 poles to the beginning.
Recorded in my office Feb. 8 1832.

Joseph H. Green C.S.

By his Dept. Thomas Gann

394
DAVID WARDEN assigned to JOHN GREGG 50 A.

By virtue of an entry made in the entry takers office for said county in the name of DAVID WARDEN and by him assigned to JOHN GREGG for value received enters the 12 day of January 1826 NO 1020. I have this 15 day of August 1831 surveyed for said Gregg fifty acres of land in said county on the waters of Meadow Creek. Beginning on a locust and chestnut thence running south 41 W. 127 1/2 poles to a white oak WARDENS line N. 15 W. 63 to a stake thence N. 81 E. 127 1/2 poles to a stake So. 15 East 63 P. to the beginning. of said survey. Recorded 8th Feb. 1832.

Joseph H. Green C.S.

By his dept. Thomas Gann

PETER I. DAVIS 200 Acres.

State of Tennessee Cocke County. Surveyors office.
By virtue of an entry made in the entry takers office for said county in the name of PETER I DAVIS the 12 day of January 1831 NO 875 I have this 10 day of May 1831 surveyed for said Davis 200 acres of land in said county laying on French Broad river. Beginning near the chimney rock running south 29 E. 60 poles to sid Davis line thence S. 75 W. 82 P. to the river French Broad on a gum then down said river N. 59 W. 44 P. to a holly ANDREW HOOPERS corner thence with Hoopers line N. 59 1/2 west 91 poles to a post oak said Hoopers corner thence Dew west 130 P. to a stake thence S. 65 W. 60 poles to a chestnut N. 70 west 54 poles to a maple Hoopers corner thence north 120 poles to a stake thence S 70 E. 445 poles to the beginning.
Recorded 8th Feb. 1832.

Joseph H. Green C.S.

By his Dept. Thomas Gann

395
GEORGE OTTINGER 200 Acres

State of Tennessee Cocke County. Surveyors office.
By virtue of an entry made in the office of the Entry taker for said county in the name of GEORGE OTTINGER the 20 August 1831 of NO 9030 I have surveyed for said Ottinger 200 acres of land in said county on the north side of French Broad river adjoining the lands of JOSEPH NEAS. Beginning on a large poplar on sd Neas entered land. running west 155

poles to a hickory is sd Neas field his own corner thence south thirty nine west one hundred and fifty poles to a poplar thence S. 65 East 200 poles to a stake and two black oaks pointers thence a direct line to the beginning.
Recorded 8th Feb. 1832.

Joseph H. Green C.S.

By his Dept. Thomas Gann.

396
WILLIAM RENNELS 25 Acres

State of Tennessee Cocke County. Surveyors office.
By virtue of an entry made in the Entry takers office for said county in the name of WILLIAM RENELS the 3 day of June 1826 NO 566 I have the 17 Feb. 1830 surveyed for said Renels 25 acres of land laying on the North side of French Broad river. Beginning on a large rock known by the name of the chimney Rock near the bank of the river thence N. 21 East 40 poles to a large rock thence north 15 East 20 poles to a hickory thence north 30 west 10 poles to a stake thence north 83 E. to the beginning.
Recorded the 8th Feb. 1832.

Joseph H. Green C.S.

By his Dep. Thomas Gann

GEORGE OTTINGER 100 acres

State of Tennessee Cocke County. Surveyors office.
By virtue of an entry made in the office of the entry takers for said county in the name of George Ottinger the 20 August 1831 NO 1024 I have this 25 day of October 1831 surveyed for said Ottinger one hundred acres of land laying in the county aforesaid. Beginning on a white oak running north 90 poles to a stake on a branch thence N. 42 E. 186 P. to a stake on GUY GAMMONS line thence N. 66 1/2 W. 64 P. to a post oak Gmmons corner thence with said Ottingers line S. 41 W. 24 P. to two white oak bushes thence with Ottingers line S. 73 W. 48 P. to a white oak thence N. 40 west seventy poles to a black oak Ottingers corner thence south 13 East eighty nine poles to a stake said Ottingers at old survey thence a direct line to the beginning.
Recorded the 8th Feb. 1832.

Joseph H. Green C.S.

By his Dept. Thomas Gann

397
GEORGE OTTINGER 50 acres

State of Tennessee Cocke County. Surveyors office.
By virtue of an entry made in the office of the entry taker of said county in the name of GEORGE OTTINGER the 20 day of August 1831 NO 1029 I have surveyed for said Ottinger fifty acres of land laying in said county on the north side of French Broad river Beginning on a large poplar on said Ottingers corner and JOSEPH NEESE running thence N. 8 poles to two white oaks Neeses corner thence N. 82 E. 10 p. to said Neeses corner on a white oak thence N. 44 E. 34 poles to a hickory and black oak thence N. 42 E. 47 poles to a white oak Ottingers corner of old survey thence south 45

East seventy five P. to a stake on his own line thence west 114 P. to white oak thence N. 80 west 18 poles to the beginning.
Recorded the 8th Feby. 1832.

Joseph H. Green C.S.

By his dep. Thomas Gann

CALVIN BUSH 50 Acres

State of Tennessee Cocke County. Surveyors office.
By virtue of an entry made in the office of the Entry taker of Cocke county in the name of CALVIN BUSH the 8th day of June 1831 I have surveyed for said Bush fifty acres of land in said county laying on the waters of Big Pigeon Beginning on a hickory near what is called the big survey line thence running S. 37 E. 90 poles to the foot of the mountain to two pines thence south 22 P. to two chestnuts thence S. 70 west 90 P. to a small white oak at the foot of said mountain north 45 W. 60 P. to a stake on said bushes older entry thence with said line E. 74 P. to a white oak said Bushes corner thence north eighty poles with said Bushes line at older entry to the beginning.
Recorded 8 Feb. 1832.

Joseph H. Green C.S.

By his Dept. Thomas Gann

398
EDOM KINDRICK 15 acres

State of Tennessee Cocke County. Surveyors office.
By virtue of an entry made in the entry takers office of said county in the name of EDOM KINDRICK the 20 Dec. 1830 No 869 I have this 30 Sept. 1831 surveyed for said Kindrick 15 acres of land in sd county and fifty poles laying on the waters of French Broad river joining the same at his old survey. Beginning on his line running South five East 150 poles to a stake on his line thence East 12 poles to the bank at French Broad river to a quanity of rock thence a direct line to the beginning. the land surveyed Recorded the 8 Feb. 1832.

Joseph Green C. surveyor

By his Dept. Thomas Gann.

399
WILLIAM P. GILLETT 100 Acres

State of Tennessee Cocke County. Surveyors office.
By virtue of an entry made in the entry takers office of said county in the name of WILLIAM P. GILLETT the 22 day of April 1821 NO 1064 I have the 19th day of May 1831 surveyed for said Gillett one hundred acres of land in said county laying on the waters of Clay Creek Beginning on a black oak and post oak running N. 8 W. 115 poles to a hickory and dogwood said Gilletts corner thence N. 54 W. 76 poles to a white oak Woods corner Due East 72 poles to a stake thence then with Rauls line N. 2 East 26 poles to a white oak thence south 80 E. 100 poles to a white near Lovells corner thence N. 76 west 72 poles to a white oak THOMAS CHRISTIANS line thence N. 65 poles to a white oak thence west 67 poles to a stake thence south 96 poles to the beginning.

Recorded the 8. Feb. 1832.

Joseph H. Green C.S.

By his Dept. Thomas Gann

THOMAS FOWLER 8 acres

State of Tennessee Cocke County. Surveyors office.
By virtue of an entry made in the entry takers office of said county in the name of THOMAS FOWLER the 7 day of December 1829 NO 784 surveyed for said Fowler the 30 day of May 1831 eight acres of land in said county. Beginning on the south side of Clear Creek on a white oak running south 4 W. 155 poles to a stake crossing said creek and the big road leading from Newport to Brownsborough thence south 86 East 66 p. to a forked hickory with O L HARVIES line thence N. 4 East 182 p. crossing said creek to a white oak SWAGERTYS line thence N. 86 W. 26 poles to a black oak sd Fowlers corner of old survey thence north 80 poles to the beginning. Recorded the 8 Feb. 1832.

Joseph H. Green C.S.

By his dept. Thomas Gann

400
WILLIAM HARRIS 50 acres

State of Tennessee Cocke County. Surveyors office.
By virtue of an entry made in the entry takers office of said county in the name of WILLIAM HARRIS the 28 Feb. 1831 NO 894 I have surveyed this August 1831 surveyed for said Harris fifty acres of land laying in said county laying on French Broad river. Beginning on a black locust P.I. CAVIS corner thence running west 118 poles to the river to a double chestnut thence up said river S. 40 E. 100 p. to a stake thence N. 30 poles to the bank of said sluice N. 42 E. to the beginning.
Recorded Feb. 8 1832.

James H. Green C.S.

By his Dept. Thomas Gann

JACOB EASTERLY 50 acres

State of Tennessee Cocke County. Surveyors office.
By virtue of an entry made in the entry takers office of said county in the name of JACOB EASTERLY the 4 day of Feb. 1831 NO 880 I have surveyed the 10 day of August 1831 for said Easterly 50 acres of land in said county laying on the south side of Chucky river. Beginning on a white oak running S. 13 with GUY GAMMONS line 95 poles to a white oak and red oak Laymons corner thence S. 41 W. 62 p. to two small white oaks thence S. 73 W. 48 p. to a white oak thence N. 40 W. 70 poles to a large black oak said Easterlys corner at old survey thence S. 70 E. 30 P. to a stake thence N.22 1/2 E. 142 poles to a stake thence N. to the beginning.
Recorded the 8th Feb. 1832.

James H. Green

401
<u>JACOB EASTERLY 200 acres</u>

State of Tennessee Cocke County. Surveyors office.
By virtue of an entry made in the entry takers office of said county in the name of JACOB EASTERLY the 4 day of Feb. 1831 NO 879. I have surveyed for said Easterly two hundred acres of land in said county laying on the south side of Chickey river. Beginning on a beech on ALFRED MIMS corner thence running N. 36 E. 20 poles to two beeches a conditional line between sd Mims and Easterly thence N. 27 W. 140 poles to a stake on the top of a knob thence S. 30 W. 70 poles to a stake on the same nobb thence S. 48 W. 27 p. to a hickory then west along said nobb to an white oak thence S. 13 W. 32 p. to a hickory thence S. 74 W. 48 p. to a locust on the side of sd nobb E. 19 W. 100 p. to a poplar in a deep hollow thence S. 53 E. 20 p. to a beech at the foot of sd nobb thence N. 72 East 68 p. to a poplar on the side of a nobb S. 47 E. 24 p. to a chestnut tree and dogwood RAYS line thence with Rays line N. 58 East 86 poles to a beech and hickory S. 34 E. 18 poles to three beeches thence a direct line to the beginning.
Recorded 8 Feb. 1832

James H. Green C.S.

By his Dept. Thomas Gann

402
<u>POLLY WARDEN 200 acres</u>

State of Tennessee Cocke County. Surveyors office.
By virtue of an entry made in the entry takers office of said county in the name of POLLY WARDEN the 25 day of Sept. 1831 NO 1037 I have surveyed for said Polly Warden on this 30 day of Sept. 1832 200 acres of land in said county. Beginning on a white oak on JOHN GREGGS line running S. 35 W. 60 p. to a locust RIDDENS corner thence with his line S. 17 East 120 poles to a pine RIDLERS corner thence 83 E. 30 poles to Renners line and Ridlers corner on a chestnut oak with Renners line N. 130 poles to a large black gum and a chestnut oak thence south 18 W. 212 poles to the beginning.
Recorded in my office this 8 day of Feb. 1831.

Joseph H. Green C.S.

By his Dept. Thomas Gann

<u>WILLIAM BLAKE 50 acres</u>

State of Tennessee Cocke County. Surveyors office.
By virtue of an entry made in the entry takers office of Cocke county in the name of WILLIAM BLAKE the 3rd day of Sept. 1829 NO 773. I have surveyed this 1st day of Feb. 1831 for said Blake fifty acres of land in the said county on the waters of little sorrel. Beginning on a dogwood and gum or near them on a stake thence running N. 4 W. 90 p. to a stake S. 80 west 54 poles to a chestnut oak under the side of a nob thence S. 37 W. 40 poles to a large black oak thence S. 45 W. 30 poles to a Red oak thence south 50 East 50 poles to a stake thence a direct line to the beginning.
Recorded in my office Feb. 8-1832.

Joseph H. Green C.S.

By his Dept. Thomas Gann

403
THOMAS WALLEN 100 acres

State of Tennessee Cocke County. Surveyors office.
By virtue of an entry made in the entry takers office of said county in the name of THOMAS WALLEN JUN. the 8th day of May 1830 NO 613 I have this day 3 of Sept. 1831 surveyed for said Wallen one hundred acres of land laying in the county aforesaid on the waters of French Broad river, adjoining THOMAS WALLEN SENR. and others. Beginning on a stake on the bank of a small branch thence running S. 36 W. to a pine thence S 60 W. 116 P. to a chestnut and black oak bush thence S. 50 East 58 poles to a white oak at the foot of a steep mountain. S. 70 E. 80 poles to a pine thence N. 51 E. 120 poles to a stake thence a direct line to the beginning.
Recorded Feb. 8 - 1832.

Joseph H. Green C.S.

By his Dept. Thomas Gann

404
JANE DAUGHTY 175 acres

State of Tennessee Cocke County. Surveyors office.
By virtue of an entry made in the office of entry taker of said county in the name of JANE DAUGHTY 4th day of May 1831 - NO 1009 I have surveyed for said Daugherty 175 acres of land in said county on nobb creek. Beginning on a beech thence south 78 E. 13 P. to a white oak on HUDSONS line live thence N. 85 E. with Hudsons line 68 P. to a black oak thence N. 5 west 66 P. to a beech N. 55 E. 68 P. to a beech on the side of a nobb thence N. 46 E. 100 poles to a white oak thence N. 70 E. 78 P. to a hickory Freshours line thence N. 23 W. 22 P. to a stake Dead black oak thence south seventy two W. 258 P. to an Ironwood thence south 88 W. 36 to a sycamore thence S. 75 W. 50 poles to a stake on a high nobb then to the beginning. Recorded 8th Feb. 1832.

Joseph Green C.S.

By his dept. Thomas Gann

CALIS WOODY 200 acres

State of Tennessee Cocke County. Surveyors office.
By virtue of an entry made in the Entry takers office for said county in the name of CARLES WOODY the 25 day of May 1831 NO. 1012 I have surveyed for said Woody two hundred acres of land in said county on the place called Meadow Creek. Beginning on a stake N. 63 E. 148 poles to the foot of the mountain to a spanish oak and post oak thence south 80 E. with the county line 141 poles to a sourwood then S. 41 W. 52 poles to a black oak thence S. 58 W. 40 P. to a poplar north 73 East 44 poles to a stake south 83 W. 80 poles to the foot of the Pink mountain on a stake then with McMAHANS line to the beginning.
Recorded the 8th Feb. 1832.

Joseph H. Green C.S.

By his Dept. Thomas Gann

405

WILLIAM P. GILLETT 200 A.

State of Tennessee Cocke County. Surveyors office.
By virtue of an entry made in the office of the entry takers office for said county in the name of WILLIAM P. GILLETT the 22 day of April 1831 NO. 1003 I have surveyed the 18 day of May 1831 for said Gillett 200 acres of land laying in said county on the waters of Clay creek Beginning on a white oak on the top of a ridge then running N. 40 W. 95 poles to a stake on THOMAS CHRISTIANS line thence with his line south 82 poles to a stake thence S. 49 E. 153 P. to a sugar tree near a small branch thence S. 46 E. 40 P. to a stake near Lowells line thence N. 68 E. 150 poles to a stake thence a direct line to the beginning.
Recorded 8th day of Feb. 1832.

Joseph H. Green C.S.

By his dpt. Thomas Gann

GREEN BANDY 200 acres

State of Tennessee Cocke County. Surveyors office.
By virtue of an entry made in the entry takers office of said county in the name of GREEN BANDY the 5 day of January 1831. Surveyed for said Bandy 200 acres of land laying in sd county on the right hand fork of Big Creek. Beginning on a hickory thence running S. 73 W. 100 poles to a black oak then north 32 East 150 poles to a stake thence a direct line to the beginning. Recorded Feb. 8 - 1832.
Joseph H. Green C.S.
By his Dept. Thomas Gann

406

JERMIAH JENKINS 50 acres

State of Tennessee Cocke County. Surveyors office.
By virtue of an entry made in the office of the entry takers of said county in the name of JERMIAH JENKINS the 16 October 1830 NO. 854 I have surveyed for said Jenkins fifty acres of land laying in said county on Cosbys creek. Beginning on a sugar tree near said Jenkins house running S. 68 W. 74 P. to a black oak thence 85 W. 112-68 W. 74 P. to a black oak saplin thence S. 70 W. 18 poles to a sugar tree crossing sd branch thence N. 85 E. along the foot of a high mountain 112 to a spanish oak thence 47 E. 18 P. to a poplar thence south 67 E. 54 P. to a hickory thence N. 53 E. 26 P. toa dogwood thence north 36 poles to a chestnut stump. JOSEPH RUNNIONS corner thence with Runnions corner N. 6 E. 66 to a white oak. Runions corner thence N. 30 East 38 poles to a pine Runions corner thence N. 61 W. 62 poles to three white oaks corner of said Jenkins old line then E. 10 W. 80 poles to a stake Jenkins corner thence a direct line to the beginning.
Recorded Feb. 8 - 1832.

Joseph H. Green C.S.

By his Dept. Thomas Gann

407
NEAHALINE RIDDLE 1000 acres

State of Tennessee Cocke County. Surveyors office.
By virtue of an entry made in the entry takers of said county I have surveyed for NEAHALINE RIDDLE 11th Sept. 1830 NO. 850 I have this 31st day of May 1831 surveyed for said Riddle one thousand acres of land in sd county laying on the waters of Meadow creek running on a line Runions thence running from the chestnut oak the beginning corner S. 83 W. 30 P. to a chestnut with Wardens line thence S. 65 W. 76 P. with Wardens line to a pine thence with the same S. 73 W. 188 poles to a white oak thence N. 17 W. 120 P. to a locust then S. 73 1/2 W. 100 P. to a black oak stake corner thence south 15 E. 90 poles to a stake Packs corner then S. 69 W. 90 P. to a white oak thence with Winters line S. 51 W. 237 P. to two gums and a dogwood then south 14 E. 222 poles to a chestnut oak on top of the mountain then north 95 E. 650 poles to a pine at the top of said mountain then N. 15 west 222 poles to the beginning.
Recorded Feb. the 8th 1832.

Joseph H. Green C.S.

By his dept. Thomas Gann

408
JOSEPH RUNIONS 25 A.

State of Tennessee Cocke County. Surveyors office.
By virtue of an entry made in the Entry takers office of said county in the name of JOSEPH RUNIONS the 23rd of August 1830 NO. 849. I have this 1st day of Feb. 1831 surveyed for said Runion 25 acres of land laying in said county on the waters of Cosby Creek Beginning on a poplar corner to said Runions thence S. 18 W. 27 1/2 poles to a pine thence N. 85 E. 96 P. to a poplar corner of said Runions thence N. 10 west 40 P. to a white oak thence N. 66 W. 100 poles to a black oak sd Runions corner thence S. 35 1/2 East 24 P. to a pine along said Runions line of old survey then south 23 poles to the beginning.
Recorded Feb. 8th 1837.

Joseph H. Green C.S.

By his Dept. Thomas Gann

PETER I. DAVIS 200 acres & STEPHEN HUFF

State of Tennessee Cocke County. Surveyors office.
By virtue of an entry made in the Entry takers office of said county in the name of PETER I. DAVIS and STEPHEN HUFF. I have surveyed for Huff and Davis 200 acres of land in said county on the waters of French Broad. Beginning on a white oak and maple thence running N. 29 W. 20 P. to a stake thence N. 9 W. 620 P. to WARDELL line thence E. 150 P. to a stake thence S. 29 E. 20 P. to a stake thence west 50 poles to the beginning.
Recorded Feb. 8 1832.

Joseph H. Green C.S.

By his dept. Thomas Gann

JOHN ELISON 400 acres

State of Tennessee Cocke County. Surveyors office.
By virtue of an entry made in the entry takers office for said county in the name of JOHN ELISON the 28th June 1830 NO. 836 I this 20 day of January 1831 surveyed for said Ellison four hundred acres of land laying in the county aforesaid on the south side of French Broad river in said mountain joining the land of GREEN BANDY. Beginning on a stake on said Bandys line thence running S. 50 west 250 P. to a spanish oak thence N. 50 East 250 poles to a stake thence a direct line to the beginning.
Recorded 8th Feb. 1832.

Joseph H. Green C.S.

By his Dept. Thomas Gann

409
JOSEPH RUNION 200 acres

State of Tennessee Cocke County. Surveyors office.
By virtue of an entry made in the office of Entry taker of said county in the name of JOSEPH RUNIONS the 26th day May 1830 NO. 818 I have surveyed for said Runions 200 acres of land in said county on the waters of Cosbys Creek Beginning on a poplar on said Runions line running N. 10 East 40 poles to a black oak S. 25 W. 40 P. to a hickory then S. 60 W. 45 P. to a pine thence S. 35 W. 38 poles to a white oak then S. 6 W. 66 P. to a chestnut stump Jenkins corner then south 35 E. 48 P. to a pine then south 50 East 160 poles to a specle oak thence S. 76 E. 96 p. to a chestnut W. 6 E. 60 poles to a white oak Runions corner then north 64 W. 38 P. to a hornbean N. 80 W. 12 poles to a poplar N. 42 W. 50 poles to a dogwood thence N. 16 W. 41 P. to a poplar thence 22 1/2 W. 39 P. to a chestnut N. 33 W. 28 P. to a black oak N. 53 P. to a stake thence to the beginning. Recorded Feb. 8th 1832.

Joseph H. Green C.S.

By his dept. Thomas Gann

410
GREEN W.L. ROSE 100 acres

By virtue of an entry made in the office of the Entry taker for said county in the name of GREEN W.L. ROSE the 10 November 1830 NO. 850 I have this 21st Oct. 1831 surveyed for said Rose 100 acres of land in said county laying on the waters of Big Creek Beginning on a poplar thence S. 20 W. 150 poles to a pine then S. 50 poles to a stake then N. 50 W. 80 poles to a stake under the foot of the chestnut ridge then N. 15 East 180 poles to a stake under the spur of the chestnut ridge thence a direct line to the beginning.
Recorded Feb. 8th 1832.

Joseph H. Green C.S.

By his dept. Thomas Gann

JOHN ROSE, JUNR. 50 A.

State of Tennessee Cocke County Surveyors office.
By virtue of an entry made in the office of the entry taker for said county in the name of JOHN ROSE JUNR. the 27 of Sept. 1830 NO. 1039 I have the 21 of October 1831 surveyed for said Rose fifty acres of land in said county on the waters of Big Creek. Beginning on a beech running south 70 west 120 poles to a stake near a chestnut on the top of a high ridge thence N. 10 W. 70 P. to a chestnut oak thence north 70 E. 130 poles to a poplar thence south 40 to the beginning. Recorded Feb. 8 1832.

Joseph H. Green C.S.

by his dept. Thomas Gann

411

GEORGE M. GRAGG 100 acres

State of Tennessee Cocke County. Surveyors office.
By virtue of an entry made in the office of the entry taker of said county in the name of GEORGE M. GRAGG the 2nd day of Feb. 1830 NO. 794 I have surveyed the 26 day of Feb. 1831 for said GREGG 100 acres of land laying on Rock Creek beginning on a pine near a small branch running up sd branch north 60 E. 142 poles to a gum dogwood and sourwood thence to the foot of the mountain thence N. 4 W. 98 poles to a locust on MOONEYHAMS line thence with said line S. 47 W. 24 P. to a poplar Mooneyhams corner thence with his line N. 49 W. 26 P. to a large chestnut and white oak THOMAS BEL??TONS line thence S. 40 W. 304 poles to a stake thence N. 60 E. 130 poles to the beginning. Recorded Feb. 8 1832.

Joseph H. Green C.S.

By his Dept. Thomas Gann

DAVID McMAHAN 50 acres

State of Tennessee Cocke County. Surveyors office.
By virtue of an entry made in the entry takers office of said county in the name of DAVID McMAHAN the 6 day of November 1830 NO. 856 I have this 3rd of Feb. 1831 surveyed for said McMahan fifty acres of land in said county laying on the waters of Cosbys Creek. Beginning on a beech running thence N. 60 E. 22 P. to a pine then N. 30 W. 120 poles to a white oak then S. 10 W. 34 poles to a black oak thence N. 35 W. 60 poles to a stake bounded all round by impossible mountains. Thence to the beginning.
Recorded Feb. 8 1832.

Joseph H. Green C.S.

By his dept. Thomas Gann

412

WILLIS LEATHERWOOD 100 acres

State of Tennessee Cocke County. Surveyors office.
By virtue of an entry made in the office of the Entry taker for said county in the name of WILLIS LEATHERWOOD the 15 Oct. 1831 NO. 1047 I have surveyed this 15 Nov. 1831 for said Leatherwood one hundred acres of land in said county laying on Capers Creek. Beginning on a dogwood on the bank of said creek running S. 47 E. 42 P. to gum near Suttons line thence East 104 poles to a black oak J. RUNIONS corner

thence with his line S. 13 west 31 P. to a stake Runions corner thence S. 83 W. with his line 21 poles to a black oak said Runions corner thence S. 24 west 34 P. to a hickory thence S. 60(?) west 35(?) to a pine Runions corner thence N. 30 W. 28 poles to a white oak N. 53 W. 26 poles to a pine thence west 20 P. to an Ironwood thence N. 57 W. 42 P. to a chestnut oak thence north thirty six W. 52 poles to a chestnut oak then the same course continued 100 poles to a stake thence N. 37 E. 20 poles to a stake thence S. 47 E. to the beginning. Recorded 8th day of Feb. 1832.

Joseph H. Green C.S.

By his dept. Thomas Gann

one page gone

415
THOMAS CHRISTAIN 100 acres

State of Tennessee Cocke County. Surveyors office.
By virtue of an entry made in the entry takers office of said county in the name of THOMAS CHRISTAIN the 15 Feb 1831 NO 885 I have the 17 day of Feb. 1831 surveyed for said Christian 100 acres of land laying on Clay Creek. Beginning on a sycamore on the bank of said creek thence south 58 E. 7 poles to a hickory on said Christians line thence north 58 E. 34 P. to a white oak Christians corner thence south 140 poles to an ash with said Christians line thence with sd line East 33 poles to a post oak thence N. 4 E. 163 poles to Christians corner on a sycamore thence N. 70 west 21 P. to a dogwood thence N. 46 W. 44 P. to a white oak corner to said Christians old Entered land thence N. 2 1/2 W. 26 P. to a post oak corner to said Christian then with his line S. 64 W. 36 P. to a black oak thence south 10 E. 122 P. to the beginning.
Recorded Feb. 8 1832.

Joseph H. Green C.S.

By his dept. Thomas Gann

416
JOHN ELLISON 50 acres

State of Tennessee Cocke County. Surveyors office.
By virtue of an entry made in the office of the Entry taker in said county in the name of JOHN ELLISON SENR. the 9 day of Jan. 1830 NO. 789 I have surveyed for said Ellison fifty acres of land in sd county laying on the waters of Big Creek. Beginning on a beech and spruce pine running East seventy six poles to a black gum on the top of Johns mountain thence N. 50 W. 30 P. to a white pine thence N. 25 W. 36 P. to a chestnut due west 36 P. to a stake on said creek thence a direct line to the beginning. Recorded Feb. 8 1832.

Joseph H. Green

By his dept. Thomas Gann

JOHN ELLISON SENR. 50 acres

State of Tennessee Cocke County. Surveyors office.
By virtue of an entry made in the entry takers office of said county in the name of JOHN ELLISON SENR. the 9th Jan 1831 surveyed for

for said Ellison survey NO 788 9 Jan. 1830, fifty acres of land in said county on the middle Fork Creek. Beginning on a small white oak S. 71 W. 130 P. to chestnut thence south 38 E. 40 poles to a white pine thence south 82 E. 90 poles to black oak thence on the top of the mountain thence south seventy six East 40 poles to a stake thence a direct line to the beginning. Recorded Feb. 8 1832.

Joseph H. Green C.S.

By his dept. Thomas Gann

417
<u>JOHN ELLISON SENR. 50 acres</u>

State of Tennessee Cocke County. Surveyors office.
By virtue of an entry made in the office of entry taker for said county in the name of JOHN ELLISON SENR. the 20th Jan. 1831 surveyed for said Ellison fifty acres of land in said county on the waters of Big Creek. Beginning on a S. pine running S. 38 W. 70 P. to a stake on top of the mountain thence south 32 East 100 P. to a stake on the side of the mountain S. 22 E. 38 poles to a spruce pine thence East 45 poles to a stake crossing sd creek or branch and thence down the ---.
Recorded Feb. 8 1832.

Joseph H. Green C.S.

by his dept. Thomas Gann

<u>JOHN ELLISON SENR. 100 acres</u>

State of Tennessee Cocke County. Surveyors office.
By virtue of an entry made in the office if the Entry Taker for said county in the name of JOHN ELLISON SENR. the 1st day of November 1830 NO. 855 I have surveyed for said Ellison the 3rd day of June 1831 one hundred acres of land. Beginning on a beech RUSSELL JONES corner north 50 W. 98 P. to KNIGHTS line thence to a dogwood HARRISES corner thence south 50 poles to a beech of chestnut sprouts on the side of the bunch ball mountain then <u>GENN</u> S. 50 E. 25 poles to a large Red oak and hickory thence south 14 E. 115 poles to a stake thence a direct line to the beginning corner. Recorded Feb. 8 1832.

Joseph H. Green C.S.

By his dept. Thomas Gann

418
<u>WILLIAM C. STORY 200 acres</u>

State of Tennessee Cocke County. Surveyors office.
By virtue of an entry made in the office of the Entry takers for said county in the name of WILLIAM C. STORY the 1th day of Feb. 1830 NO 798 I have this 23rd day of August 1831 surveyed for said Story 200 acres of land in said county laying on Clear Creek in part joining said Storys other entry. Beginning on a white oak foiled then running west 280 poles to a stake the center of Clear Creek on KINDRICKS line S. 34 E. 100 poles to a hickory and dogwood thence East 54 P. to a stake on sd Storys line thence north 83 1/2 P. to a white oak corner to sd Storys line thence

to Storeys old survey then E. 126 1/2 poles to two post oaks Storeys corner thence south 63 1/2 poles to the beginning. Recorded Feb. 8 1832.

Thomas Gann by Dept. pf C.S. Joseph H. Green

419
WILLIAM C. STORY 386 Acres

State of Tennessee Cocke County.
By virtue of an entry made in the entry takers office of said county in the name of WILLIAM C. STORY the 23rd day of August 1831 NO. 1033 I have this 26 day of August 1831 surveyed for said Story three hundred and eighty six acres of land in said county joining the lands of Byers and Atlars. Beginning on a large white oak corner of said Storeys fifty acres thence E. 160 P. to a stake and black oak pointed Denn N. 19 poles to a stake with sd Storys line thence N. 77 E. 54 poles to a post oak MOSES FAUBIONS line then with FORLEYS line N. 128 p. to a stake and oak pointers FORBIES corner thence N. 35 W. 195 P. to a black oak BOYERS line thence with Boyers line S. 112 poles to a stake Boyers corner thence with the same west 76 poles to a hickory on Boyers field then S. 34 poles to a stake Boyers line west 118 poles to a hickory thence N. 36 W. 76 P. to a stake on J. BOYERS line thence a direct line to the beginning. Recorded Feb. 1832.

Joseph H. Green

By his dept. Thomas Gann

420
THOMAS HOLLEN SENR. 198 acres

State of Tennessee Cocke County. Surveyors office.
By virtue of an entry made in the entry takers office of said county in the name of THOMAS HOLLEN SENR. the 2nd day of June 1831 NO 894 I have this 12 day of June 1831 surveyed for said Holland one hundred and ninety eight acres of land in sd county Beginning on a stake on top of a ridge running N. 45 E. 100 poles to a bunch of chestnut sprouts thence with said Hollands line of old survey S. 85 E. 270 poles to a stake thence with the same S. 50 E. 150 poles to a stake thence with Hollands line N. 74 W. 150 poles to a stake Hollands corner with the same S. 36 W. 14 P. to a pine thence with the same 100 acre entry S. 60 W. 116 poles to a chestnut and black oak bush thence N. 50 W. 76 P. to a double pine thence N. 38 W. 46 poles to a chestnut oak then N. 37 W. 26 P. to a pine thence a direct line to the beginning. Recorded Feb. 1832.

Joseph H. Green C.S.

By his dept. Thomas Gann

421
JOHN YEAROUT & ARCHIBALD D. NELSON 600 Acres

State of Tennessee Cocke County. Surveyors office.
By virtue of an entry made in the office of Entry taker of said county in the name of JOHN YEAROUT & ARCHIBALD D. NELSON the 8 day of October 1831 NO 1041 I have this 25 day of November 1831 surveyed for said NELSON & YEAROUT 600 acres of land laying in said county on the waters

of Oven Creek beginning on a white oak near D. BORDINS line running south 27 W. 110 p. to a post oak and black oak on the top of high nob thence N. 85 W. 30 P. to a black oak on SWAGERTYS line thence N. 42 W. 48 P. to an ash thence N. 48 W. 162 to a post and hickory DASSONS corner thence N. 8 W. 38 poles to a red oak thence S. 70 E. 40 P. to a stake a direct line to the beginning. Recorded Feb. 8th 1832.

Joseph H. Green C.S.

By his Dept. Thomas Gann

ARCHIBALD D. NELSON & JOHN YEAROUT 300 Acres

State of Tennessee Cocke County. Surveyors office.
By virtue of an entry made in the office of the entry taker for said county in the name of ARCHIBALD D. NELSON & JOHN YEAROUT the 15 day of November 1831 surveyed for said Nelson and Yearout 300 acres of land in said county on the waters of Oven Creek. Beginning on a stake on sd Nelson and Yearout 600 acre entry running N. 14 E. 100 P. to a stake on OTTINGERS line thence S. 65 E. 24 poles to a stake thence S. 70 E. 70 P. to a white oak and red oak and hickory thence with the same course continued 400 poles to a stake corner at said Nelson and Yearouts six hundred acre entry thence a direct line to the beginning. Recorded Feb. 8th 1832.

Joseph H. Green C.S.

By his dept. Thomas Gann

422
THOMAS GANN 50 acres

State of Tennessee Cocke County. Surveyors office.
By virtue of an entry made in the office of the entry taker of said county in the name of THOMAS GANN and by him assigned to WILLIAM GANN entered the 1st day of August 1831 NO 1023 I have this 2nd August 1831 surveyed for said Gann fifty acres of land laying on Big Creek Beginning on a stake at the upper end of what is called long bottom under the spur of John Mountain thence running S. 12 E. 20 P. to a stake near a lynn under the fork ridge then S. 30 W. 56 P. to a stake near an ash tehnce S. 55 W. 22 P. to an Elm under the side of said mountain thence south 80 W. 10 poles crossing said Creek to an ash thence 75 W. Down said creek West 28 P. to an ash on the bank of said creek thence N. 75 W. 32 poles down said creek to a spruce pine thence N. 20 W. 30 Poles to a stake under the side of a mountain thence along under the foot of said mountain up said creek and crossing sd creek to the beginning. Recorded Feb. 8, 1832.

Joseph H. Green C.S.

By his dept. Thomas Gann

423
RUBEN BLACK 100 acres

State of Tennessee Cocke County. Surveyors office.
By virtue of an entry made in the Entry takers office of said county in the name of RUBEN BLACK assigned to him by RICHARD PRICE entered the 27 of August 1830 NO 847 I have this 21st day of August 1831 surveyed for said Black by assignment from Price one hundred acres of land in said

county on the waters of Grassy Fork branch which Empties into Big Creek Beginning on a maple and white oak thence N. 10 W. 10 P. to a stake at the foot of the Grassey fork Creek mountain on the Grassey fork creek to a bunch of pines on the fork of sd Creek thence up the meanders of sd creek S. 80 E. 80 poles to a stake thence south 78 1/2 W. 125 P. to the beginning. Recorded Feb. 8 1832.

Joseph H. Green Surveyor

By his dept. Thomas Gann

424
JOHN THOMAS 50 acres

State of Tennessee Cocke County. Surveyors office.
By virtue of an entry made in the office of entry taker of said county in the name of JOHN THOMAS the 15 November 1830 I have surveyed for said Thomas fifty acres of land laying in said county on the waters of Clay Creek. Beginning on a white oak of place where HOLTS line joins JOHN GILLETTS running with said line S. 35 E. 20 P. to a white oak Gilletts corner then S. 65 East 14 P. to a dogwood on said Gilletts line thence S. 85 E. 20 poles to a post oak and pine thence N. 28 P. to an ash thence N. 28 P. to an ash thence S. 85 E. 74 P. to a white oak NATHAN JENKINS corner thence N. 39 P. to a white oak on said JOSHNOR JENKINS line thence west 80 poles to a Red oak Jenkins corner thence west 80 poles to a Red oak Jenkins corner of old deeded land thence S. 60 W. 26 poles to a red oak and dogwood said Thomas corner of deeded thence a direct line to the beginning. Recorded Feb. 8th 1832.

Joseph H. Green C.S.

By his dept. Thomas Gann

JOHN FRESHOUR 50 acres

State of Tennessee Cocke County. Surveyors office.
By virtue of an entry made in the office of the Entry taker for said county in the name of JOHN FRESHOUR the 10 day of Oct. 1828 NO 729 I have this 30 day of April 1831 surveyed for said Freshour fifty acres of land in said county on the waters of Slate Creek. Beginning on a stake JOHN WORTHS line thence running south 87 E. 140 poles to a spanish oak Freshours corner of old survey thence with said Freshours line of old survey NO 40 W. 68 P. to a white oak corner of same tract thence N. 16 W. 32 poles to a black oak near said Freshours line thence S. 74 W. 64 P. to a white oak on THOMAS SMITHS line to the beginning. of old survey. Recorded the 8th Feb. 1832.

Joseph H. Green

By his dept. Thomas Gann

425
JOHN FRESHOUR 12 acres

State of Tennessee Cocke County. Surveyors office.
By virtue of an entry made in the office of the Entry taker for said county in the name of JOHN FRESHOUR the second day of Feb. 1829 NO 758 I have this 30 day of April 1831 surveyed for said Freshour twelve acres of land in said county on the waters of Slate Creek Beginning on a stake running East 30 poles to a hickory thence N 72 poles to a stake thence west 30 poles to a stake near a chestnut oak at said Freshours field thence with said Freshours (field) line of old survey seventy two poles to the beginning. Recorded Feb. 8th 1832.

Joseph H. Green C.S.

By his dept. Thomas Gann

ANDREW HOOPER 150 acres

State of Tennessee Cocke County. Surveyors office.
By virtue of an entry made in the office of the Entry taker of said county in the name of ANDREW HOOPER 1st day of March eighteen hundred and thirty one no 899 I have this 19 day of March eighteen hundred and thirty one surveyed for said Hooper one hundred and fifty acres of land in sd county on the waters of bresh creek. Beginning on a stake thence running with said Hoopers line south thirty five East fifty poles to a maple thence south fifty eight East thirty two poles to a chestnut stump thence north 68 - forty poles to a black oak thence north 85 East fifty six poles to a maple and sweet gum said Hoopers old corner thence north 3 East twenty poles to a black oak stump thence East one hundred and thirty poles to a black oak stake along said Hoopers line of old deeded land then south fifty nine East ninety one poles to a stake Hoopers corner then N. 45 East one hundred and eighty poles to a stake on the side of a mountain thence south eighty west four hundred and fifty poles to a hickory and oak thence a direct line to the beginning. of said survey on brush creek. Recorded Feb. 8 1832.

JAMES NEELY) C.C.
Joseph H. Green C.S.
ABRAHAM HOOPER)
By his dept. Thomas Gann

427
BENJAMIN BRYANT 100 acres

State of Tennessee Cocke County. Surveyors office.
By virtue of an entry made in the entry takers office of said county in the name of BENJAMIN BRYANT the 10 day of November 1830 NO 861 I have this 29 day of July 1831 surveyed for said Bryant one hundred acres of land in said county on the waters of Clay creek Beginning on three lynns running south forty W. sixteen P. to a hickory then N. fifty on a nobb thence S. thirty five E. two P. to a hickory then N. fifty E forty eight P. to a stake then N. 75 East forty poles to a lynn THOMAS CHRISTAINS corner on a stake then south 12 W. 30 P. along said line to a stake then south forty five E. 20 poles to a beech then S. twenty four P. to a stake on the side of an Nobb near a hickory then S. 76 E. 80 P. to a white oak then north twenty six E. twenty poles to a Ironwood then S. sixty six E. twenty eight P. to a beech on a branch thence south twenty five E. forty P. to a stake on natural Boudary thence East 20 poles to a stake

on natural boundary at a clift thence N. 20 W. 40 poles to a stake near said Bryants corner thence N. 20 East forty five poles to a stake along said Bryants line thence N. 12 East twenty four P. to a black oak thence N. 23 west 110 west poles to a black oak on the side of a clift impasible thence a direct line to the beginning. Recorded Feb. 1832.

WILLIAM DEAN) C.C.
Joseph H. Green C.S.
SAMUEL BRYANT)
By his dept. Thomas Gann

428
SAMUEL WILSON 100 acres

State of Tennessee Cocke County. Surveyors office.
By virtue of an entry made in the office of the entry taker of said county in the name of SAMUEL WILSON and by him assigned to SAMUEL GARRETT & JOHN GRIFFIN entered the 21st day of July 1828 NO 718 I have this 22nd day of March 1831 surveyed for said Wilson and Garrett one hundred acres of land laying on the waters of Indian Creek Beginning on a poplar NOAH GRIFFINS corner thence running with Griffins line S. 36 E. 72 poles to a dogwood thence south 71 W. 48 poles to a hickory Garretts corner of old survey thence south twenty E. 126 poles to a poplar and dogwood thence north seventy E. sixty three poles to a stake on Garretts corner of old survey thence south thirty four poles to a black gum near FRANCES line of deeded land thence with his line south fifty five west sixty poles to a stake on said line north 30 west 156 poles a dogwood thence N. 83 west twenty poles to a chestnut oak thence north thirty west one hundred poles to a stake thence a direct line to the beginning. On Griffins corner. Recorded Feb. 8th 1832.

NOAH GRIFFIN) C.C.
Joseph H. Green C.S.
--- GARRETT)
By his dept. Thomas Gann

JERMIAH MURR 100 Acres

State of Tennessee Cocke County. Surveyors office.
By virtue of an entry made in the entry taker of said county in the name of JEREMIAH MURR the 17 day of May in the year 1830 NO 817 - I have surveyed for said Murr one hundred acres of land in said county laying on the waters of Bogerd. Beginning on a stake on the side of the mountain running south 21 East 124 poles to a chestnut north fifty East 44 poles to a black oak near GANNS corner of older survey thence East 100 poles to two black oaks near a drean thence north 8 west 72 poles to a black oak on the side of the mountain thence north sixty seven west 100 poles to a white oak on the side of the mountain thence a direct line to the beginning. Recorded Feb. 8 1832.

JOEL DENNIS) C.C.
Joseph H. Green
JOB MURRELL)
By his dept. Thomas Gann

429
ABRAHAM ALLEN 100 acres

State of Tennessee Cocke County. Surveyors office.
By virtue of an entry made in the office of the entry taker of said county in the name of ABRAHAM ALLEN the 10 day of January 1831 of NO. 873. I have this 18 day of April 1831 surveyed for said Allen one hundred acres of land in said county laying on the waters of Cosbys Creek. Beginning on a post oak JOHN ALLENS corner running north twenty one west thirteen poles to a black oak said Allens corner then with Allens line south seventy eight west thirty eight poles to a white oak and post oak thence north thirty six west seventy three poles to a hickory on NAITHS line thence with said line north seventy five East fourteen poles to a post oak NORTHS corner 38 East 56 poles to a stake on ELDRIDGES line near a post oak thence with norths line near a post oak thence with Norths line south fifty three East forty eight poles to a black oak ELDRIDGES & JACK ALLENS corner thence a direct line to the beginning on a post oak. Recorded Feb. 8, 1831.

THOAMAS DENTON) C.C. James
H. Green C.S.
JEFFERSON DENTON)
By his dept. Thomas Gann

430
JOHN CARNEY 50 acres

State of Tennessee Cocke County. Surveyors office.
By virtue of an entry made in the office of the entry taker of said county in the name of JOHN CARNEY the 10 of November 1830 NO. 858. I have this 8th July 1831 surveyed for said Carney fifty acres of land in said county on the waters of big creek. Beginning on a large white oak running north 10 west eighteen poles to a sourwood then north forty west thirty six poles to a white pine under the foot of the mountain north twenty east thirty poles to a chestnut on the side of said mountain north seventy East thirty eight poles to three maples north thirty five East fifty poles to a stake thence East thirty poles to a stake then to the beginning.

REUBEN BLACK) C.C.
Joseph H. Green C.S.
JOHN CARNEY)

431
ANDREW HOOPER 50 Acres

State of Tennessee Cocke County. Surveyors office.
By virtue of an entry made in the office of the Entry taker of said county in the name of ANDREW HOOPER the 1st day of March 1831 NO 897 I have surveyed the 19 March 1831 for said Hooper fifty acres of land in said county laying on the river of French Broad Beginning on a spruce pine on bank of said river running south twenty seven poles to a stake said Hoopers corner thence south eighty East twenty three poles to a stake thence south seventy three East twenty two poles to a beech under side of mountain thence south fifty seven East 127 poles to a poplar and an ash thence south 66 East 57 poles to a beech Hoopers corner of older survey thence south twenty five west thirty poles to a stake on the side of the mountain thence north 27 west two hundred and seventy

poles to a stake thence a direct line to the beginning. Recorded Feb. 8th 1832.

ABRAHAM HOOPER) C.C.
Joseph H. Green C.S.
JAMES FREDY)
By his dept. Thomas Gann

REUBEN BLACK 50 Acres

State of Tennessee Cocke County. Surveyors office.
By virtue of an entry made in the office of the Entry taker of said county in the name of REUBEN BLACK the 18th day of October 1828 NO. 735 I have this 19th July 1831 surveyed for REUBEN BLACK fifty acres of land in said county on the waters of Big Creek on the Grassy fork branch Beginning on a large chestnut thence running south fifty east one thirty poles to a poplar thence south fifty west sixty five poles to a beech on a drean the waters of Big Creek then north forty west one hundred and thirty poles down said branch to a white oak thence a direct line to the beginning of said survey. Recorded Feb. 8th 1832.

JAMES BLACK) C.C.
Joseph H. Green C.S.
GREEN W. ROSE)
By his dept. Thomas Gann

432
WILLIAM C. COLLIAR 50 acres

State of Tennessee Cocke County. Surveyors office.
By virtue of an entry made in the office of the entry taker of said county in the name of WILLIAM C. CALLION then 25 day of January 1831 NO. 877 I have this 15th March 1831 surveyed for said Colliar 50 acres of land laying in said county on the waters of Neelys creek Beginning on a white oak on JOHN TURNERS line running with said line East one hundred and twenty eight poles to a small dogwood near said COLLIERS corner of old survey thence N. 5 west 87 poles to a dogwood then south 83 west seventy one poles to a hickory on a small branch thence south thirty three west eighty four poles to the beginning. Recorded in my office Feb. 1832.

JOHN WAYMYERS) C.C.
Joseph H. Green C.S.
OWEN WILLIAN)
By his dept. Thomas Gann

433
JOHN BAILEY 100 Acres

State of Tennessee Cocke County, Surveyors office. Surveyors office.
By virtue of an entry made in the office of then entry taker of said county in the name of ALLEN BEARD and by him assigned JOHN BALEY for value received entered the 15th day of January 1830 NO 790 I have this 1st day of August 1831 surveyed for said Baley one hundred acres of land in said county laying on the waters of french Broad river beginning on a locust running north seventy East one hundred and eighty six poles to a stake on the side of the mountain north twenty west ninety three poles to a stake near a small stream thence south seventy west one hundred and eighty six poles to a stake near a clift thence a direct line to the beginning. Recorded Feb. 8th 1832.

JAMES BALFY) C.C.
Joseph H. Green C.S.
THOMAS GANN)
By his dept. Thomas Gann

434
WILLIAM PALMER 75 Acres

State of Tennessee Cocke County. Surveyors office.
By virtue of an entry made in the Entry taker of said county in the name of WILLIAM PALMER the 21st day of February 1831 NO. 887 I have this 18th day of March 1831 surveyed for said Palmer seventy acres of land in said county on the waters of Clay Creek Beginning on a walnut bush running north seventy seven E. thirty six P. to a hickory Palmers corner thence N. 51 E. eighty eight poles to a red oak on said Palmers line of old deeded land S. 43 E. sixteen poles to a white oak thence N. fifty two west forty two poles to a white oak on said Palmers line thence south fifty five west one hundred and ----- eight poles to a black oak Palmers corner thence with said Palmers line north fifty west twenty eight to two white oaks Palmers corner thence north seventy three west eighteen poles to a stake thence along the same south ten East fourteen poles to a beech thence S. sixty five W. 26 poles to a stake on the branch thence south forty west fourteen poles to a walnut thence with said Palmers line south twenty west twenty four poles to a walnut Palmers corner thence with Palmers corner running through his field north forty two west seventy two poles to a small white oak Palmers corner thence a direct line to the beginning. Recorded Feb. 8, 1832.

JAMES DAUGHTY) C.C.
Joseph H. Green C.S.
DAVID GRGORY)
By his dept. Thomas Gann

435
JOHN DRISKINS 75 acres

State of Tennessee Cocke County. Surveyors office.
By virtue of an entry made in the office of the Entry taker of said county in the name of JOHN DRISKINS the 16th Nov. 1830 NO 863 I have surveyed the 14 March 1831 for said Driskins seventy five acres of land in said county laying ---------- Beginning on a sugar tree on FOWLER LEACH branch one fork of Clay Creek running north ten west seventy eight poles to a hickory then north seventy one East one, fifty poles to a hickory on a drean thence south ten East seventy eight poles to a dogwood thence to the beginning of said survey. Recorded Feb. 8 1832.

JEBEDEE HOLT) C.C.
Joseph H. Green C.S.
JOHN THOMAS)
By his dept. Thomas Gann

436
JOHN HAMPTON 50 Acres

State of Tennessee Cocke County. Surveyors office.
By virtue of an entry made in the office of the Entry taker for said county in the name of JOHN HAMPTON the 23rd day of August 1830 NO 845 I have this 9th day of March 1831 surveyed for said Hampton fifty acres of land in said county. Beginning on a white oak Hamptons corner of

old survey running south forty five E. 90 poles to a white oak Hamptons corner thence N. fifty East twenty poles to a dogwood then north thirty six poles to a hickory then East with Swagertys line twenty poles to a white oak thence north sixty three west fifty six poles to a post oak on Swagertys line thence north forty eight west twenty eight poles to a stake thence a direct line to the beginning. Recorded Feb. 8th 1832.

JOSEPH HAMPTON) C.C.
Joseph H. Green C.S.
WM. HOLT)
By his dept. Thomas Gann

437
ISSAC FOWLER 80 Acres

State of Tennessee Cocke County. Surveyors office.
By virtue of an entry made in the office of the Entry taker of said county in the name of ISSAC FOWLER Dec. 23rd 1830 NO 870 I have this 8th day of March 1831 surveyed for said Fowler Eighty acres of land in said county adjoining the land of WILLIAM PALMER. Beginning on a small white oak running north 32 west forty poles to a black oak on said Palmers line thence S. sixty E. three poles to a hickory thence N. fifty three E. sixty two poles to a hickory red oak thence N. 37 W. ten poles to a hickory and white oak on said line then N. forty six E. fifty six poles to a large white oak on said line then south forty four East three poles to a large white oak on said line then south forty four East three poles to a white oak a conditional line between DAWSON & FOWLER thence south sixty three west eighteen poles to a hickory on a conditional line thence south twenty four west sixteen poles to a white oak then south fifty three East thirty three poles to a hickory on the said conditional line thence south fourteen East thirty two poles to a poplar on said Fowlers corner of old survey land then to the beginning. Recorded Feb. 8 1832.

WM. FOWLER) C.C.
Joseph H. Green C.S.
JORN DEAN)
By his dept. Thomas Gann

GEORGE HOLT 15 Acres

State of Tennessee Cocke County. Surveyors office.
By virtue of an entry made in the entry takers office of said county in the name of GEORGE HOLT the 18th day of August 1828 NO 770 I have this 9th of March 1831 surveyed for said Holt fifteen acres of land in said county on the waters of Clay Creek. Beginning on a beech running East five poles to a beech Hamptons old corner under the side of a nobb thence south fifty two East twenty two poles to a beech thence north eighty East thirty seven poles to a stake on said branch thence East seventy poles to a lynn. Corner of said Holt thence twenty two poles to a dogwood on Holts and Hamptons line thence West eighty eight poles to a beech thence N. seventy six west sixteen poles to a dogwood thence a direct line to the beginning. Recorded Feb. 8th 1832.

JOSEPH HAMPTON) C.C.
Joseph H. Green C.S.
WM. HOLT)
By his dept. Thomas Gann

438
DANIEL STEPHENS 175 acres

State of Tennessee Cocke County. Surveyors office.
By virtue of an entry made in the office of the Entry taker of said county in the name of DANIEL STEPHENS on the 10th day of November 1831 NO 370 I have this 10th day of November 1831 surveyed for said Stephens one hundred and seventy two acres and fifty poles of land in said county in the fork of French Broad and Pigeon river adjoining the land of ISSAC SMITH and the NETHERTON tract and the WILEY tract. Beginning on a locust near a hickory ISAAC SMITHS corner thence with said Smiths line south forty East one hundred and seventy nine poles to a stake Smiths corner thence south fifty one East two hundred and eighteen poles to a stake a corner of five hundred acre tract to WM. JOBE thence with said line of the five hundred acre tract west two hundred and eighty poles to the beginning. Recorded Feb. the 8th 1832.

Joseph H. Green County Surveyor

By his dept. Thomas Gann Surveyor

of Cocke County.

439
DANIEL STEPHENS 172 Acres & 30 poles

State of Tennessee Cocke County. Surveyors office.
By virtue of an entry made in the office of the Entry taker of said county in the name of DANIEL STEPHENS on the 10th day of November 1831 NO 730 I have this 10th day of November 1831 surveyed for said STEPHENS 172 acres and 30 poles of land in said county in the fork of FRENCH BROAD and Pigeon river adjoining the lands of ISSAC SMITH and the NETHERTON tract and the WILEY tract. Beginning on a locust near a hickory ISSAC SMITHS line south forty East one hundred and seventy nine poles to a stake Smiths corner thence north fifty one East 218 poles to a stake a corner of a five hundred acre tract granted to WM. JOBE thence with said line of said five hundred acre tract west 280 poles to the beginning.

Joseph H. Green C.S.

By his dept. Thomas Gann

440
ISSAC GANN assigned to JAMES SWAGERTY 12 acres

State of Tennessee Cocke County. Surveyors office.
By virtue of an entry made in the office of the entry taker for said county in the name of ISSAC GANN and assigned by him to JAMES SWAGERTY entered 15th day of December Eighteen hundred and thirty one of NO 1056 I have this eighteenth day of December eighteen hundred and thirty one surveyed for said Gann assigned to Swagery twelve acres of land lying in sd county on Big Pigeon river joining the land of Issac Gann deeded land including one sluice on the foot of the river at the lowerend of sluice. Beginning on a horn bean on the bank of the river at the lower End of said Sluice thence running up said sluice on the East side south twenty west one hundred and ten poles to a stake at the upper end of the sluice then west thirty poles to a stake on the bank of the river near ALLENS spring under a clift thence north twenty East one hundred poles to a stake thence down sd river with HOWELLS line and same on to GANNS line thence thirty poles to the beginning of said survey. Recorded Feb. 8th 1832.

Joseph H. Green C.S.

441
TIPTON JENNINGS- assigned to WILLIAM GANN 75 Acres

State of Tennessee Cocke County, Surveyors office.
By virtue of an entry made in the office of said county in the name of TIPTON JENNINGS and by him assigned to WILLIAM GANN for value recieved Beginning on a beech JAMES JENNINGS upper corner entered the 13 of October 1827 NO 666 and surveyed the 21st of October 1831 for said Gann seventy five acres of land in said county on the waters of Big Creek. Beginning on Jennings upper corner north thirty poles to the creek to a double spruce pine on GARRETTS line thence south seventy two East one hundred and eighty poles to a chestnut REUBEN BLACKS corner thence with BLACKS line south sixty five west eighty poles to a white oak Blacks corner thence with Blacks line south sixty five East forty poles to a poplar then south forty five west fifty poles to a spanish oak on top of said ridge thence a direct line to the beginning.

REUBEN BLACK) C.C.
Joseph H. Green C.S.
GEMS(?) B. ROSE)
By his dept. Thomas Gann

GEORGE GRAY 50 acres

State of Tennessee Cocke County. Surveyors office.
By virtue of an entry made in the entry takers office for said county in the name of GEORGE GRAY the 20th day December 1831 of NO 1059 I have this 20 day December 1831 surveyed for said Gray fifty acres of land in said county adjoining the land of BOYERS and others. Beginning on a dogwood on said Grays line running with Boyers line North 8 west 32 poles to a pine thence south sixty two west forty poles to JOHN BOYERS line on sourwood thence south thirty five west thirty six poles with Boyers line on sourwood thence south thirty five west thirty six poles with Boyers line to a hickory and white oak Boyers corner thence with sd line west forty two poles to a hickory bush Boyers corner thence south thirty three west four poles to a walnut on SNEEDS line south forty one East fifty six poles to a hickory and white oak Sneeds corner thence north eighty two East twenty four poles to a hickory thence a direct line to the beginning. Recorded Feb. 8th 1832.

Joseph H. Green C.S.

By his dept. Thomas Gann

442
WILLIAM JENNINGS assigned to WILLIAM GANN 50 acres

State of Tennessee Cocke County. Surveyors office.
By virtue of an entry made in the office of the entry taker of said county in the name of WILLIAM JENNINGS and by him assigned to WILLIAM GANN enterd the 13th day of December 1827 NO 665. I have surveyed this 21st day of Oact. [sic] 1831 surveyed for said Gann fifty acres of land in said county laying on the waters of big Creek. Beginning on a large white oak on the north bank of the Indian Cabin branch fork of big Creek thence running north seven west ten poles to a maple at the foot of the mountain thence north seventy eight west fifty six poles to a chestnut at the foot of the

same mountain thence with the foot of the mountain south thirty five west twenty poles to a beech then north eighty four west seventy poles to a large spruce pine at the foot of said mountain thence north fifty poles to a stake thence south eighty five east one forty poles to a stake near a chestnut thence a direct line to the beginning. of survey Recorded --- 1832.

Green Rose) C.C.
Joseph H. Green C.S.
REUBEN BLACK)
By his dept. Thomas Gann

443
JAMES JENNINGS 10 acres

State of Tennessee Cocke County. Surveyors office.
By virtue of an entry made in the office of the entry takers of said county in the name of JAMES JENNINGS and by him assigned to WILLIAM GRAY entered the 21st of March 18-- surveyed numbered six hundred and eighty six surveyed the 21st day of December eighty hundred and twenty one for said Gray ten acres of land laying in said county joining the land of ABRAHAM FINE and others. Beginning on a black oak on said FINES and GRAYS corner running north fifty five west twenty five poles to a stake near BOYERS corner thence running north twenty six east with BOYERS line to MCSWEENS corner sixteen poles thence north thirty seven east seventy poles to a stake thence south twenty East twenty two poles to a black oak FINES line thence a direct line to the beginning.

WM. GANN)
Joseph H. Green C.S.
THOMAS GANN) (I believe the above to be Gann not Gray. A.M.)

444
JESSE JENNINGS 100 acres

State of Tennessee Cocke County. Surveyors office.
By virtue of an entry made in the office of the entry takers of said county in the name of JESSE JENNINGS and by him assigned to MELTON and from him to REUBEN BLACK for value recieved from him entered the -- day of -- of NO four hundred and eighty three I have this day surveyed for said Black one hundred acres of land in said county on the waters of Cosbys Creek. Beginning on a spanish red oak on a ridge near an old flatt on WILLIAM WILHITES thence north seventy East forty poles to a stake thence south fifty one East forty six poles to a stake thence south forty East sixteen poles to a stake thence south twenty seven west one hundred and nine poles to a stake north twelve west sixty poles to a stake thence north seven East thirty one poles to the beginning.

Joseph H. Green C.S.

By his dept. Thomas Gann

445
GILBERT BAXORS assigned to EZIKILL BIRDSEYE 5000 acres

State of Tennessee Cocke County. Surveyors office.
By virtue of an entry made in the office of the entry take of said county in the name of GILBERT BAXORS for five thousand acres of number 834 dated 21st June 1830 and by the sherriff of Cocke County assigned

to EZIKILL BIRDSEYE became the purchers I have therefore surveyed for EZIKILL BIRDSEYE by virtue of levy on exicution and said entry of sd E. Birdseye I have surveyed for EZEKIEL BIRDSEYE three thousand acres of land it being all that could be had for older titles laying in said county on the waters of Cosbys Creek. Beginning at a heap of stones near the south west corner of ADAM BENJIMON ELLIOTT, NICHOLAS HAWKINS, LOONEY WALLICE & HENRY PECK five thousand acre grant and running from thence with said Pecks line north forty five degrees East Eleven hundred poles to a rock with stones filled around it on the top of a spur of said mountain on the south west side of the fallinf branch then to the chestnut to bearing north thirty five degrees East also to the highest point of English mountain north twenty one west thence running down said spur north forty five degrees west crossing the middle of Green brier Fork of Cosbys Creek at one hundred and didty two poles opposite to the End of said spur same course continued crossing the INDIAN CAMP FORK of Cosby Creek at four hundred and seventy poles then crossing and recrossing said creek at five hundred poles same course in all six hundred poles to a small double chestnut on the west side of the big ridge thence north fifty five degrees East four hundred poles North forty five degrees west five hundred and eighty poles to the Sevier county line thence with said Sevier county line to the place of beginning. Having such form as is represented by the above platt. Surveyed the 29th Sept. 1841.

Alexander Mathes

Surveyor Cocke County

UNICE BIRDSEYE 5000 acres

State of Tennessee Cocke County. Surveyors office.
By virtue of an entry made in the office of the entry takker for said county of NO 1881 dated the 18th day of January 1839 I have surveyed for UNICE BIRDSEYE five thousand acres of land lying in said county on the waters of Big Creek and Big Pigeon river. Beginning on MATHEW BLACKS line running from thonce south forty five degrees East six hundred and forty poles south seven hundred and twenty poles to a white oak OSBORN BALLS corner south forty five degrees west four hundred poles ELI BONE EMERYS north west corner of a five thousand acre survey same course continued nine hundred poles further to a stake north forty eight degrees west four hundred and fifty north twenty three deg. west eight hundred and forth poles to a white oak JOHN MCNABBS upper corner East twelve hundred poles to a black oak OSBORNE BALLS corner north thirty five degrees East two hundred poles to a white pine OSBORNE BALLS corner with five hundred poles to the beginning. Having such as is represented by the above platt. Surveyed Sept. the 1st 1840.

Ezikill Birdseye)
Alex Mathes
------ -------) C.C.
Surveyor Cocke County

WILLIAM HUFF 1000 acres & ALEXANDER MATHES

State of Tennessee Cocke County. Surveyors office.
By virtue of an entry made in the Entry takers office at Newport for said county of NO. 1699 dated this 5th day of February 1839 in the name of WILLIAM HUFF for one thousand acres and the said Wm. Huff hath assigned the one half of said one thousand acre entry to ALEXANDER MATHES I have therefore surveyed for WM. HUFF and ALEXANDER MATHES one thousand acres of land laying in said county on the waters of Big Pigeon river. Beginning on a chestnut oak near the buffalo lick and running thence south forty degrees East thirty poles to a stake on said Huff and Mathes two thousand tract thence with the same two courses East three hundred and eighty poles north three hundred and sixty poles to a black oak corner of OSBORNE BALLS fifteen hundred acre tract south seventy five deg. East two hundred and fifty poles to 2 chestnuts said Balls corner south twenty nine deg. East two hundred and fifty two poles said Bolls corner south forty five deg. west four hundred poles to the north west corner of ------ EMBREES six hundred acre tract and with no. the same course continued six hundred and forty poles to said Embrees south west corner thence north forty Eight deg. west four hundred and fifty poles thence twenty three deg. west eight hundred and forty poles to a white oak corner to JOHN MCNABB and the Ruff and Mathes two thousand acre tract then with do. a direct line to the beginning. Having such forme as is represented by the above platt. Surveyed the 16th day of August 1840.

MATHEW DAVIS) C.C. Alex
Mathes
ALEX DAVIS)
Surveyor of Cocke County.

WILLIAM HUFF & ALEXANDER MATHES 2000 acres

State of Tennessee Cocke County. Surveyors office.
By virtue of an entry made in the office of the entry taker at Newport for said county of NO 1609 dated the 29th day of November 1838 in the name of WILLIAM HUFF for two thousand acres and the said WILLIAM HUFF hath assigned the one half of the two thousand acres entry to ALEXANDER MATHES I have therefore surveyed for the said WILLIAM HUFF & ALEXANDER MATHES jointly two thousand acres ofland lying in said county and on the waters of Big Creek and big pigeon river. Beginning at a stake painted by a chestnut and hickory WILLIAM BALLS corner and running from thence with said Balls lines two courses south twenty two and an half dig. west one hundred and seventy four poles to a stake said Balls corner south west corner thence west with JONATHAN BIRDSEYE line four hundred poles to a stake said Birdseye corner same course continued in all five hundred poles to a stake south ten deg. west one hundred and eighty poles to a white oak JOHN MCNABBS upper corner on JOSEPH MCMILLENS line thence with said McMillens line East twelve hundred poles to a stake north three hundred and sixty poles to a black oak corner to OSBORN BALLS fifteen hundred acre tract thence with the same two corses north five degrees East one hundred and three poles to a chestnut north fifty six degrees East one hundred and three poles to a chestnut north fifty six degrees East one hundred and fifty poles to a pine corner to said Ball and JONATHAN B. BIRDSEYE and with said Birdseyes line north sixty degrees west four hundred poles to the beginning. Having such form as is represented by the foregoing platt. Surveyed the 15th day of August 1840.

WILLIAM HUFF 1000 acres & ALEXANDER MATHES

State of Tennessee Cocke County. Surveyors office.
By virtue of an entry made in the Entry takers office at Newport for said county of NO. 1699 dated this 5th day of February 1839 in the name of WILLIAM HUFF for one thousand acres and the said Wm. Huff hath assigned the one half of said one thousand acre entry to ALEXANDER MATHES I have therefore surveyed for WM. HUFF and ALEXANDER MATHES one thousand acres of land laying in said county on the waters of Big Pigeon river. Beginning on a chestnut oak near the buffalo lick and running thence south forty degrees East thirty poles to a stake on said Huff and Mathes two thousand tract thence with the same two courses East three hundred and eighty poles north three hundred and sixty poles to a black oak corner of OSBORNE BALLS fifteen hundred acre tract south seventy five deg. East two hundred and fifty poles to two chestnuts said Balls corner south twenty nine deg. East two hundred and fifty two poles said Bolls corner south forty five deg. west four hundred poles to the north west corner of ------ EMBREES five thousand acre tract and with do. the same course continued six hundred and forty poles to said Embrees south west corner thence north forty Eight deg. west four hundred and fifty poles thence twenty three deg. west eight hundred and forty poles to a white oak corne to JOHN MCNABB and the Huff and Mathes two thousand acre cract then with Do. a direct line to the beginning. Having such forme as is represented by the above platt. Surveyed the 18th day of August 1840.

MATHEW DAVIS) C.C. Alex Mathes
ALEX DAVIS)
Surveyor of Cocke County.

WILLIAM HUFF & ALEXANDER MATHES 2000 acres

State of Tennessee Cocke County. Surveyors office.
By virtue of an entry made in the office of the entry taker at Newport for said county of NO 1609 dated the 29th day of November 1838 in the name of WILLIAM HUFF for two thousand acres and the said WILLIAM HUFF hath assigned the one half of the two thousand acres entry to ALEXANDER MATHES I have therefore surveyed for the said WILLIAM HUFF & ALEXANDER MATHES jointly two thousand acres ofland lying in said county and on the waters of Big Creek and big pigeon river. Beginning at a stake painted by a chestnut and hickory WILLIAM BALLS corner and running from thence with said Balls lines two courses south twenty two and an half dig. west one hundred and seventy four poles to a stake said Balls corner south west corner thence west with JONATHAN BIRDSEYE line four hundred poles to a stake said Birdseye corner same course continued in all five hundred poles to a stake south ten deg. west one hundred and eighty poles to a white oak JOHN MCNABBS upper corner on JOSEPH MCMILLENS line thence with said McMillens line East twelve hundred poles to a stake north three hundred and sixty poles to a black oak corner to OSBORN BALLS fifteen hundred acre tract thence with the same two courses north five degrees East one hundred and three poles to a chestnut north fifty six degrees East one hundred and three poles to a chestnut north fifty six degrees East one hundred and fifty poles to a pine corner to said Ball and JONATHAN B. BIRDSEYE and with said Birdseyes line north sixty degrees west four hundred poles to the beginning. Having such form as is represented by the foregoing platt. Surveyed the 15th day of August 1840.

MARTIN DAVIS) C.C. Alex.
Mathes
ALEX DAVIS)
Surveyor of Cocke County

448
DAVID PALLARD(?) 75 acres

State of Tennessee Cocke County. Surveyors office.
By virtue of an entry made in the entry takers office of the aforesaid county at Newport of NO--dated--day of--1855. I have therefore surveyed for DAVID PALLARD seventy five acres of land lying in said county on Neelys creek and Nola Chuckey river. Beginning on a beech in a hollow on a line of the heirs of WILLIAM SMITH deceased running thence with the same north forth one and one half degrees East twenty poles to an ash & white oak on ----- REAMS line thence with the same north twenty one poles to an ash in a hollow corner to said Reams & JOHN HALL thence with Balls line north forty deg. west sixty five poles to a beech thence north twenty six Degrees East eighteen poles to a beech corner to HOLLOWAY R. BRAGG then with Braggs line north fifty nine degrees west sixty poles to a dogwood corner to JAMES HOLLOMANS then with Hollomans line south sixty five west one hundred and twenty poles to a lynn in the mouth of the Cod branch corner to ABRAHAM FRANK HAGNERS then with his lines south sixty five degrees east one hundred and twenty poles to a stake then south fifty nine degrees east sixty poles to a stake on a line of said heirs then with the same to the beginning/ Having such form as is represented by the above platt. Surveyed the 16th Nov. 1855.

SCI HEAD(?)) C.C.
George Sisk
JAMES B. WALFORD)
Surveyor of C.C.

449
State of Tennessee Cocke County.
Personally appeared before me M.H.BIBEE Dept. Clk, of said Allen Bryant Reg. who takes oath in due form of law that he has transcribed the foregoing book delivered---without any deviation---change to the best of his--acknowledged sworn to and subscribed before me this June 28th 1898.

M.H.Bibee Dept. Co. Clk.
Allen C. Bryant

www.ingramcontent.com/pod-product-compliance
Lightning Source LLC
Chambersburg PA
CBHW070106290526
45789CB00005B/1947
9781500132262